SCOTLAND UNDER MARY STUART

(*Frontispiece*) Mary Queen of Scots, by Jean le Court

SCOTLAND UNDER MARY STUART

An Account of Everyday Life

BY MADELEINE BINGHAM

London
GEORGE ALLEN & UNWIN LTD

First published in 1971

© *George Allen & Unwin Ltd 1971*

ISBN 0 04 942084 4

Printed in Great Britain
in 10pt Baskerville type
by T. & A. Constable Ltd
Edinburgh

CONTENTS

ILLUSTRATIONS

NOTE:

Nos. 3, 4 (*top*), 5, 6, 7, 11, 15 are reproduced from R. W. Billings, *The Baronial Antiquities of Scotland*, 1848. The remainder of the illustrations are by courtesy of The Mansell Collection.

ACKNOWLEDGEMENTS

I would like to express my thanks to Mr Stuart Maxwell of the National Museum of Antiquities of Scotland, Edinburgh, for his help in connexion with this book, and also to the Curator of the West Highland Museum, Fort William.

CHAPTER ONE

BACKDROP TO SCOTLAND
IN THE SIXTEENTH CENTURY

A true picture of a disturbed and remote country in the sixteenth century will be a picture of contrasts and contradictions. Much of the background is sombre, and most of Scotland's history in this century was played against a dark backdrop of unrest and assassination. Yet, side by side with this, ordinary people carried on their daily lives. Courtiers wrote lyrical poetry, merchants traded and amassed wealth, and the peasants sowed and reaped. Women sat at their spinning wheels while their husbands were killed in clan feuds. At the court, assassins wore rich velvets imported from abroad, while far away in remote valleys wolves threatened village life.

Scotland, in the turmoil of this century, was a country in transition between the medievalism of the Roman Church, which had long passed its apogee and was on the decline—a Scotland of agriculture and crafts, many of them with the monasteries as a focal point—and the new Scotland which was to be controlled by the great lords who became the inheritors of the Church's riches. The rising merchant and trading classes who adopted the new religion also began to exert their influence on the shaping of events.

But in spite of the ferment of the Reformed Religion, with its self-appointed 'Saints', and the changes they were to bring to the country, it brought no amelioration to the poor or to the sick, and little to the unlettered.

It did not change the primitive state of agriculture, the rapacity of the landlords, or the worst features of the clan system. The peasants were still periodically plundered by the lairds gathering the fruits of heavy toil, and the lords were no less grasping in the Reformed present than the abbots and bishops had been in the medieval past.

The basic hardships of the country were rooted in its poverty,

bad communications, and in the lawlessness of many of the clan chiefs. While in theory the clan chiefs owed their allegiance to the sovereign, the practice was very different. This discrepancy, in some measure, caused the downfall of Mary Stuart. An additional factor was, of course, her allegiance to the Roman Catholic religion which, by the time Queen Mary arrived in Scotland, was already fighting a losing battle with the parallel fanaticism of the Reformers.

In the years immediately preceding Mary Stuart's birth, Henry VIII had sacked Edinburgh, and he continued to alternate between policies of seeking a royal marriage between his son and Mary Stuart, the infant Queen, and either waging outright war and devastation, or resorting to threats of war. In this he was helped by the clan system and its factions.

The fact that the Scottish peers were often in the pay of the English king did not lead to improved relations with clans who were not, or to the general pacification of the country. Bribery was, and continued to be, even in the age of Elizabeth, a plank in England's Scottish policy.

On the Borders between England and Scotland, and in the Highlands, a system prevailed which, in many respects, fell little short of anarchy. The clan system led to bloody feuds which continued from generation to generation, and it was only when these rose to intolerable, anarchic heights that the sovereign of Scotland intervened and was compelled to lead a punitive expedition against the warring chieftains.

Officially, the clan chiefs were responsible for the actions of their followers, but when, as was often the case, the chiefs were engaged in the same depredations against the farmers as their followers, there was no material benefit for them to be on the side of the law in general, or on the side of the sovereign in particular. The reavers or plunderers continued to seize cattle or crops as and when the opportunity arose.

The method employed by the sovereign against the chiefs at this time showed a classic simplicity. When it became obvious that action would have to be taken, the sovereign would muster a force and lead a raid against the plunderers, and, if caught, the chiefs and some of their followers were hanged on the spot, and that, for a while, was that.

The following incidents show the difficulties which at this period beset the sovereign and law-abiding citizens, and the often piece-meal methods employed in an attempt to cope with them.

Shortly after her marriage to Darnley, Mary Stuart and her husband were obliged to set out to suppress a rebellion. The way of raising troops for the crown was by proclamation.

'There was a proclamation at the Market Cross of Edinburgh, commanding all and sundry earls, lords, barons, freeholders, gentlemen, and substantious yeomen to address them with fifteen days victuals, to pass and convoy the King and Queen to the parts of Fife, under the pain of loss of life, lands and goods, and also commanding all and sundry the inhabitants of the burgh of Edinburgh between sixteen and sixty to address them in the same manner, under the pains aforesaid.'

The net was flung wide and, as Edinburgh was one of the most prosperous of the trading towns, this kind of interruption and general disruption of the work of the city added in its turn to the impoverishment of the general exchequer, as well as causing certain disputes.

In the autumn of 1565, the Queen and her husband tried to make some of the notables of the city of Edinburgh lend them money, 'which they refused to do'. Subsequently they were 'commanded to remain in ward within the old tower where my lord of Moray lodges, wherein they remained'.

Eventually a compromise was reached, and the notables were allowed to go free on producing ten thousand merks 'upon the superiority of Leith under reversion'. This presumably meant that they had demanded some collateral for their loan. They also made another deal—they would pay £1,000 so that the whole town should be allowed to remain at home.

This sovereign's troubles with her recalcitrant subjects were not only in the realm of minor rebellions but she had, in addition, to contend with constant lack of money. There were no actual revenues accruing to the crown and, although at the time of the Dissolution of the Monasteries an attempt was made to secure crown revenues, this was not successful, owing to the opposition of both the Lords of the Congregation and the Reformers, twin opposers of the power of the crown.

An additional difficulty, which did not add to the prosperity of the Border territories, was that the country in the Lowlands was fertile, and that the 'moss troopers' from the less favoured country over the border in Northumberland were in the habit of carrying out raids against cattle and crops. The peasants were therefore threatened not only by raids from their own countrymen but also by raids from England. Bothwell was badly wounded in an affray of this kind when leading an expedition against 'a small fierce tribe called the Elliotts', who inhabited territory near the frontier with England.

Nor did these raids cease with the flight of the Queen, and in October 1567, when Scotland was ruled by the Regent Moray, 'there was a proclamation to meet the Regent in Peebles upon the 8th November next, for the repressing of the thieves in Annandale and Eskdale, but my Lord Regent, thinking they would get advertisement [i.e. might be warned] he came over the water secretly and lodged in Dalkeith'. Rather cannily the Regent decided to set out earlier than planned and as a result 'he came both secretly and suddenly, and there took thirty-four thieves, whom he partly caused to hang and partly drown; five he let free upon caution, and upon the 2nd day of November he brought another ten with him to Edinburgh, and there put them in irons'.

Although the 'small fierce tribe called the Elliotts' are not specifically referred to in this case, the Lord Treasurer's Accounts record a payment to Andrew Lindsay, the keeper of the Tolbooth prison, for 'furnishing of meat and drink to Robert Elliott (alias Clement's Hob), Archy Elliott (called Archy Kene)'. Further disbursements are recorded for 'Robert Elliott alias Mirk Hob, Gavin Elliott called Gavin of Ramsiegill, Martin Elliott called Martin of Heuchous, Robert Elliott son to Elder Wil, and Robert Elliott called The Vicar's Rob, and another Robert Elliott called Hob of Thorlieshope'. Obviously the habit of thieves operating under aliases is not new.

In November 1567 an act of the Privy Council refers to the habit of the thieves of Liddesdale of holding people to ransom. Their methods seem to have borne certain resemblances to the present day Mafia. The Privy Council states 'that many persons are content to pay blackmail to these thieves and sit under their protection permitting them to reave, harry, and oppress their neighbours in their sight without contradiction or stop'. It was a case of money paid for a little peace and quiet, even if the neighbours suffered.

14

The Privy Council forbade such practices under pain of heavy penalties and stated that,

'when any companies of thieves or broken men comes over the valleys within the in-country, all dwelling in the bounds shall incontinent cry on hie, raise the fray, and follow them, as well in their in-passing as out-passing, in order to get back the stolen goods or beasts'.

Many of these decrees were ignored, for the physical forces did not exist for the general pacification of the country. During the Regency of Mary's mother, Marie de Guise Lorraine, further attempts were made to restore order, but the Government could neither raise sufficient forces to achieve this, nor even find generals who were willing to attempt the herculean work. For example, in 1553, the Master of Maxwell very sensibly declined the honour of being Warden of the Western Marches. He was offered £500 a year, an immense sum at the time, and various other tempting rewards to induce him to take on the pacification of the Borders. He still declined, because the Government could not muster sufficient forces to make the task a healthy proposition. Sir James Douglas accepted the post, but after some months gave up. The disorders in the region became steadily worse and continued into the reign of Mary Stuart, and on into the Regency of Moray. The peaceful growing of crops, or raising of beasts was fraught with heartbreak. The fruits of agriculture, carried out with primitive tools, and the beasts, reared in a difficult, damp climate, were always at hazard. The hard toil of the Lowland peasant was set against these seemingly endless border raids, the depredations of the clans, and the general hazards of a life which was often short as well as brutish and hard.

In the Highlands life was no less difficult, with added special features, and the climate was more harsh. Here the crown delegated its powers of life and death to the local overlord, the Earl of Huntley in the north, or the Earl of Argyll in the west, thus saving a good deal of highly uncomfortable travelling and hazardous campaigning.

It can easily be seen that such methods, though convenient, did not eradicate the inner evil of factions. Indeed, in many cases it extended the possible cabals of chiefs and earls against the sovereign, because by transferring their allegiances they could often out-number the sovereign's forces with their own clan followers. Nor did

SCOTLAND UNDER MARY STUART

the execution of summary justice by the sovereign, or the sovereign's delegates, pacify the country. Even less did it put down the blood feuds, since each hanging gave serious cause for revenge against the sovereign, or against other clan chiefs.

Blood feuds were indeed a major curse. Hundreds of years of internal wars and raids had augmented this evil. One murder by an opposing clansman, a hanging by a sovereign, a killing in a Border raid, was never forgotten either by the surviving members of the immediate family, or the kinsmen in the clan. On a simple basis of arithmetical progression, the numbers of blood feuds must have grown at a terrifying rate with resultant bitterness and disorders.

The main difference between the Borderers and the Highlanders was the complete loyalty which the latter owed to their chiefs. The Highlanders were bound in honour to love and respect their chiefs and to stand by them in prosperity or misfortune, to die for them in battle, if need be, and to support them—even against the sovereign or the law—should that prove necessary.

The contemporary pictures painted of the Highland Scots often refer to them as savages or 'wild Scots'. Sebastian Munster of the University of Heidelberg in his famous *Cosmographia*, a standard reference book in the sixteenth century, says: 'In the other part, which is mountainous, dwell a kind of people much tougher and fiercer who are called the wild Scots. These are dressed in such a manner as the Irish and go with legs bare to the knee. Their arms are a bow and arrow with a very large sword, and a dagger.'

Loyalty is an admirable quality, but the loyalty of the 'wild Scots' to their chieftains was of such an extended nature that it certainly did not benefit the country or diminish the difficulties of the ruling sovereign. This background of loyalties, indeed, explains in some measure the sea of troubles against which the two queens, Marie de Guise Lorraine and Mary Stuart, had to contend. They were both in essence French queens, dedicated to the proposition that the sovereign's writ ran paramount. But they were ostensibly ruling a country where, as we have seen, normal law and order did not prevail, and where their pretensions to power, over their nobility in particular or the countryside in general, had no validity.

In many of the nations of Europe at this time, kings and emperors were increasing their own power by curbing that of the nobles, but in Scotland this process had not even begun. The Scottish nobility, by their clan system, had actually increased their power over more

16

than two centuries. In addition, when the coming of the Reformed religion threw the estates and lands of the Church into their laps, their power was augmented still further, and at the accession of Mary Stuart they had reached the summit of their influence and riches, although as far as the general state of the country was concerned the term 'riches' was comparative. All were poor by standards prevailing in many other countries, but some were poorer than others.

The fact that some of the Scottish peers were not resplendent figures is made plain by this description of them at the coronation of James VI and I (quoted by John Aubrey):

'And at the erse of them marches the Scottish peeres
With lowzie shirts, and mangie wrists, went pricking up
    their eares.'

As with the nobility, so with the majority of the community; for against the background of lawlessness it was impossible not only for the peasantry, but even the ordinary trading community, to increase their well-being, though there were certain pockets of prosperity. These were mainly around the ports which were connected by trade and culture to the Continent.

Where internationalism touched Scotland—in the court, in the circles of the rich trading merchants, in the ambience of the princes of the Church and the monasteries before their ultimate decline— different standards did prevail. But these were circles which contained only small numbers of people. Their prosperity did not even begin to reach vast tracts of the countryside and the mountainous districts.

Symptomatic of the wretched state of the kingdom was the number of vagrants and beggars which was constantly increasing. Special laws were passed in certain towns against alien beggars, for while these towns and villages were reluctantly willing to undertake a modicum of support for characters they considered to be well-known 'no goods' from their own district, they were not willing to undertake any form of responsibility for beggars from other districts. This situation was brought about by the fact that the cities and towns were autonomous. They ruled their own area independently, and they were often entirely uninterested in the effects of their policies on adjacent towns, or the district in general.

As always, in times of reform and upheaval, the decay of the old ideas of religion and order led to certain dislocations. The monasteries had been the guardians of culture. They often ran schools, universities and centres of learning for poor clerks and scholars. They provided a certain relief for the armies of beggars, and support for their own tenants when they fell on evil days. They were the nucleus of an organized system of farming. Admittedly it was based on a method of tied feudal labour, but at least the abbot or prior had some responsibility for his 'men'.

The abbots and bishops, with their great wealth, their mistresses, and their rich attire, had given open scandal, but many of their more humble followers had provided much humanitarian relief. With the seizure of the monastic and church 'biens' by the nobles, all these sources of primitive social security disappeared.

The clerics had taken tithes from their tenants, and had in addition exacted a primitive form of military service from them. It could be said that this was a 'protection' racket, and that it was to the advantage of the churchmen to have a small field force to protect their broad lands against raiders and the general lawlessness of the country.

Yet once the dismantling of the apparatus of the Church had taken place, the lawlessness was not decreased. The general condition of the peasantry was not improved. Nor was the Reformed Church able to supply the financial deficiency, for they were not the inheritors of the Church's wealth.

The lack of communications between castles, towns, and villages made the general lawlessness even more difficult to remedy than it might have been. The condition of the roads was so bad as to make wheeled traffic useless. A few carriages were known, but only among the very rich. Queen Marie de Guise is known to have imported one.

Even horses, though extensively used, were expensive, costing £10, a huge sum when it is set against a wage as low as six or seven shillings a year. Saddles and bridles were unknown to the general run of the people, and farmers rode to church or to the market on pillions made of hair. Only the forefeet of their horses were shod.

It was no wonder that Mary Stuart, on her arrival in Scotland, wept when she saw the horses provided for her French relatives and courtiers who had accompanied her from France. It was a far cry from the milk-white palfreys with fine leather saddles and bridles to which she was accustomed in France.

In the broad historical context, the peasantry were to achieve little progress over the centuries between 1300 and the beginning of the eighteenth century, and this was certainly partly due to the poor communications.

Yet Sebastian Munster paints an almost lyrical picture of the potentialities of Scotland.

'Scotland is not equal in fertility to England except that it has more fish and white beasts, because the harbours are good and safe, and the tide enters more easily. The lakes, marshes, rivers and springs are full of fish so that the salmon there are so large they sell for a crown apiece. In many places, Scotland is mountainous, and above the mountains is an even plain which gives abundant pasture to cattle. Near the city of Aberdeen there is much forest, and it is thought that this is the Caledonian Forest of which Ptolemy makes mention. It begins about two leagues where is the palace of the King of Scotland. Beyond Scotland towards the North are the Orkney Isles which in our time are all inhabited, and oats and barley grow there but no wheat. They have very good pasture, and many white beasts.'

Sir David Lindsay, in his poem 'The Dreme', paints a very similar picture, and speaks of

'the abundance of fishes in our seas, fruitful mountains for our beasts, for our corn many a lusty vale, the rich rivers pleasant and profitable, the lusty lochs with fish of sundry kinds, hunting, hawking for nobles "convenabill", forests full of deer, roe, harts and hinds, the fresh fountains whose wholesome crystal strands refresh the flourishing meads, so lack we nothing that to nature needs. Of every metal we have the rich mines, both gold, silver and precious stones—although we lack both spices and wines, and other strange delicious fruits, we have meat, drink, fire, clothes that might be made abounding. More fair people of greater ingenuity and of more great strength great deeds to endure. I marvel greatly I assure you considering the people and the land that riches should not in this realms abound.'

He might well marvel considering the picture he had painted.

But Sebastian Munster puts his finger on the troubles besetting Scotland.

'Between England and Scotland there is perpetual war, and there is no hope of composing it unless the two kingdoms should be united by royal marriage. The Scots do not differ in manners and customs from the Irish from whom they originated; when the sky is clear one can see Ireland from Scotland. Further their language, their customs and their dress are alike. They are very intelligent as their learning shows for whatever subject they apply themselves to they readily profit by. They are proud, quick to revenge, strong in war, and to endure hunger, thirst and wakefulness. Those who dwell in the southern part, which is the best are very courteous, and more highly civilized than the rest; they use the English language. Because there is hardly any forest, they make fire of black stones which they extract from the ground.'

What Munster did not mention was that the difference between the 'wild Scots' and those of the Lowlands was not only a difference of language but a difference of background and a difference of blood.

The northern Scots had been invaded from Ireland, and by the ninth century, with the Picts, they eventually formed one Gaelic-speaking nation. This nation started to spread southwards by conquest, first into the British kingdom of Strathclyde, which spoke Welsh. Then the great Anglian capital of Edinburgh fell to them. Finally, under Kenneth III, in the tenth century, the Lothians came into the possession of the 'wild Scots' from the north.

But one of the conditions which the conquered managed to exact from the ruling of their country by the conquerors was that they should keep their own laws and their own speech. This speech was 'Inglis', descended from the speech of the German tribes which had conquered parts of Britain in the fifth and sixth centuries. It bore many resemblances to the speech of Bede and Caedmon, and was the original speech of many of the northern territories in Britain. From the conquered Lowlands 'Inglis' gradually spread northwards, and eventually only the Highlands preserved their original Gaelic in daily speech. Right up until the sixteenth century the main Scottish tongue was known as Inglis.

But as the various wars with England caused bitterness between the countries the name of the old speech of the Lowlands changed from Inglis to Scottis, and by the time Mary Queen of Scots ascended the throne the Scottis language had separated itself from the mainstream of the developments in the true English tongue.

It was the internationalism of the Reformation and the joining together of the two kingdoms under James I and VI which caused the Scottis tongue to join again with the mainstream of English literature and speech, although the Scottis language lived on in lyrical poetry to the age of Burns, and has echoes in the prose of Scott and even of James Barrie and other Scottish writers.

Another force for linguistic change was the spread of the Bible in the vernacular. Owing to the fact that there were innumerable delays over the publishing of the Bible in Scottish, by the time it came to be printed more widely in Scotland it was printed in current English and so caused the gradual decay of the original 'Inglis' tongue. Furthermore, the Reformers considered English to be a grander, more rhetorical form of speech, well suited to the great perorations and rolls of verbal thunder to which John Knox and the 'Saints' were addicted.

Munster goes on to say: 'The Scots differ in law and government from the English, for they use the Civil Law like other folk, and the English have nothing but their statutes and customs.' Although Scottish law was based on Roman law, what Munster failed to mention was that often, in effect, law was non-existent in large areas of the country.

The population of Scotland in the sixteenth century numbered about 700,000, and the bulk of this population were the peasants, at first toiling for the Church, and then for the nobility, their lives spent in smoke-filled hovels, which they shared with their cattle.

Although shoes were one of the few items which could easily be made in Scotland, as hides were one of the country's exports, they were a luxury to be worn only to kirk or to market. Women's dress was of the simplest kind, a loose garment of linsey woolsey hanging from the shoulders, worn over a petticoat.

Against this background of intense and grinding poverty among the great mass of the people, it was not surprising that John Knox should have been able to rouse resentment against the luxury of Mary Stuart's court. While peasant women dragged men and hay wains across rough rivers and rougher country, the court at the summit seemed full of frivolity, soft music, dancing, and ladies dressed in velvet robes and hung about with gold chains.

To contrast the Penicuik jewels, those intricate pieces of Renaissance work set with pearls and rich stones, with the primitive state of the general lives of the people is to see illustrated, in telling reality, the gulfs between rich and poor. These gulfs have existed in every country and century to a greater or lesser degree, but in Scotland they existed against a background in which the powerful could guarantee, as recompense, neither justice nor sufficient food nor physical security.

The huge fortresses and castles which stood as sentinels in the Marches, and at strategic points all over the country, were not the guarantees of the safety of the people, but a physical expression of the power of the sovereign or the nobility. When Mary Stuart travelled across the country, she rode from strong-point to strong-point. In the sixteenth century the castle or fort could be equated with the possession of a strong fleet in the nineteenth century.

At the height of his power over the country—and over the Queen —Bothwell was awarded the possession of the castles of Dunbar and of Edinburgh. It is difficult at this distance of time to understand the importance of such gifts. Yet the whole history of the period illustrates it, for the reduction of the local fortress by siege was a paramount necessity to gain power over the surrounding countryside.

Scottish castles were built on a more primitive pattern than the English ones, and because of the troubled state of the country, they retained their importance far longer. During the sixteenth century they began to take on some of the features of the French *châteaux-forts*, adding turrets, gables, dormer windows, and decorated mouldings. Some of the improvements made by French architects can be seen in Stirling Castle, which was largely reconstructed in the reign of Mary Stuart's father. But these evidences of civilization were in the interior of the fortress, and the walled gardens in Stirling and Craigmillar were still protected by stout stone defences and steep inclines.

The romantic pictures of sixteenth-century ladies tending their herb gardens, and watching the flight of doves from dovecotes have charm, but ignore certain practicalities. The herbs were used in primitive medicine and for flavouring unappetising meat. The doves were for the table. And although the interior walls were often hung with tapestries, or in some cases protected by wainscotting, the castles were neither comfortable nor warm.

They still remained fortresses and were used as such.

Sanitation was almost non-existent. Bothwell, who was suffering from dysentry, asked his servant, 'French Paris', to show him some place where he could go, and was shown 'an embrasure between two doors'. This stark fact brings into prominence the reason why the court moved so frequently from one castle to another. After a few months residence the living quarters had become untenable. Nor was it surprising that pestilence raged in the cities, for the ordure was thrown out of the windows, and passers-by took their chance.

In spite of the massive buildings which surrounded the castles and towers of the period, the private rooms were very small, possibly due to the fact that they were easier to heat. John Knox's study is little larger than a modern hanging cupboard, and even the chamber in which Riccio was murdered at Holyrood Palace is only twelve feet by ten, less than the size of many a modern suburban sitting room.

Much of the furniture was portable, and noblemen had their beds carried into their apartments each evening. They were removed before breakfast, so that the bedroom then became a reception room. The bedrooms of other less well-endowed persons were nothing but recesses in the wall.

Like the Romans, the Scottish nobles lived in public, and their reception rooms were used to impress. The painted gallery of Pinkie House was 120 feet long, and the public rooms in Stirling and Holyrood are very large chambers.

This is understandable. The nobility and the sovereign were constantly accompanied by armed men, and it was thus a matter of convenience that the public rooms should be able to accommodate numbers of halberdiers and servants. There was a dual necessity for this, to impress upon the people the power of the sovereign, and to save him, if possible, from assassination. It did not, of course, preclude death from treachery, owing to the halberdiers and servants having changed their clan allegiances.

The lords and lairds copied the sovereign in being accompanied by bodies of their followers. But the presence of large bodies of armed men does not necessarily make for prosperity. Side by side with the fact that neither commerce nor agriculture made real progress during the sixteenth century in Scotland, the value of money against silver fell.

In 1544 the value of a pound of silver in Scotland was £9 10s od and by 1565 it had risen to £18. In England, a more prosperous country, a pound of silver was valued at this time at between £2 and £3.

This alone gives an idea both of the poverty of Scotland at this time, and of the shortage of currency. Laws were passed to try to stabilize the currency and to forbid both the importation of false coins, and the export of silver coins. That death was the punishment for refusal to accept certain currencies issued by the Government gives an idea of the distrust felt by the people in their debased coinage. According to the old Chinese adage, death and taxes are the only certainties in life, and it is equally sure that when times are disturbed, and government either unstable or distrusted, the currency declines and the value of goods rises in proportion.

Life held other perils in sixteenth-century Scotland. A social evil was the belief in witchcraft which seems, curiously enough, to have grown parallel with the spread of the reformed religion. As Our Lady and the old saints fell from their niches, smashed by the zeal of the new 'Saints', as the candles, lights, and flowers were banished from the high altars, so witches were found to be the cause of everything evil which stalked the land from murrain in cattle to aborted children.

In 1563, witchcraft was made punishable by death, and the reformed clergy were assiduous in seeking out and destroying witches. When alleged witches were caught, they were deprived of rest, food, and water, and finally tortured until they confessed. They were subsequently tried, and burned or drowned.

The belief in witches was not confined to the peasantry. Thomas Randolph, the English envoy to Scotland, when writing to William Cecil of Mary Stuart's supposed infatuation for Darnley, puts it down to a posset, and proceeds to give further details as to what the court believed in the matter of the Queen having been attainted by witchcraft.

One witch was indicted for 'common awaytaker of women's milk in the whole country and detaining the same at their pleasure, as the whole country will testify'. Nothing was too extraordinary to be believed, and in one account of a trial, it was stated that a hundred-strong General Meeting of Witches was addressed by a devil wearing a fine black gown and a hat. This story has a strong flavour of *Mr Bolfry*, by James Bridie, but in the context of the tortures and the death, it was not comic.

The Reformed Religion had been spread in Scotland not only by word of mouth, but also by means of the printed word. The coming of the Bible in the vernacular, and the works of Knox and others, had helped to discredit the Roman Catholic Church, which now no longer had the monopoly of learning.

The Reformers sought to mitigate one result of their policies against the monasteries by decreeing the retention of the schools attached to them. Like the rule of law, the ability to read and write was not widespread. Most people were illiterate. There was only one printing press and that was in Edinburgh. Bibles cost more than the year's wages of a servant. And there were only three universities in the whole of the country, at Glasgow, St Andrews and Aberdeen.

The nobility attached to the court of Mary Stuart may have been graceful and accomplished in the arts and literature, but as a general rule they were educated abroad. Thus most of their art was a borrowed culture, from France or from Flanders.

Walter Scott of Harden, one of the Border chiefs and an ancestor of Sir Walter Scott, was married in the year 1567 to Mary Scott of Dryhope, called romantically the 'Flower of Yarrow'. Less romantic was the fact that the marriage contract was signed by a notary because neither of the contracting parties could write their names.

Because of the illiteracy of the population the Reformers used readers and instructors to spread the new religion. The old churches had relied on the abbacies and the monasteries, and picture stories in stained glass and wood, to tell the Bible tales. Bereft of these 'visual aids' in their stripped churches, the Reformers therefore used their lay readers to spread the Word.

But as with so many other reformers, these Reformers soon set about suppressing the views of their opponents. The General Assembly of 1563 passed an act which prohibited the publication of any book, printed or written, if it had any bearing on religion, unless it had been censored by the local churchmen. By 1574 the Privy Council had progressed to the prohibition of the printing of any book at all without a licence from the Government. The penalty for the contravention of this act was death and the confiscation of goods.

The Reformers, while they had encouraged the publication of scurrilous ballads and books against the abuses of the Roman Church, were not disposed to be tolerant to ballad mongers who dared to make fun of the 'Saints'. They were well aware of the influence which popular songs and plays in the past had had on the minds of the people, and how much it had advanced the Reformation in Scotland. They were not going to allow their opponents to counter-attack with the same weapons.

Although the Reformers, having brought the corruption of the church to an end, failed to bring prosperity to Scotland, or pacify the country, they were admittedly dealing with a violent people, accustomed to settle their disputes by violent means. While it is easy to appreciate the graceful well-expressed letters and poems of Mary Stuart in the context of a European culture, it is less easy to reconcile them with the conditions which prevailed in the wild country beyond the towns and the court. It is only in snatches that it is possible to form an opinion of how the ordinary people and even the rough lairds lived.

For example, towards the end of the sixteenth century, Stewart of Ardvorlich, a laird, married the daughter of the King's Keeper of the Royal Forest. Some members of the Clan Macgregor who happened to be passing through the Royal Forest killed off a few of the King's deer. Summary justice was meted out to them for this infringement of the royal hunting rights. They lost their ears, and were sent home bloody, but far from bowed. In their rocky fastnesses the rest of the Macgregors brooded on the evil done to their clansmen.

They made their plans, captured the Royal Forester, and cut off his head.

At this time in Scotland, and especially in the Highlands, it was the custom that hospitality must be given to travellers, either if they claimed kinship or if they were genuine wayfarers in need of a roof or food. In view of the robbers, reavers, and beggars who swarmed across the countryside, it seems to have been a charity which had its dangers.

The Macgregors happened to hear that the laird of Ardvorlich was absent from home. So they set off carrying the head of his father-in-law wrapped up in a plaid. They knocked at the house, and requested hospitality. (A recent writer suggests that the laird's wife must have known about the feud between the clans, and have recognized the Macgregors by their tartans. But some writers on Scottish costume say that many of the clans did not at this early date wear distinctive tartans, and that many of them wore saffron kilts which served as a form of camouflage, like khaki, which blended with the heather and made concealment easier.)

Whether the laird's lady recognized them or not, the custom of Highland hospitality demanded that she should offer them food. Like any good housewife she produced cheese and oatcakes and bread. While she was out of the room, perhaps producing drink to wash the simple meal down, the Macgregors perfected their revenge.

When the lady returned, she saw as the centrepiece of the table the bloodstained head of her father with bread and cheese in its mouth.

The wretched woman shrieked and rushed from the house. When the laird returned his wife had disappeared. Subsequently the cottagers found that their cows seemed to be giving no milk. This was possibly one of those cases where witchcraft might have been suspected, but the peasants kept watch, and found that the laird's wife had been milking their cows. She was followed and discovered near the shores of a loch, and taken home demented, later to give birth to a son who, in his turn, committed a murder.

Meanwhile, the murdering Macgregors, perhaps having second thoughts about their neat revenge, set out for the headquarters of their clan chief, Alasdair of Glenstrae, and demanded protection. The clan was called together and they met in the church where the gory head was set as a decoration on the high altar. The young chief, placing his hands on the head, swore to defend the murderers with his life.

The Government in Edinburgh heard of these bloody doings, and 'the Lords of the Secret Council, being credibly informed of the cruel and mischievous proceedings of the wicked Clan Gregor so long continuing in blood, slaughters, herships, manifest reifs and stouchs' outlawed the whole clan, and they were condemned to death.

Lord Drummond was granted 'letters of fire and sword' against the clan, and subsequently he was joined by the dead man's son-in-law, Stewart of Ardvorlich. Together they killed twelve of the Clan Macgregor. But, judging by the history of feuds in the Highlands, it is quite probable that this was not the end of the story of revenge of the exchange of ears and a head.

The Macgregors were known as 'Children of the Mist' and it is indeed easy to see that the mist and the mountains were the allies of violence. They came from the mist, and, their deeds of violence done, they faded into the mist again.

This story could stem from one of the more violent scenes in *Macbeth*. Shakespeare did not take a rosy or lyrical view of Scotland as is shown by his reference to it in the *Comedy of Errors*.

Antipholus.   In what part of her body stands Ireland?
Dromio.   Marry, sir, in her buttocks: I found it by the bogs.
Antipholus.   Where Scotland?
Dromio.   I found it by the barrenness; hard in the palm of
              the hand.

It was in the context of the poverty and ruthlessness of the people of the country that the Reformers were able to blame all the ills of the country on the capon-fed churchmen and the claret-swilling abbots. Every century sees a reform as a new beginning, and the sixteenth-century Scots cannot be characterized as more gullible than people in any other century. It is in the nature of human endeavour to see the disappearance of night and the rise of a rosy dawn in the mouthings of politicians. It is also in the nature of the oppressed and the ill-fed to believe that any change must be a change for the better.

John Knox proclaimed against Mary Stuart,

'Let men patiently abide and turn unto their God, and then shall he either destroy that whore in her whoredome or else he shall put in the hearts of the multitudes to take the same vengeance upon her that has been "tane of Jesabell and Athalia . . ." for greater abominations was never in the nature of any woman than is in her, whereof we have but seen only the buds, but we will after taste of the ryip fruit of her impiety, if God cutte not hir days schort.'

Although Mary's days were cut short, and she was driven from her kingdom, the ryip fruit of the Reformation was not always to the taste of all the people, nor could it be.

Scotland was a harsh, turbulent and dangerous country for all its inhabitants, and rich and poor suffered equally in different ways. The poor could lose their cattle and their crops, but the rich might as easily lose their lands by confiscation and their heads by the axe.

CHAPTER TWO

THE ORGANIZATION OF SOCIETY

It is not possible to refer to the 'organization' of society in sixteenth-century Scotland. It would be more accurate simply to draw attention to attempts on the part of various governing bodies to suppress the general turmoil.

In every country the organization of society is like a section of a rock face, with new layers and old layers built one upon the other. The decay of old ways of behaving and old laws does not take place within a few years; it is a gradual process of erosion. The Scots' kings of the twelfth and thirteenth centuries brought the feudal system to Scotland, and attempted to put the whole country into the orderly shape demanded by the feudal structure. But this was done gradually and over a great number of years; the feudal system was superimposed on the old system, and sometimes worked in conjunction with it. The old laws and the old customs were eroded very slowly.

A general picture of feudal society was that the sovereign stood at the head of the kingdom. Under him were the earls and barons who held their lands under him. Equal to them, and sometimes richer and more powerful, were the princes of the Church and the abbots. These were the first two of the Three Estates, and finally there were the burgesses in the Royal Burghs. But apart from these three classes, there were other gradations in society. There was a class holding certain rights over their own land; there were independent freemen; and there were the peasants who actually tilled the soil, whether they worked the land for the lord or laird or whether they were attached to a monastery, or worked for a wealthy burgess.

Originally the peasant class had been serfs or villeins, and the early charters of the great abbeys show records of the transference of these serfs, called 'nativi'. For example, the prior of Coldingham bought from one laird a man called Hog with his sons and daughters for three merks of silver (about £1). Some of such serfs were attached to the abbeys for three or four generations.

The same system applied to the great lords. The peasants were his chattels, they were his labour force, and the generating power of his military strength, and while the vassals were bound to serve their lords as soldiers, the lord was bound in his turn to supply soldiers to the sovereign on demand.

Although a great distinction was made between the freemen and the villein, they were both vassals of the lord. He was responsible for administering the laws amongst them and in return they could claim his protection.

Parts of this system were still in evidence in the sixteenth century, but the whole structure was undergoing a process of change, and vassals were gradually evolving into new classes of freemen, tenants, and sub-tenants. In many cases it was difficult for some of these classes to claim any rights to the land, but a different system and a different view of the rights of the peasant class was gradually evolving.

Nevertheless, in the sixteenth century the essential idea of the lord having rights over his followers, and he in his turn owing duties to them, still pertained.

An idea of the interrelated duties can be gauged from some negotiations carried on between the peasants attached to an abbey in Tweeddale and the abbot. The 'men' were anxious to have their rights clarified with the abbot. They wished to appoint a bailiff of their own race to represent them—perhaps the equivalent of a modern shop steward.

They asked for the support of the abbey should any of them fall into poverty or old age. The abbot said that the abbey was not bound to give support, but would do so 'out of affection for its men'. The other question asked was whether they could receive sanctuary if they were fugitives from the law. The abbot said they would receive the same sanctuary as if they were strangers. The final question was, would the abbey pay the fines for a serious crime of one of its 'men'?

The answer to this last question was an unqualified no.

The little exchange highlights the fact that the rights of the lord abbot and his duties towards his men, although shadowy in essence, were often quite strong in fact. In the same way, the duties of the lords towards their vassals were founded on a basis of mutual loyalties, help and protection. If they committed crimes he was bound to protect them, as they were bound to give him support in war, whether local or national. This paternalism existing between the lords or abbots and their peasants would explain the endurance of a system which very often seems harsher on paper than it was in practice.

A good deal was still expected of the underlings in the sixteenth century. They could be asked for payment if the eldest son of the lord was knighted, and they must contribute to the marriage of an eldest daughter. It was said to be doubtful whether tenants could be forced to help him in purely personal feuds or help out with the marriages of younger daughters.

The original grant of land to a knight was supposed to give him a reasonable way of life, and in exchange for the land he was expected to supply defenders for his own land and for the country. Sometimes rent for the land was demanded by the sovereign, or at other times the land was given away for services rendered to the sovereign. The grant included every kind of right in the land: rights to grow crops and to pasture cattle, the rights to exclude people from using the roads and paths; rights over moors, marshes, running water and ponds, fish ponds, parks for game, as well as brushwood and heaths; the right to cut turf and peat; the right to salt-pans; exclusive rights over mills and to impose dues for grinding corn. His rights over the free tenants meant that he could demand help with the harvest, rights to demand messengers, to convey goods, to labour on the roads, and this included the labour of their bondmen and their services.

Other rights of the overlord were still a cause of great unrest. The cattle of underlings could be impounded, and his goods distrained on for non-payment of dues, and 'if any dwells upon land pertaining to a free man, and as a husbandman holds lands of him' dies, then the master can demand the best beast of his cattle.

The lord might take over the land if the tenant died without heirs, or even take it from his heirs. He could also resume ownership if the tenant committed murder and fled from the country, or if the tenant did not give the labour which was demanded under the contract for the land. Fines were levied on tenants who did not keep their land free of weeds. Many of these old 'service' tenancies were still being exacted as late as the eighteenth and nineteenth centuries in Scotland.

It is not possible to make overall assumptions about the power of the feudal overlords in Scotland, however, because this system was superimposed on the old Gaelic laws and customs, and some of them, like the clan system, survived this feudalization.

All through the later history of Scotland, the clan system was interwoven with the feudal system. The younger brothers, cousins, and cousins-once-removed, are found in old rent rolls as sub-tenants of the clan chief in such a way as to make it apparent that, although the feudal system worked on the surface, underneath the old clan loyalties were still of paramount importance to the working of society as a whole.

Although the clan system was an institution which stemmed from ancient Ireland, it spread from the Highlands into other parts of Scotland, even into those parts of the Lowlands where the people were Anglian and the nobles Scoto-Norman. In 1587, in laws dealing with the unruly subjects in the country, it mentions 'the Clans that have Captains, Chiefs and Chieftains upon whom they depend . . . as well on the Borders as in the Highlands'.

The partial erosion of the feudal system in Scotland was due to the fierce wars of independence against England. This meant that the peasantry was freed from the feudal system without any great struggles, and there grew up a different system of landlord and tenant relationship. The Scots peasantry may not have suffered some of the greater hardships of the feudal system in some districts, yet the clan system produced other disadvantages.

Scotland under the Queen Regent, Mary of Guise Lorraine, and under her daughter, Mary Queen of Scots, was a country without effective central government, dominated by lords, because the grant of a barony or earldom to a landowner made him not only the owner of the land but the virtual king of it. He was the military leader of the land under his sway, he was the judge of the men under him, and had powers of life and death over his followers and peasants. The greatest lords not only had these powers, but they had barons, heralds and pursuivants and councils of retainers, and their armed followers gave them a private army.

Their forces were not inconsiderable.

During the reign of James IV, the Spanish Ambassador noted that there were some thirty-five powerful barons, and most of them were able to raise some five or six thousand men, while the Lord of the Isles had followers numbering ten thousand.

During the reign of Mary Queen of Scots, Huntley, Governor of the North, had between six and seven thousand men under his

James Stuart, Earl of Moray

John, Earl of Mar

James Hamilton, Earl of Arran

3. *Top:* Falkland Palace, the courtyard;   *bottom:* Holyrood Chapel and Palace, north side

command, Bothwell and Home had a thousand men each, and when Arran was Governor his followers amounted to eight thousand men.

The powers of Huntley, as Lieutenant of the North, extended not only over the whole of the north of Scotland, but included the Isles. Responsible for law and order, and raising armies, he could bear the royal banner, make statutes and ordinances, and invade the land of those who rebelled not only against the Queen but against himself.

He could imprison the rebels, seize their castles, imprison and execute them, or pardon them.

Two royal castles were in his possession, as well as five of his own, and he was in control of the many other strong points of his sub-chiefs and supporters.

These great lords also had the power of fire and sword. A proclamation issued in 1528 gives this power to heads of clans, commanding them to 'pass upon the Clan Chatten and invade them to their utter destruction by slaughter, burning, drowning and other ways and leave no creature living of that clan except priests, women and bairns'. This order for slaughter was undertaken by the Earl of Moray, but although he executed a number of the leaders of the clan, he by no means succeeded in killing them all.

The legal powers were given to the lords simply because they were powerful, and although these commissions giving sweeping powers to the lords were common between the years of 1545 and 1550, they became even more common in the troubled times between 1568 and 1579.

Mary of Guise Lorraine tried to mitigate the powers of the nobles by proposing a paid army of mercenaries, but her idea was cried down, because, as we have seen, the absence of absolute power in the hands of the sovereign meant, in effect, that the crown was in the hands of the nobles. They could give or withdraw their support at will. Although their grants of land were tied to their liability to put men in the field at the disposal of the sovereign, this support was not always forthcoming.

During the regency of Mary of Guise Lorraine an English spy reported: 'Item, the Earl of Huntley's country, his friends and tenants are straightly commanded to repair to Haddington to the wars, but it is doubtful whether they come or not because the Earl himself is prisoner.'

B

The report shows that the raising of armies by the local lords was still essentially feudal: 'thirty-nine gentlemen would be able to put five thousand men in the field.' The followers of the gentlemen numbered from one thousand to twenty-seven men per gentleman.

An army was gathered together on a somewhat casual basis. One account says:

'The nearest chief gathers the neighbouring folk together and at the first word of the presence of the foe each man before midday is in arms for he keeps his weapons about him, mounts his horse, makes for the enemy's position and whether in order of battle or not rushes on the foe.'

It was not surprising in view of this loose method of assembly and attack that the better organized English were so often able to defeat the Scots in battle.

An additional hazard, as far as the sovereigns of Scotland were concerned, was that very often the Border lords were in the pay of England.

The sixteenth-century statutes made it clear that 'every baron and freeholder must answer at justice ayres (assizes) for his own men upon his own land'. The records of the Privy Council show that there was a 'band', a firm legal bond, by which the landowning classes were held responsible to the sovereign for the rule of law and order in their own territories.

They were responsible for catching and delivering the criminals to the courts, and if they did not do this they were held responsible for the crimes, and could be fined. If a criminal escaped they were forced to evict his family from his farm and stop the criminal returning to his land. They had to raise their followers to catch rebels of the crown and bring them to justice and kill them, or arrest any people who had been 'put to the horn', that is, declared outlaws to justice.

Such was the law in theory. To imagine that it was applied in practice over most of Scotland is the equivalent of thinking that disinterested brotherly love and affection was widespread in England at the time of the appalling Wars of the Roses.

The power of the lords was supreme in their own territories because the possession of the land was the main source of economic wealth. It supplied not only the means of physical subsistence but also supplied the men to keep the population in subjection, and to prevent complete anarchy. Most of the lesser clan chiefs were dependent on the great lords for the physical possession of their own land and for the security of their tenants and peasantry.

The sovereign would sometimes reward his followers with even more land to ensure their loyalty, which often led to the nobles becoming even more powerful. That the government of the country became largely impotent as a result of this vicious circle is undeniable.

The ineffectiveness of the sovereign was not only due to the lack of a standing army but also to the poverty of the crown. Mary Queen of Scots' father, James V, was so poor that his expenses could not be met from his revenues. The method of raising revenue was extremely primitive and the factions against the crown did not make it any easier to collect taxes. Very often the court moved about in order to consume their dues on the spot—eating their way around the country.

Under James V, the Spanish Ambassador recorded that the crown revenues from land and pasture were 40,000 ducats, from customs 28,000, from fines etc. 25,000, and other revenues only 20,000 ducats. It can be seen that the value of agriculture to the crown was far higher than that of trade. This illustrates the power of the nobles, the possessors of the land.

It may now be convenient to consider certain aspects of Scottish society separately.

Rise of the Burghs and Burgesses

Although industry was comparatively unimportant in sixteenth-century Scotland there was nevertheless an increase in trade, and with the increase the power of the Royal Burghs made some progress.

The sixteenth-century town was a small collection of thatched houses. These were grouped around the castle, or the abbey, which formed their physical and economic protection.

The burgesses held their trading rights direct from the sovereign and in this way formed a gradually-growing balancing factor in the Scottish economy. Flanders was a rich country at this time, and her burgesses obviously had a growing influence on the manners and modes of the countries with whom they traded, and whose merchants traded with them. This was true of their influence on trade in Scotland.

35

Among the Royal Burghs were the towns of Aberdeen, Berwick, Dunfermline, Edinburgh, Elgin, Haddington, Perth, Roxburgh, and Stirling. Bishops ruled in St Andrews, Glasgow, Brechin and Dunblane, while Jedburgh, Kelso, Dunfermline, the Canongate, and Paisley were attached to the monasteries, who ruled them.

The Officers of the Crown

Under the King was the Chamberlain, the Constable, and the Chancellor. The Chamberlain was at once a court official and the supervisor of the Royal Burghs.

The sheriffs, who also operated under the crown, supervised the shires. Originally, when the sheriffs were appointed, they had been intended to take over the whole organization of the country, and they were to have had powers over the collection of revenues, as well as the dues which the Church had to pay to the crown. But the powers of the nobility intervened between the plan and its fulfilment. As a result, though the old pattern of government by the chiefs still remained, the sheriffdoms were superimposed on the old pattern.

One outcome was that more and more Royal Burghs were formed, and in the burghs the officials were merely the servants of the crown. Over the years the organization of the burghs very often became stronger and freer of interference by the great lords. The Mayor and Bailies became the governors of the town. These were chosen by the whole community of the burgh, and if there was any dispute about their election, then twenty-four 'good men of the said burgh' elected to choose 'one person to rule the said community'.

The powers of the burghs were not clearly defined, but these were the beginnings of true civic organization in Scotland.

The sovereigns of Scotland took an interest in the burghs, partly because they were sources of income from the dues which could be collected from them, and partly because they made a focus of prosperity. They were stable centres, like the monasteries, and were in touch with outside culture, and with the more prosperous centres of the south and overseas.

The sovereigns of Scotland approved of the burghs as centres of economic life, partly perhaps because their Royal Officers were able to put their hands on the revenues of more organized communities. Dumbarton, for example, is referred to as a centre of civilisation, and as a 'protection against a lawless and wild kind of man dwelling in the neighbouring mountainous parts'.

In spite of their comparative stability the burghs only paid one-fifth of the levies on the general wealth of the country. This may in part explain why the merchants were richer in goods and movable assets than the nobles. They were better placed, certainly, to trade 'in kind' with other countries—but was it a form of tax evasion?

The burgesses were a higher and better regarded class than the people who worked with their hands, and a clear distinction is made between the guild merchants and the others. By the terms of the burgh laws no dyer, shoemaker, or butcher might become a guild merchant unless he could guarantee that he did not work with his hands, and was an employer of labour.

The privileges of these guild merchants were well defined. No one except a member of the guild could buy hides, wool, or sheep-skins. No foreigner could trade in these commodities. No butcher was allowed to buy wool or hides 'unless he abjured his axe'.

In this way the guild merchants had the monopoly of handling the richest export from Scotland. Even the powerful lords and lairds had to trade through the guild brethren. In addition to this all the landowners, whether they were free or attached to someone else's land, could only buy and sell at the fairs in the burghs. For, in addition to other monopolies such as the importing of wines, and the making and selling of dyed cloth, the burghs held the monopoly to hold fairs.

The upshot of the monopolies being handled by the town guilds was, that at a time when foreign trade was commencing to become more generalized, the whole of the wealth from this overseas trading fell into their hands. Another result of the establishment of Royal Burghs, meant that trade was concentrated in a few centres round castles and abbeys, or along the eastern seaboard which traded not only with the adjacent seaboard of England but also with the Low Countries.

Right up until the sixteenth century, Brechin had the only market which was outside the jurisdiction of the Royal Burghs. A side effect was that very few industries and very little trade could flourish away from the burghs, which resulted in a certain back-wardness in industry. Another result was that small towns and villages did not grow up in Scotland until well into the eighteenth

37

century, and the Scottish weaving and cloth industry remained very backward until the same date.

The guild merchants also enjoyed other privileges. They were often exempt from paying tolls and customs dues, and this encouraged them to move about their business in Scotland and abroad.

The merchants in the burghs seem to have been amongst the first to have attained to some degree of autonomous government, for although the chamberlain could enquire into the behaviour of the bailies, his was merely the right of inspection, and the bailies themselves carried out their duties, and 'did justice to rich and poor alike'.

In his turn, the chamberlain had to see that the privileges of the burgesses were looked after, especially in connexion with 'strangers and other outsiders'. These rights of burgesses *vis-à-vis* 'outsiders' were considerable. For not only was a 'stranger' not allowed to trade in commodities in the burghs, but he was treated with the gravest suspicion. A burgess was not allowed to harbour him for more than one night unless he was willing to act as a guarantor for the foreigner. Should a burgess trade with a foreigner's money he was liable to a heavy fine. In addition should a foreigner contract a debt which he was unable to pay, all the other foreigners currently in the burgh could be made liable for his debt.

But these wretched foreigners did have a few safeguards. Should there be a lawsuit between a burgess and a foreigner, the burgess had to have a foreigner on his side as guarantor, and the foreigner one burgess.

Castle and Town

Although most of the Royal Burghs grew up around the castles, an absolute distinction was made between the garrison at the castle and the townsmen. If disputes arose between them and the men from the castle were the alleged offending party, then judgement would be carried out at the castle gates, and if the burgesses happened to be the accused parties then the burgh courts would settle the dispute.

The burgesses also had fairly summary powers against what was known as 'upland men'. From these raiders the burgesses were able to take any questionable goods, and they had to ask no one's permission to do so. Even their own bailies did not have to be consulted. It can be seen clearly that the 'wild men' from the hills were regarded as a menace and treated as such. Unfortunately for the burgesses it was often impossible either to catch them or repossess the goods or beasts they had stolen.

The Monasteries as a Civilizing Influence

Although the end of the sixteenth century saw the sudden destruction and decline of the abbacies and monasteries, at the beginning of the century they still had great power and influence. When the monks had first come to Scotland they had been, and were seen to be, a great civilizing force. The Cistercians were famed for their knowledge of agriculture, and all the other orders, from Benedictines, who were the first to come to Scotland, to the White Canons, the Carthusians, and the Augustinians, brought various kinds of knowledge and education.

Sometimes these monks came directly from their mother houses abroad, and at other times they were under the control of English abbeys in the south. In this way they were not only a focus of civilization, but also an international force which linked Scotland to the outside world. There was a constant exchange of information and knowledge between the various houses of the monasteries and many monks journeyed from one foreign monastery to another.

They were cultured, and they were also international.

In the beginning, the kings of Scotland had seen the Church as a useful adjunct to their royal power. As a rule, the churchmen were a useful support for the crown. They had in their hands the weapon of the written word, and this could be used in the service of the sovereign.

Unlike the great lords the abbots, the bishops, and their followers were peaceful men. They had much knowledge of agriculture, kept their flocks and herds in great numbers, cultivated their farmlands, and generally added to the wealth of the country. They formed a more easily ruled and less turbulent element in the state than the lords. Very often they treated their vassals better than the clan chiefs, and, if they used them for any form of military service, it was purely in self-defence, and not against the sovereign.

In the north of Scotland, in Moray, and in the south-west during the twelfth and thirteenth centuries, the Church had been actively used to establish the royal writ.

Caithness and Sutherland, owing to the invasions from the

Norsemen, were virtually no longer under the control of the king at that period. Here a bishopric was established, and the bishop was given the land by the king. This land was subsequently gifted, leased, and generally spread about amongst his own family and retainers. Eventually, this meant that the district was pacified and fell under the general rule of the king, but that he no longer owned it. As a result of this policy of pacification by land gifts, some of the abbots and bishops became much richer than the governing sovereign.

Cardinal Sermoneta, writing to the Pope in 1556, noted that the Church in Scotland 'far surpassed the laity in the wealth and substance of its resources'.

A dozen of these abbeys and priories had been founded by the sovereigns of Scotland, and many of the nobles had been generous in encouraging their growth and endowing them. In proportion to the total wealth of the country, indeed, Scotland contributed much more to the enriching of the Church than other European countries. In this way, because of the backwardness of Scottish agriculture and industries, the Church came to play a larger part in the economic development of Scotland than she did elsewhere.

This, in the end, contributed to her downfall.

The extent of the lands owned by the abbeys and monasteries was enormous. Scone, for instance, had over 3,000 acres in different districts. Dunfermline, also rich, had received twenty-three royal gifts of land. This did not mean that the monks were exclusively occupied with their flocks and crops, for the monasteries had other rights.

They owned fisheries and salt-pans, they took tithes of brushwood, and the skins of animals killed for the royal table. They enjoyed freedom from tolls and had a share in other dues collected for the crown.

At Kelso, beside their sheep and cattle pastures, the monks had other lands from which they drew rent as farms, or which they rented to other workers on the abbey lands. They had fourteen granaries with cottages attached to them, as well as houses for brewing and mills. If the cottagers grew crops on the abbey land, they had to use the abbey mill for grinding it, or the abbey brewhouse for brewing their ale. The abbey was in effect an enormous self-supporting and interrelated industrial unit.

But sometimes the rights of the Church and the burgesses could be in conflict. Special permission was obtained by the abbey of Kelso for their 'men', the labourers and tenants attached to their estate, to sell fuel, timber, bread, and beer 'out of their windows'. Even there an exception was made—they were not to do this on the Roxburgh market-day. The burgesses were keeping a close eye on their rights.

Reasons for the Decline of the Church in the Sixteenth Century

During the twelfth and thirteenth centuries the Church was established in Scotland, and by the fifteenth century she had achieved her maximum power and riches. But the Scottish kings, like many other monarchs, needed money and they saw the constant drain of money to Rome as an evil to be combated. In addition to this they did not agree with the appointment from Rome of the princes of the Church in Scotland. The result was that the Scots began to take a hand in appointing bishops and abbots. Furthermore, because of the immense riches of the Church, laymen started to intervene in its government. A typical example of this occurred in the early part of the sixteenth century.

The archbishopric of St Andrews fell vacant. There were not one, but three people appointed to this rich picking—one by the Queen Mother, Margaret Tudor, another by the Chapter of the Cathedral, and another by the Pope. The Queen's candidate, Douglas, seized the castle of St Andrews. Hepburn, the Chapter's nominee, took the castle and garrisoned it with his followers. The Pope's choice, Forman, went about it a different way: he managed to get Lord Home on his side by giving him the priory of Coldingham.

As a result of this sweetener, Home managed to raise 10,000 men in order to re-take the castle of St Andrews. Unfortunately for Home he did not succeed, and some compromise was reached.

The pickings were then shared out amongst the various members of the warring lords 'to mitigate the minds of the nobility'. Forman, the Pope's choice, managed to get the archbishopric, and also the abbey of Dunfermline in his stewardship. Hepburn got a pension to be paid out of the moneys, and his brother was made Bishop of Moray.

Other characters were then drawn into the general *distribution des biens*. A Gordon relative was made bishop of Aberdeen, a Hamilton, Abbot of Kilwinning. Beaton, then Archbishop of Glasgow, added the abbey of Arbroath to his kingdom, but on the other hand he had to pay a pension to Forman; and one of the Ogilvies became

41

Abbot of Dryburgh. It was said these riches were given to them 'to each one as he was noble, and not conform to his virtue'.

Not only were totally unsuitable people sometimes given these high positions in the Church, but they also very often managed to duplicate or triplicate their rich appointments.

Originally, if a Church post fell vacant a steward could be appointed to administer it in the interim. This was supposed to be a purely temporary arrangement until the new appointment had been confirmed, but the arrangement of stewardships led to abuses. In 1540 to 1558 the Bishop of Orkney also held the abbacy of Kinloss and the priory of Beauly. The Bishop of Moray was also Abbot of Scone.

Finally, this policy of stewardships was carried a stage further, and high positions in the Church were transferred to laymen. Three of James V's illegitimate children were given church positions while they were still infants. James Stuart, afterwards Earl of Moray, half-brother of Mary Stuart, was Prior of St Andrews. The Hamiltons managed to obtain the abbeys of Paisley and Arbroath for relatives.

The practice of appointing stewards was called 'in commendam', and their official name was commendators. It was said that 'of the twenty abbots and priors that sat in the Parliament that effected the Reformation, fourteen were commendators'.

Other reasons for the decline of the Church were the lawlessness of the sixteenth century, and that fact that owing to her riches she was a prey to raids, destruction, envy, and criticism. She was unable to call on the support of either the nobility or the laity to help her. The nobility had a predatory eye on her riches; the laity disapproved of them. Her wealth had made her both weak and vulnerable.

The Administration of the Law

The development of law administration in Scotland was complicated at once by the conflicting interests of the Church, the nobles, and the crown.

There were several kinds of justice, that administered by the sheriffs, who had wide powers, that administered by the Church courts, and yet other laws which only pertained in the burgh courts. In addition, barons and freeholders had the right to hold their own courts.

The sheriff lived at the royal castle, and was theoretically the head of the administration of the district. Originally, it had been intended that his office should be one of the most important in the country under the supreme legal head, the Justiciar, and he was supposed to administer both civil and criminal justice. The barons were obliged to refer certain cases to him, and he had a supervisory role over the courts of the nobles.

The sheriff was also supposed to be responsible for the military organizations of the country under his control—he had to keep the castles in repair, he held 'wappenschawings', when the men under arms in the district had to produce their arms and to exercise, and he had to see that the noblemen under his control produced their quota of armed men when they were required.

Among his other duties was to see that the crown moneys were collected, and to collect the fines amassed by the high court of the Justiciar, as well as those collected in his own court. These fines formed the second largest source of revenue for the crown. Very often noblemen were quite willing to undertake the offices of Justiciar and of Chamberlain, because in the course of their duties, administering justice all over the country, they could feed and maintain their followers who lived from the land.

The office of the sheriff was therefore very important, and his castle as well as being a means of defence was also a focus of law and order.

But the state of the country and the complications of the various different courts made laws difficult to administer. The burgh courts, for example, dealt with both civil and criminal cases, and they could administer the death penalty. But although the Church courts employed the 'visnet', or trial by jury, the burgh courts had different methods. They preferred the trial in which the accused man could establish his innocence by the evidence of his friends as to his character.

Ordeal by battle was a recognized institution, and many of the punishments inflicted were of a harsh and brutal nature. The accusers were themselves often made responsible for carrying out the sentence of death or mutilation, and if they did not do this, they were themselves punished.

Further complications occurred in the realm of property, owing to the different ways in which land was leased or let. In the burghs, local laws allowed the citizen to bequeath his property, and should he die leaving a minor as his heir, then the relative could administer the inheritance. But a distinction was made between land which had been bought, and land which had been inherited. The inherited land must be passed on to the burgess's children. In this way the burgesses in the burghs had more freedom to do what they liked with their wealth than other people, who might hold their land under feudal laws. It could be said that in legal matters the burgesses formed a spearhead of a more modern method of the distribution of wealth and the administration of justice.

Although attempts were made at a uniform system of justice all over the country, the whole organization foundered in the general disorder and lawlessness which accelerated the poverty of the country, and was added to by the destruction of the monasteries.

In the sixteenth century, despite the theoretical framework, the total lack of law and order was much worse than in the previous centuries. Bishop Leslie says, 'the realm was in such deformity that justice was pulled up by the roots'. An anonymous author who wrote the *Complaynt of Scotland* says that he is left desolate without defence among the hands of wrongful oppressors calling themselves brothers and defenders, 'for I endure more persecution by them than by the cruel oppressions of England'.

Although the courts might award the ownership of land to an aggrieved party, getting possession of the actual land itself was quite a different matter. In 1578 a bailie in Edinburgh bought land in Lothian, but he was never able to use it because the Laird of Dalhousie killed the servants he sent to till it, and destroyed his oxen.

The Laird Gordon of Avochy drew a band of local thugs around him and terrorized the neighbourhood for twenty years. He stole, murdered, and forced the local peasants to work for him without payment, and even made them dismantle the wooden fittings in their own houses, and then re-install them in his own. The courts were presumably powerless to touch him.

This type of situation was not at all unusual. There were many cases in which land was held in this way, and if a neighbour had more physical power than the actual owner of the land, he might make it impossible for the land to be used, or even to be lived on. Land held from the crown on a lease was useless if the local laird had the idea that he had a better right to it, or even no right at all.

The actual administrators of the law were sometimes no better.

In Perth, the bailies had a dispute with a laird, Bruce of Clackmannan. Some of the laird's servants had been arrested by the bailies for non-payment of customs dues. The laird took action against the bailies, and the bailies then destroyed the corn in his field. This was too much for the laird, who carried the bailies off forcibly. This, in turn, was too much for the Privy Council who were brought into the dispute. They decided that everybody was wrong and clapped them all in gaol.

At the root of these evils were the conflicting claims of the clan system and the feudal laws. The feudal lord was not only responsible for his own lands, but he was also responsible for all the lands and goods of everyone who lived under his protection. Should any raid or personal injury against one of his vassals or tenants go unavenged, both his honour and his authority were at risk. If he could not defend his 'men' then his great position was without point.

Sometimes, of course, he was acting in defence of his own property and then he could call on his followers to help him. They were bound to do this under the bonds of 'manrent', by which they bound themselves in honour to defend the lord and his possessions.

Sometimes the crimes committed against his vassals would give him a good excuse to pursue some private vendetta. Between the almost totally lawless Highlands and the Lowlands, stood the two great lords Huntley and Argyll. They acted as a buffer state between the Highlands and the Lowlands, and were constantly appeased by further grants of land given to them as guardians of order. This only increased their power and their intransigence. Mary Queen of Scots was forced to attack Huntley, and yet after his death his heirs were restored to their estates. The noble lords Oliphant and Caithness fought a battle round the market cross in Wick in 1569. In Clackmannan, the Earl of Mar and Lord Oliphant were carrying on a private war.

Unfortunately for the general state of administration, it was impossible to carry out the laws except by physical force. After the defeat of Bothwell, the ruling faction wrote to Queen Elizabeth asking her if she would like the Earl to be delivered into her hands. She, realistically, took the view, that before she could make him her prisoner it was necessary to catch him. This in fact was never done for he escaped to Norway.

In 1570, during a raid on the Hamilton Clan, recorded by the *Diurnal of Occurrents*, their opponents carried off 400 cattle, 600 sheep and other animals. It was said that the tenants' lamentations were great enough to 'make a stone-hearted man to greet and bewail. But cry what they would cry and lament as they pleased there was none that obtained comfort at the unmerciful hands of the raiders.'

The constant internecine wars between the various nobles kept the crown weak, and meant that it was impossible for the sovereign to exercise absolute power over the country. Although Carlyle called the Scottish noblemen 'a selfish, ferocious, unprincipled set of hyenas', from their actions some good ensued for England. Under the regency of Albany, under James V, and under the Regent Mary of Guise Lorraine, they refused to carry out the pro-French and anti-English policies of the governing body.

It is a moot point whether the bribes they were constantly receiving from England, or whether the attraction of carrying on their own private wars were the principal reasons for this. The unknown writer who commented that he was more oppressed by his fellow countrymen than the English was probably right.

In other countries the feudal system led to a servile lower-class population, but in Scotland this did not happen because the clan loyalties and the obligations expected between the ruler of the territory and his people were effectively binding on both sides, and were respected as a dignified arrangement. One writer says, 'The Scots farmers keep a horse and weapons of war and are ready to take part in the laird's quarrel be it just or unjust with any powerful lord, if they only have a liking for him, and, with him, if need be to fight to the death.' On the other hand, should the farmer in his turn be wronged by another lord, then the laird had an equally binding duty to see that the farmer was revenged in his turn.

In this way the clan relationship between landlord and tenant, lord and vassal, was not a purely mercenary one, not merely a question of one paying rent and the other receiving it. It bound the two parties together with ties of loyalty for their mutual benefit and with ties of blood, too.

One example of this was the attitude of the Gordons to their leader, Huntley. When their rebellion against Mary Stuart ended in defeat at Corrichie, and even later during their troubles with James VI, although all their allies deserted them the Gordons remained fiercely true to the Huntleys against the government.

Another case was the family of Home. David Home, of Wedderburn, who died in 1574, was hymned by his son who said, 'Not the least of his virtues was said to be his love of the House of Home'. When Lord Home turned against Home of Wedderburn, and was imprisoned by the Earl of Morton, then Regent, his loyalty remained unshaken and he managed to secure Lord Home's release. Even following these betrayals, the next Lord Home, whose estates were forfeited, was supported by George Home of Wedderburn. The Regent Morton logically pointed out that the Wedderburns had not been very well served by two generations of Homes. But George Home retained his simple belief in the clan system: 'If his chief should turn him out of the front door he would only come back through the back door.' Come imprisonment, putting 'to the horn', betrayals and wars, the clan name held more magic in Scotland than anything else. It cut across national and feudal duties and held like a rock in all circumstances.

Owing to this system, and the virtual splitting up of the country into territories governed by different and sometimes warring lords and lairds, the Scottish people developed a certain independence of spirit. It has been pointed out that there was never a 'peasants revolt' in Scotland.

Among the ills which sprang from the general decay of the rule of law was that the legislature fell into the hands of the ruling faction, which during the century was a constantly shifting factor with disastrous results for the great mass of the people. The lords were not only the administrators of the law, but they were also responsible for collecting the taxes and dues, and in the general state of the country the combination of these two offices led to massive abuses.

Naturally the abuses were not confined to the governing classes, and there is no doubt that many of the general run of the people joined in the general murdering and the general plundering. Most of the more glaring cases which have come down to posterity were concerned with well-known people indicted at the high courts or 'justice ayres'. The smaller people and their crimes were dealt with at the sheriffs' and barons' courts, and little is heard of them.

The most common form of crime was plundering, and although redress might be sought for this, it was more often than not impossible to obtain. 'Letters of Slains' were instituted. This was, in legal form, an attempt to prevent violent reprisals for this kind of wrong. Another device which was used was an Act of Caution. The

47

Privy Council records contain pages and pages of Acts of Caution. These were sureties to prevent feuds and constant reprisals. But possession being nine-tenths of the law, it was very often impossible to enforce them, especially if the misdeeds of vassals were backed up by the military power of the local lord, who was bound by his loyalty to his 'men' to join in the local quarrels and, no doubt, plunderings.

Mary Queen of Scots was involved in constant pitched battles with various factions of the nobles. During the minority of James VI, the country was governed successively by the Regent Moray who was assassinated, the Earl of Lennox who was killed, the Earl of Mar who died worn out by the country's troubles, and finally by the Earl of Morton who was executed in 1580.

The imprisonment of the 'Queen over the Border' led to even more complicated manœuvres among the factions of the lords. It was said in 1571 that

'the whole realm of Scotland was so divided into factions that it was hard for any peaceable man as he rode out on the highway to profess himself either to be a favourer of either the king or queen. All the people were casten so loose and were become of such dis-solute minds and actions that none was in account but he would either kill or reive his neighbour.'

By the end of the century, following these regencies, under James VI the position had not been ameliorated. In 1595, the King decided to end the lawlessness that 'was shaking loose the common-weal'. He called more than thirty of the lords to try to settle the disputes, but until the end of the century and the joining of the two crowns of England and Scotland, the evils continued.

CHAPTER THREE

THE PEOPLE IN THEIR SETTING

Physical Type, Clothes, Houses, and Furniture

It is very difficult at this distance of time to form an idea of the physical type of the ordinary people who lived in Scotland in the sixteenth century. Those few portraits which have survived are mostly of the ruling classes—regents, kings, and courtiers, painted by Flemish or French artists. Like most members of the Renaissance governing class, they show hard men and women with the wary eyes which characterized the period. Considering the conditions of violence and treachery in which they lived, it is not particularly surprising that they do look carefully about them. There could always be an assassin behind the arras.

Another point which has to be taken into account is that fashionable painters of all periods are inclined to paint their sitters according to the physical type which is contemporarily admired. It is only necessary to think of the portraits of Lely and Kneller to see that portrait painters tend more often to depict a type rather than the true appearance of the person painted. There are very few early prints of Scots, and again most of these are of outstanding people.

The general run of the populace goes unrecorded.

The linguistic differences which cut the Lowlands off from the Highlands were matched by physical differences and appearances. The Highlanders, or 'wild Scots', were Celts, dark haired, and dark eyed, while the eastern seaboard showed a mixture of Viking and Norse blood. It has also to be remembered that the kings and queens and the ruling classes not only intermarried with foreign races, but were subject to foreign influence in their manner of dress.

Dress

There are, of course, many portraits of Mary Stuart, but none of these was painted in Scotland. Brantôme described the Queen as

49

looking magnificent in the costume of 'her savage people', and there is supposed to have been a portrait of her wearing it but it has unfortunately vanished. There is no doubt that Mary Stuart, who was nearly six feet tall, must have looked splendid in the simple dress of the Highlander and, with her innate French good taste, have enhanced and beautified it.

Bishop Lesley described a Highland lady's dress in the sixteenth century:

'The dress of the women among them is most becoming, for over a gown reaching the feet, and very richly adorned by the Phrygian art [embroidery], they wear very full cloaks of several colours, loose and flowing and yet gracefully drawn into folds. With their arms tastefully adorned with bracelets, and their throats with necklaces they have great grace and beauty.'

It is curious that, in a portrait painted by a Scottish artist of Mary Stuart when she was imprisoned in England, she wears a jet necklace of a very similar pattern to an ancient one that can be seen in the Scottish Museum of Antiquities. Possibly this may have been a traditional necklace which she had been accustomed to wear with her Highland costume. The shape of the dress of a court lady was simpler than that worn in England. It consisted of a fitted bodice, and a tight sleeve with a trailing edge. It is possible that the sleeves were detachable as the household accounts of the period often refer to a 'pair of sleeves'. A white shirt was worn under the dress, and sometimes a small white collar. On their heads they wore small velvet caps, sometimes trimmed with gold embroidery, or jewelled.

Class differences were brought into focus with equal differences in dress: the nobility wore the velvet cap and the middle classes a hat; the peasants and farmers often had to make do with draping their plaids over their heads.

Another class difference was brought out by the wearing of jewellery and gold chains. The crude Scottish portrait of Mary Queen of Scots in black and white gives an idea of the quantity of jewellery worn by a great lady of the period. This picture shows jet earrings, two jet necklaces, a large pearl and gold cross, a silver chain belt, besides various other small pieces. Quantities of jewellery were the status symbol of the period.

One of the things remarked on by contemporaries when describing the murder of Riccio was the manner in which he was dressed—

in a richly furred robe, a doublet of satin and velvet breeches, with a cap on his head.

Word pictures are painted of the fashionable lady by an early Scottish playwright in a scene where a go-between is trying to get a nubile young lady to marry an old man.

'What wealth, ease and honour await you with him—your fire shall be burning clear before you rise, your maidens shall put all your "gear" in order, lay out your mules, put on your petticoat before it cools, you sit on your velvet stool, two maids come to comb your hair, put on your headgear, take your glass to see that it is set aright, and so goes on your gown . . . you may have coifs and headgear, ruffs, and furbelows, a cloak with double garnishings of gold, a velvet hat, your hood of state, your mask when you go out to protect you from the sun and air and keep your skin white. Your gowns shall be in the latest mode of pan velvet, raised and figured or plain, silk, satin, damask or grosgrain, the finest that can be found. Your clothes shall be slashed and embroidered, your stockings of silk, worn with velvet shoes and an embroidered petticoat. At your wrist will hang a jewelled jotting book, gold bracelets, your fingers shall be full of rings, set with pearls and precious stones—you will be so careless of your jewels you will fling them in heaps.'

Here is the contemporary picture of great luxury for a great lady.

Naturally the lower classes tended to emulate the rich, and Sir David Lindsay writing around 1540 satirizes the bourgeois women and the lower classes for imitating the robes worn by the Queen and her ladies. These trains or 'side tails' are even worn by servants, he says scornfully, women who have scarcely two marks wages. He thinks it 'very scorn that every lady of the land should have a long train trailing behind, whether they be of low or high estate; the Queen they must counterfeit, and wherever they go it can be seen, that church and street they sweep cleane'. But even he gets a little fun out of it. 'But the thing I like best to see is a Nun, carrying her train above her bum, so that her lily white hose can be seen.'

The satirists of the period never missed a trick when it came to getting in a crack at the Church.

Sir Richard Maitland, also, lets himself go about female fashions, and voices the age-old male complaint that women are spending too much money on their backs. As well as the unhygienic trains, he takes exception to the long sleeves of the period 'hanging down like jelly bags.' He complains that the women picked up their skirts to show their petticoats. Possibly this was very necessary, considering the unsanitary state of the streets, but maybe these gentlemen found the 'gear' of the ladies upsetting to their growing puritan principles. Even an embroidered petticoat could probably be inflammatory to the male thoughts in those days.

An unknown author, who might possibly be female, satirizes the clothing of the male dandy:

'Their neat well-fitting doublets rejoice their eyes and they spread out their padded breeches. They take delight in needlework, they glory in their ruffed shirts, their little bonnets or braid hats, sometimes high and sometimes flat (no one can guess how they stay on their heads). They hold perfumed gloves in their hands, everything *à la mode de France*. Their pattens are trim and neat, and their embroidered mules glitter on their feet, their garters are knotted with a rose putting all the girls at their disposal, they only blow their noses so that they can flourish their embroidered handkerchiefs, of the gold tassels shall show its grace.'

But all this finery was imported, and the farmers, the peasants, and the Highlanders had to make do with less flashy gear. Fynes Morison, who travelled in Scotland towards the end of the century, decribed the husbandmen, the servants, and 'almost all in the country' as wearing coarse cloth made at home of grey or sky colour with 'flat blue caps—very broad'.

By contrast, 'the merchants in cities were attired in English or French cloth of pale colour, or mingled black and blue'. He makes it clear that Scotsmen were dressed much less finely than the equivalent class in England.

'The inferior sort of citizen's wives and women of the country did wear cloaks made of a coarse stuff of two or three colours of checkerwork vulgarly called ploddan [plaid]' and ends by saying that Scotsmen of all classes followed the fashions of France, while the women were dressed after the fashion of Germany with naked heads and close-fitting sleeves.

Because of the low wages of the times, clothes were a luxury, and it was an accepted fact that part of a servant's wages would be paid in clothing and shoes. The court records of Elgin make this plain when 'Madge Pakman was ordered to pay Issabell Kemp eight shillings in money, an ell of cloth, half an ell of linen cloth, one pair of mended shoes and an old shirt for his bounties in service to the said Henre and Madge between the feasts of Whitsunday and Martinmas last'.

Religion and the Outward Man

There is a distinct difference between the clothes worn by the Queen's men and the rising puritan lords. The early puritans, like the Roundheads who succeeded them, preferred to show the solidity of their principles by the sombre cut and colour of their garments. In the picture of the Regent Moray he wears a black silk suit trimmed with velvet. His jewellery is discreet. The contrast with the glittering scarlet costume worn by the fifth Lord Seton, heavily encrusted with golden thistles and the monogram of Mary Stuart, is striking. Lord Seton's costume is thought to be French in design and shows him as Master of the Queen's household.

The two companion portraits of the Earl of Moray (Mary Stuart's half-brother) and his wife Agnes also show a French influence, and the costumes are much more elaborate than the simpler picture of the Earl in the National Gallery of Scotland, where he wears a simple flat cap, a dark doublet, and a small white ruff. Possibly these Puritan lords kept their finery for their visits abroad.

The portrait of Lady Helen Leslie, wife of Mark Ker of Newbattle, also shows the Reforming influence. She wears a small puritan bonnet, a black velvet overdress, with sleeves of a mauvy purple— possibly the cramoisie colour so often mentioned in the accounts of the period. The simple collar and cuffs are of white *broderie anglaise*. This lady was the daughter of the fourth Earl of Rothes, and her brothers were both involved in the murder of Cardinal Beaton. Her dress would seem to indicate the fervour of her family principles.

Highland Dress

Pictorial evidence of the dress worn in the Highlands in the sixteenth century is almost non-existent. There exists a drawing in Ghent University which shows a man wearing short trousers, with a check jacket and a plaid. His hair is long; he wears beard and moustache, and carries a long sword and short dagger.

The written evidence about the populace of the Highlands at this time is also very scanty. A French traveller says that 'several savages followed the Scottish army and they were naked except for their dyed shirts and certain light coverings of different colours'. However, he did add that their swords, shields, and bows were similar to those carried by the Lowlanders. It was remarked by Aeneas Silvius, later Pius II, when he visited Scotland, that the men had bare legs, a mantle instead of an upper garment, and a shirt dyed with saffron. In war the Highlanders wore a linen garment sewn together and daubed with pitch, with a covering of deerskin.

Travellers passing through Scotland seem to take all these facts as evidence of the extreme poverty of the people, but John Elder, writing to Henry VIII in 1542, gloried in the fact that he was described as a 'Reddshanke':

'We of all people can tolerate, suffer cold for both summer and winter—going always barelegged and barefooted. Our delight and pleasure is not only in the hunting of red deer, wolves, foxes and grays, whereof we abound and have great plenty but also in running, leaping, swimming, shooting and throwing of darts.'

He goes on to say that because the Highlanders always go barelegged the 'tender delicate gentlemen of Scotland' call them Redshanks.

On a more practical note he says that

'frost we cannot suffer barefoot so well as snow which can never hurt us—when it comes to our girdles we go a-hunting and after we have slain the red deer we flay them of the skin, and setting our barefoot inside for need of cunning shoemakers, composing and measuring so much as shall reach up to our ankles, pricking the upper part with holes that the water may repass where it enters and stretched with a strong thong of the same, the rough hairy side outward.'

But just in case the king to whom he wrote might think that Scotland sounded an unlikely subject for a union of the crowns, he goes on: 'But when we come to Court, the King's grace our master being alive, waiting on our Lords and Masters we have as good garments as some of our fellows which give attendance in the Court everyday.' This might seem to indicate a double standard amongst the Highland lairds, or possibly John Elder was looking on the bright side.

Bishop Lesley, writing in 1578, remarks of the Highlanders that, 'their clothing was suited chiefly to war. All—both nobles and common people wore mantles of one sort (except that the nobles preferred those of several colours).'

There was a distinct difference between the dress worn by the clan chief and his followers. As late as 1592, Angus Mackintosh, of Clan Chattan, was identified by his yellow coat and killed.

The word 'plaide' means blanket in Gaelic, and the plaids worn by the 'wild Scots' were obviously used for a double purpose, as a cloak, or as a blanket. Bishop Lesley makes this clear.

'There cloaks are long and flowing, but capable of being gathered up into folds. Wrapped in these they would sleep comfortably . . . the rest of their garments consisted of a shirt, woollen jacket with sleeves open below for the convenient of throwing their darts, and a covering for the thighs of a simplest kind.'

Their coarse linen shirts are described as being large and loose flowing to their knees. 'These the rich coloured with saffron and others smeared with grease to preserve them longer clean among the toils and exercises of a camp.'

All this gives a picture of fighting men, unencumbered, and simply dressed in a way to make them tough and warlike, and to keep them very mobile, for the main purpose of their lives—fighting.

The Bishop remarks condescendingly, 'In the manufacture of their garments, ornament and certain attention to taste were not altogether neglected, and they joined the different parts of their shirts together very neatly with silk thread chiefly of a red or green colour.'

Tartans

No costumes of the Highlands have survived from the early period. The earliest pictorial evidence is a print by Lucas de Heere, who lived in England from 1567, which depicts a man and a woman wearing tartan. But there is no early indication that particular weaves of tartan or plaid were purposely associated with different districts, or with different clans. It is possible that different districts achieved different results using the same ingredients. The very first evidence of the association of a tartan with a particular district can be found in a series of crown charters from 1587.

The fact that the peasants and country people are reported to be wearing blue costumes is probably because strong dyes were expensive and imported, and one of the native dyes used was the Devil's Bit Scabious which did produce a blue dye.

Many of the complicated clan tartans date only from the eighteenth century. Since all cloth was spun and woven by the cottagers, the weaving of cloth was a formidable task. This meant that any form of clothing would be difficult to obtain, and difficult to make. Such clothing as was worn in the Highlands at this period would have been strictly utilitarian.

The Reformers and Fashion

The Reformers, as so many men of solid principles, were against any form of fashion, and in 1575 they instituted orders against fripperies. Their ordinance condemned all manner of finery as unsuited to ministers, and those who 'bear function in the Kirk, including all kind of light and variant hues in clothing as red, blue, yellow and suchlike which declares lightness of the mind, their wives to be subject to the same order'.

Whether the wives paid any attention is not recorded.

But the Assembly did its best and went into detail about the things they disapproved of. Embroidery was unseemly, and all facings of different colours on gowns, breeches and coats were frowned on. They were against the wearing of rings, bracelets, buttons of silver, gold and metal, as well as velvets, satins, taffetas, and 'silken hats of divers and light colours'. They expressed the pious hope that clothes worn should be of a 'grave colour'— and listed their preferences as 'black, russet, sad grey, or sad brown'.

They took exception to the wearing of plaids and forbade their readers or ministers to wear them when carrying out their duties. There was not much sartorial fun to be had in sad brown.

It is quite possible that the Reformers' admonitions about fashion were not, in fact, necessary except in the large towns, for in general fashion did not exist save in those districts which were in touch with the Continent; and as most manufactured cloths were expensive and imported they were not in widespread use beyond the main centres of court and trade.

This would explain the enormous contrast between the rich attire of the court and to some extent the bourgeois ladies, both satirized by the writers of the period, and the 'gear' of the redshanks and peasants living by hard physical endeavour, whether the endeavour was wringing a living from the soil or plundering their fellow men.

Houses and Furniture

If there were three estates in social and political life in Scotland at this time, there were also three estates in houses. There were the castle and 'towers' of the clan chiefs, the small town houses of the bourgeoisie and the trading classes, and the primitive huts of the peasants.

Many of these castles still exist, either in ruined or in reconstructed form, and it is easy to form an estimate of their enormous size, the thickness of their walls, and their possibilities of defence. When danger threatened, peasants took refuge in the outer defences, often driving their cattle into the courtyards, for even in normal times the courtyards were used for the stabling.

In Scotland, as elsewhere, castles were built at points which commanded extensive views of the surrounding countryside. The view from the top of Stirling or Edinburgh castles gives a very good idea of the use of a castle in watching the movements of troops or marauders from long distances. But to stand at the bottom of the outer defences of a castle and look up is to form an estimate of the disadvantages of the attackers against the defenders. This was often the reason that famine and lack of water were the sole means of driving the defenders out. Edinburgh Castle held out for Mary Queen of Scots long after she was imprisoned by Elizabeth and her cause lost.

This kind of seige warfare only disappeared when gunpowder became powerful enough to demolish the castle walls. The splendour may have fallen on castle walls, but their final usefulness was made obsolete by gunpowder, and gunpowder alone.

The castles may have had reception chambers of a large dimension, but in Craigmillar for example the private rooms used by the Queen were most modest, and reached by winding turret staircases from the inner courtyards. Falkland and Stirling are more attractive, but even there the bulk of the architectural space is given to reception rooms, or chapels.

In Falkland, the state bedroom is high rather than of great size. The absence of glass and the necessity of hanging tapestries on the walls, to stop the damp penetrating through the thick stone, must have made even small rooms excessively dark and cold.

In Falkland, leading from the state bedroom, is the royal garderobe or privy closet, which has a primitive method of drainage attached to an underground sump. It is possible that when Bothwell was shown a place 'between two doors' it could have been a privy of this type. At Ferney Castle, in a similar space between the walls, there is a lead bath dating from the same period. It is a good six feet long and fairly deep. There is a step leading down to the bathing place itself. Whether this step was used to sit in the bath, or whether it was just a means of access, it is difficult to say. The outlet for the water is a hole at the bottom of the bath which was presumably plugged with wood.

The towers or 'mottes' of the clan chiefs and lairds started, like the castles, as a mode of defence. The ground floor was a large hall or assembly room which could also be used as a strong point. As with the castles the heights of the towers enabled the upper floors to be used as look-outs. The central section served as living quarters for the family.

Doves being good to eat, many of the old castles incorporated dovecotes in their walls. There is a dovecote in the ruins of Craig-millar and another very large one can still be seen at Dirleton.

The houses of the bourgeoisie, as a rule, were huddled in a few streets round a central castle, or in alleys and wynds as in Edinburgh. John Knox's house in Edinburgh must have been large compared to many of the tradesmen's houses, some of which only had a couple of rooms. As in the castles, the rooms were small, and although built somewhat after the fashion of Elizabethan houses in England, they were neither so numerous or so richly decorated.

The evidence of travellers in Scotland in the early days seems to have varied considerably.

In the fifteenth century, Aeneas Silvius wrote that the towns were without walls, the houses put together without lime, and the roofs made of turf or covered with skins. But at the end of the century, Don Pedro de Ayala was reporting happily to his king, about to try to marry one of his daughters to the king of Scots, telling a different story: about good houses, glass windows, and innumerable chimneys, as well as excellent furniture. Yet at the beginning of the sixteenth century a traveller dismissed the houses as badly built, and another writer even a century later, was still commenting on the primitive nature of bourgeois houses, and that the king's palaces had few glazed windows. It seems likely that the realists about Scottish housing at this period took a correctly unfavourable view.

Although the town bourgeoisie were often richer than the country lords and lairds, the houses of these trading merchants often consisted of only two or three rooms built of wood, or partly of wood and partly of undressed stone. Many of the smaller town houses in Glasgow and Edinburgh at this period were in effect stone houses with wooden balconies and boarded fronts. An outside staircase led up to the living quarters of the family, while ground floor served as a shop, office or workshop for the merchant, tradesman or artisan.

One writer describes the houses in Edinburgh as having many balconies, built out over the streets, which made the streets narrow and dark, and also increased the risk of fire, a habitation defect which was, of course, found in many countries. A fire in one house could soon set the whole street ablaze. Some houses had iron chimneys as a form of fire prevention, but even so in these huddled houses cheek by jowl, with their projecting wooden balconies, fire was a constant hazard, for the roofs were usually thatched with straw or heather. The lower half of the windows was shuttered, and in the shutters were cut decorative holes to watch the passers-by in the street below. There was no glazing of windows.

Some time later, in the seventeenth century, a writer describes the fronts of Scottish houses in the principal towns as still being boarded up with 'firr' boards into which round holes had been cut. Obviously the building methods had not changed very much in fifty years. Even at the end of the seventeenth century, acts were being passed to try to discourage town-dwellers from thatching their houses. The last thatched house in Edinburgh was not pulled down until the nineteenth century.

The ground floors of these simple bourgeois houses, apart from being used as shop or office, often housed agricultural implements; a plough, a pair of harrows, a cart, and a sledge are listed amongst the goods and chattels of one prosperous merchant. The merchants sometimes farmed stretches of agricultural land on the outskirts of the town on a co-operative basis, so that they still had a stake in farming although on a minor scale. This could also have been a hedge against the vagaries of foreign trade.

It is possible that some parts of Edinburgh may have been built on a more grandiose scale, and mostly of stone. Alexander Hailes, a Scotsman, who described the city for *Cosmographia*, writes that it was set in a fertile land with pleasant fields, groves, lakes, burns, and more than a hundred 'castles' within the space of three miles. Whether this Scotsman, writing for an international audience, was penning an unduly rosy picture is difficult to decide, though

Edinburgh, being connected to the Continent by trade and education, must have been more in line with other international cities
than the rest of the towns in Scotland.

He goes on to say that the houses are built of stone 'both hewn
and unhewn'. The Royal Mile is stated to have been built of
dressed stone, and from this main street 'stretched an infinity of
small streets, all adorned with tall houses in which dwelt the gentry
. . . there is nothing humble or rustic but all is magnificent'.

Perhaps, as with most towns, the city centre was more grandiose
than the rest, and the streets described were the dwellings of the
richer classes, giving way to smaller streets where lived the smaller
merchants, and then tailing off into alleys and wynds with the
dwellings of the lesser tradesmen or artisans. As most of these
dwellings served the double purpose of house and shop, or workshop, it is unlikely they would have been found in the centre of the
city.

There was unfortunately no Hogarth in Scotland at this time to
bring these houses and streets to vivid life in painting. But reports
about the hard fight against dirt give a picture of what it must have
been like.

In 1574 the town of Glasgow was trying vainly to rid the town of
the effects of its own insanitary habits. A statute laid it down that
there were to be no middens in the 'front street'—which presumably
meant in front of the houses, and that butchers were not to throw
offal in front of their shops. Stones and timber were not to be left
at front gates for more than a 'year and a day'. The last order seems
to denote a certain dilatoriness in building and repairs.

Little was done to get the filth from the streets as is proved by the
fact that three years later the city fathers were still trying to remove
the middens from the streets, and even trying to stop people digging
on the highways, though whether this digging was part of an attempt
to rid themselves of the rotting rubbish is not made clear.

The keeping of horses and cows in the centre of the towns cannot
have helped matters. Glasgow, like other towns, had its herds of
cows, each citizen keeping his private cow on common land beyond
the walls. These cows were tended by herdsmen appointed for a
year. But decrees against the keeping of pigs in the vicinity of houses
prove that attempts to separate farming from town life were not
easy to achieve.

If the town houses were insanitary and unhealthy, the cottages of the peasantry were worse. These were mere hovels of clay, covered with turf or thatched with straw.

As late as the eighteenth century the normal cottage of the Scottish peasant had not changed, it still had no chimney, only a hole in the roof.

'There houses were hovels built of stone or turf without mortar and stopped with straw to keep the wind from blowing in upon them. In such houses they lived in a constant cloud of smoke, enough to suffocate them had they not been habituated to it from infancy. They slept on peat covered with the coarsest blankets, and kept their cattle in the same house with themselves tied to stakes at one end of the house.'

so writes one traveller, and another in 1704 thus describing a village in Crawfordjohn:

'The houses are either of earth or of loose stones . . . the roofs are of turf and the floors of the bare ground. They are but one storey high, and the chimney is a hole in the roof, the fireplace in the middle of the floor . . . seats and beds are of earth turfed over and raddled up, near the fire place, and serve for both uses.'

The cottages sometimes had thatched roofs of straw or heather. Apart from the earth, the family might also sleep on a pile of straw or heather. Sometimes the thatch was kept in place by stones held down by heather ropes to prevent the roofs being carried away in rough weather. The beasts were kept at one end of the cottage, partly for warmth and partly as a protection against raiders.

Thus the general picture built up of the countryside at this period is of small huddled groups of houses in small townships, built round a castle or motte, interspersed with solitary cottages or groups of cottages in a bleak landscape.

Obviously, in a country which had been in a state of unrest for so many years, the building of solid houses of even a modest nature was not a practical proposition. Simple dwellings were easily rebuilt using the stones and sticks which could be found in the surrounding districts, and if such cottages were burned by marauders they could be replaced in a few days.

It was not only the scarcity of good materials and the poverty of the people which produced these rough dwellings, but also the uncertainty of their lives.

It was in the homes of the burgesses that the most progress in domestic articles was made in this century. Not only were the merchants prosperous, but they were influenced by one of the great trading peoples of the period, the people of the Low Countries. British bourgeois culture can be said to stem from the Low Countries and when one thinks of the pictures of the Dutch and Flemish painters, the domestic interiors and the furnishings, it is clear that this prosperity and *Gemütlichkeit* would have had an immense influence on merchants from a Scotland less favoured financially, and having a much lower standard of living.

The burghers of Holland and Flanders set an example which the Scottish merchants tried to emulate.

Francis Spottiswood, who died in Edinburgh about the time of Mary Stuart's birth, was a rich merchant trading with Flanders, and on his death a careful inventory was made of his goods and chattels. Although his house was small, only two or three rooms, it contained many evidences of prosperity. A court cupboard, or aumrie, from the French word armoir, on which were displayed a silver cup, a silver salt-cellar and silver spoons, to make plain to the world that he was a 'warm' man. A mirror, an ivory seal, a gold signet ring, and a gold image of St John the Baptist. He had a fine bed with serge curtains and a serge cover, a clothes press, chests for storing goods, a trestle table, with a bench for his wife and children, and a chair for himself.

This presents a picture of a small house in which furniture was kept to the minimum. The silver ware had a dual purpose, it was an investment, and a mode of display, rather than mere utensils to be used at table—though the 'salt' was a ceremonial item, and often used on the long trestle table as a focal point which divided the family from the hired hands.

The merchant's aumrie was an item much coveted at this period, and was often used to display plate on three shelves. These cupboards came originally from Holland, and were frequently inlaid after the Dutch fashion, and often appear on inventories as 'a dresser for the setting of Stoups'. Stoups were bowls. This word only survives today in the phrase 'holy water stoup', which is still used in the Catholic Church.

In a rich merchant's house the ordinary plates and dishes would have been of pewter, though wooden platters were also much used. Some eating utensils were made of horn, as were the drinking vessels ('cuaches'). In many cases, guests brought their own knives and spoons. Forks were unknown. An early reference to silver tableware occurs in the inventory of Sir David Lindsay, who died in 1555, where it is recorded that he owned a dozen silver spoons which were marked with his arms. This is a very early record of the engraving of silver with the arms of the family, although it is also recorded that Mary Stuart engraved the arms of England on her silver. But this was before she came to Scotland, so possibly it was originally a Continental fashion, or just a canny way of discouraging thieves. Her action certainly did not endear her to Queen Elizabeth.

Glass was practically unknown for drinking vessels, and cups were a rarity, although they are referred to as early as 1526.

During this period carpets and rugs began to displace rushes for the floor and are mentioned as being embroidered, so presumably they were rugs of tapestry work.

The fact that mirrors were so specifically mentioned in the inventories proves that they were an imported luxury, as were clocks, first brought in by merchants. There is also a very early reference to an alarm clock which arrived in the ship *Neptune* at Burntisland. This alarm clock was 'taken in piracy' and is lovingly described as being gilt 'having a little knock with a wakener'.

Many novelties and luxuries occur amongst the 'gear' of the Queen: a parasol, 'a little canopy of gold and cramoisie satin furnished with fringes and tassels, and many little painted buttons, all serving to make shadow before the Queen'.

In spite of the Queen's fancy parasols it is unlikely that her apartments were furnished very differently, though possibly more grandly, than those of her prosperous subjects. Furniture at this period was at a minimum, and the fact that the Queen sent furniture down to Darnley's lodgings proves that if this house was furnished at all it had little or nothing to make it a lodging for a king. The list of the furniture which disappeared in the explosion was later presented to the Queen for her signature, and it included a bed of violet velvet, a small table with a green velvet cloth, a chair covered with violet velvet, sixteen pieces of tapestry, a high chair covered with leather, a *chaise percée* fitted with two basins, a little turkey carpet and a chamber pot.

Although the merchant's serge hangings are replaced by velvet, it does not seem as if the King's main furnishings were more numerous than the merchant's.

On the other hand, considering the poverty of the country, the Church and its churchmen did themselves very well. At this time, immediately before the Reformation, many writers believe that almost half the revenues of the country were in the hands of the Church. Although it can be fallacious to argue from the particular to the general, the inventory of the Parson of Stobo, who died in the year 1542, is not without interest.

Master Adam Colquhoun was a kind of sixteenth-century absentee parson—on the English eighteenth-century model—in that he paid someone else a small fee to do his work while drawing a large benefice for himself. Stobo yielded the parson £2,000 a year, at a time when servants drew five or six shillings annually. The parson of Stobo was also attached as a canon to the Chapter of Glasgow, and as there were thirty-two other canons enjoying similar benefices, it can be seen that canons in general, and, as we shall see, the canon of Stobo in particular, were a fairly heavy drain on the general exchequer of the country.

It has been suggested that the wealth of the Church attracted the cupidity of the nobles and inflamed them against the corruption of the Church. Others allege that it is only the catholic writers who blame the greed of the nobles. But when it comes to greed and cupidity, these vices are not as a rule governed by political alliances, but by the individual greed and cupidity of actual people. There were dedicated men toiling in the fields of souls for the Reform of the Catholic Church. Some of these were inside the Church. No one side has the monopoly of virtue or of vice.

However, it must be said that the goods and chattels of Master Adam Colquhoun, the parson of Stobo, probably give a good idea of the abuses which had crept into the Church, especially when his wealth is set against the general conditions of the country.

His manse was built of stone, and was possibly on the tower houses or 'mottes' favoured by the upper classes. The entrance had a spiral staircase which led to the upper floors, and the doors of the various rooms opened directly from the staircase. The large fireplaces were on the Elizabethan pattern. The rooms would, as usual, have been dark, lit by small windows cut into the walls, which were a yard thick. Any of the Scottish castles would give an idea of the rooms. Like the town houses described in Edinburgh, the manse had a wooden gallery. This ran round the back of the house, and afforded a view of the countryside and the river.

4. *Top:* Holyrood Palace, Queen Mary's Chamber

left: Holyrood Palace, Queen Mary's Closet

5. *Left:* Bedroom at Craigievar Castle

right: The Great Hall at Glamis Castle

In his bedroom he had a bed of carved wood, decorated with gold. A comfortable feather mattress consisting of 140 pounds of down, with down pillows to match, covered with holland (a linen cloth), and sheets of similar material. On top of these were laid a pair of plaids, and two blankets of fine fustian. The bed had damask curtains—'many coloured with embroideries and gold tassels'—as well as a silver water pot for other needs.

During the day the bed was covered with a velvet cover, and the walls were hung with tapestries depicting scenes of the countryside with hunting and animals. Presumably this bed served as a place to repose during the day. From the ceiling hung a chandelier with white wax candles. No rush lights for the parson.

In his bedroom he also had a carved oaken settle, a carved oak press for clothes, with a damask curtain to screen his clothes from curious eyes.

His clothes make jolly reading. As there was no recognized clerical dress, they include a doublet of 'cramoisie' velvet lined with scarlet, a scarlet waistcoat, stockings of black Paris silk, garters with gold tassels, a silk belt with gold tassels, velvet shoes, and a rich housegown of damask lined with marten sable to keep out the winter cold. This was equipped with a gold fastener. His bonnet and his gloves were also sewn with gold. His dagger, or 'whinger', was chased with gold, and for the protection of his teeth he owned a silver toothpick.

His valuables, kept in his bedroom, consisted of a set of rosary beads, possibly also gold as they were valued at £63, a tablet with a relic of the true cross, valued at £200, and a gold chain valued at £500, as well as various gold rings and sundry other bits and pieces picked up on his journey through life and religion. These valuables were kept in strong boxes.

His dining room was also well furnished and included an 'eating board' and trestles, and his aumrie, which displayed forty silver vessels and a flagon weighing about 65 ounces. A double 'counter', probably used as a buffet or serving table, came from Flanders. There were a settle, a chair, a stool of carved wood, as well as a number of feather cushions to soften the discomfort of sitting when eating.

His kitchen was equally well served with a table, dresser, and many large and small pots, as well as saucepans for cooking fish, meat, and poultry.

c

In his stable he boasted a riding saddle, as well as the cloth trappings with which a horse would be decked on ceremonial occasions. His riding gown was of damask, with a velvet hood, a black cloak lined with velvet, and in case anyone should take a fancy to his 'gear', he also owned a suit of armour and a two-handed sword. The fact that the clergy were not supposed to bear arms does not seem to have deterred the parson of Stobo. His other arms included a bow and arrows, and a single-handed sword.

He was also a sporting parson as is proved by his owning coursing equipment: a silk dog-lead, and a dog-collar with silver studs. Amongst the other animals he kept for his amusement were a tame hind and a crane.

Stobo seems to have been a little island of culture and prosperity in the surrounding desert.

The list of the parson's belongings was put in as evidence in a lawsuit brought by his nephew. For the parson had not neglected other appurtenances of life, and was blessed with a mistress who had fruitfully produced two sons. After his death the sons were legitimized, and the nephew contested this post-death-bed regularizing of the situation. Unfortunately for the nephew, in spite of his careful list, he lost the case.

But in case he might be accused of neglecting his holy work, the parson had provided himself with splendid appurtenances for the job in hand. In his private chapel he boasted an altar with silver furnishings, a chalice, patten, and a silver plate with two cruets for wine and water, as well as his chasubles, maniples, stoles, amice, and alb, and a portable altar stone to be used when travelling. His other ecclesiastical costumes included: a biretta; three surplices, one of lawn, one of crêpe, and one of holland; a hood of purple satin with a draw string of gold; and a cap with ermine fur and tails.

The parson of Stobo was furnished and dressed on a princely scale, and the contrast between this ecclesiastical magnificence and the list of household goods given in a sixteenth-century poem, called 'The Wooing of Jok and Jynny', is sharp indeed.

Jynny's mother, to tempt the young man, sings of the wealth of Jynny's dowry. She boasts that her daughter owns a sheet, a meal chest, a cupboard, two ladles, a milk strainer, a rusty knife to cut kail, a large wooden bowl, a bench, a wooden platter, and a porridge stick.

Jok, not to be outdone in worldly goods, lists the farm implements which he can bring, as well as his own ramhorn spoon. These ramhorn spoons were carried everywhere, often in the bonnet of the owner. One end was formed into a whistle, from which came the old saying: 'Better the supping end nor the whistle end!'

Jok also owned a bag, a pedlar's wallet, and, as a more practical inducement to the susceptible Jynny, 'two lusty lips'. The list given by Jok and Jynny would indicate that this was regarded as a fair marriage portion with which to set up a home, and therefore presumably many peasants were much worse off than this happy pair.

Pockets of poverty and riches existed side by side, and the Highlands in general presented the poorer picture, dependent as they were on local manufactures and local materials for their clothes and household goods.

Scott, in a note to his novel *Marmion*, says, 'The accommodation of a Scottish hostelry or inn in the sixteenth century may be recollected from Dunbar's admirable tale of the Friars of Berwick, where Simon Lawder, the gay hostler, seems to have lived very comfortably and his wife decorated her person with a scarlet kirtle, a belt of silk and silver rings on her fingers.' Obviously this picture of jolly inn life in the Lowlands did not apply to the Highlands, where inns were non-existent. Fynes Morison who travelled in Scotland at the end of the century says that there were no regular inns with signs hanging out, but that private householders would entertain passengers 'on entreaty, or where acquaintance was claimed'.

The general picture presented of the furnishings of the houses of the period is that the peasantry lived with the bare necessities for cooking and tilling the land. A cupboard was a luxury. A bed was unknown. Even a stool was something to be proud of.

The merchants and the priests owned silver plate, furniture, and even a chair or two. But most of the furniture seems to have served two purposes. There were chairs of which the backs could also serve as tables, and the dining table proper was always a trestle which could be cleared away so that the room could be used as a sitting room.

In the castles of the nobles, the lord's table was called the 'hie Burd', because it was raised up above the level of the common herd. The lord had a carved chair, and this in particular denoted his status. Presumably the idea of the king on this throne stemmed originally from the fact that only the head of the household owned the chair.

Other differences, apart from the 'salt' which divided the family from the hired hands in the merchant's house, were made plain in the castle of the baron. Those privileged people sitting at the high board kept their hats on, the servants wore no hats. At the high board, pewter plates were used; on the lower level there were wooden platters. And it was not only the class of Jynny and Jok who brought their own spoons and knives, for even at the baron's table guests were expected to supply their eating utensils.

Manners were strict. Meat was handed round on skewers after having been carved by one of the attendant squires. Eating must have been a fairly difficult business without forks, and it is not surprising that table napkins were used, and that pages circulated among the guests with ewers and basins.

Even at court it is possible that trestle tables were used. The way in which Mary Stuart's supper table was overthrown at the time of the murder of Riccio probably indicates that it was a light trestle table covered with a cloth. Although the pictures which have been painted of the incident in Victorian times present a heavy carved oak table being overthrown, this was possibly to make the incident more 'olde worlde' and dramatic.

All real household luxuries, whether furniture, silver, velvets, clocks, or pictures, were imported from France and Flanders. In Edinburgh and around the sea coasts some noblemen and merchants astonished the invading Englishmen. Protector Somerset, on landing at Leith, was surprised at the elegance of the 'table appurtenances which included some of the best continental craftsmanship. Dishes were commonly pewter and drinking cups were of tree with pewter or silver bases or pedestals.'

Some of these drinking cups or quaiches (from the Gaelic *cuach*, a cup) survive, and although the horn and silver ones are of a later date they must have followed the traditional patterns, as do so many of the objects made by Scottish craftsmen.

Luxury at Court

John Knox was constantly inveighing against the luxury of Mary Stuart's court, possibly because the luxuries were brought in from abroad. And he had, after all, done a turn in French galleys as a prisoner.

The list of Mary Queen of Scots' wardrobe includes dresses of all colours, cramoisie, blue, grey, carnation colour, cloth of silver and cloth of gold, a mantle bordered with ermine, and a dressing gown of chestnut velvet trimmed with silver cord.

These dressing gowns or 'nightgowns' were house-coats which were usually trimmed with fur, and Sir James Melville, when speaking of one of his trips to England, gives as an instance of hospitality that he was lent a 'nightgown'.

But if the distinction between the man in the street and the great noble was made by the gold chains the latter wore round his neck, this was even more true of the great lady. Mary Stuart's jewels were world famous. With each dress she would have worn a parure. A parure, besides the necklace, earrings, and bracelets, included a jewelled belt, chains from shoulder to shoulder, brooches, clasps, and jewels for the velvet cap.

She had several sets of jewels: three of diamonds; one of rubies and diamonds; one of rubies and pierced pearls; one of rubies, diamonds, and pearls; another of sapphires as well as great ropes of black pearls, filigree gold ornaments, diamond crosses, a 'table' of diamonds in a ring, and cabochon rubies. But the *pièce de resistance* was the 'Great Harry' diamond, an enormous faceted stone, set with a large cabochon ruby in an H which had been given to her by Henri II King of France when she married the Dauphin.

Mary Stuart had it mounted in the Scottish crown, but later it became, like so many heirlooms, a jewel of dispute, and Parliament had a great deal of trouble to prise it from the clutches of the Earl of Moray's widow, Agnes. Widows are notoriously unhappy at parting with the family heirlooms.

Later, James I and VI mounted it into a royal jewel which was called the Mirror of Britain. Under the Commonwealth it disappeared, never to be traced. It remains a reported and fabulous jewel.

Mary Stuart's black pearls were sold by Moray to Queen Elizabeth. It is perhaps odd that Reformers, whether puritan, republican, or Marxist, ever aim at the destruction of luxury, yet are never averse to the proceeds of its disposal.

After the Reform

Once the 'Saints' had accomplished their Reforms, the climate of clothing, furniture, and Church appointments changed. Luxury both in clothing and church furnishings disappeared. The carved reredos gave way to the plain wooden pulpit of Mr Knox, the missals with their jewelled clasps disappeared in favour of the large leather-covered bible, and the original gilded and painted saints were banished forever. Clothing became sober, and the paucity of furniture in the manse could be seen as evidence of virtue and high-minded living. 'Sad brown' and 'sad grey' became the order of the day, and were recommended for high-minded use.

Naturally, this sad-brown mood did not last, and by the time the thrones of England and Scotland were joined, luxury had begun to raise its head again, at least among the aristocracy.

CHAPTER FOUR

FAMILY LIFE

Marriage and Courtship

Marriage, being the centre of family life, shows certain discrepancies in early Scotland. Before the eighth century there were no church ceremonies, but there had been a Celtic custom of 'handfasting'. It was, in essence, a system of trial marriage and endured until the Reformation.

A young man and a girl would engage themselves to live together for a year, and at the year's end they could either marry or agree to separate. This custom was not confined to the lower strata of society. For one contemporary writer records of Alexander Dunbar, (the son of James, sixth Earl of Moray) and Isobel Innes, that 'this Isobel was but handfast with him and deceased before the marriage'.

Another case was recorded of Queen Margaret Tudor who sued for a divorce from the Earl of Angus. One of the reasons she gave was that he had been 'handfasted' to Jane Douglas, who had borne him a child, and that for this reason her marriage was not valid as he was already contracted to the other woman. The Pope granted the divorce, but the child of the Earl and the Queen was nevertheless declared legitimate.

The practice of handfasting was very widespread, and one of the duties of the itinerant friars was to persuade the 'handfasts' to enter into legal ceremony.

Most of these 'handfasts' met at the local fairs which were obviously times of fun and games, and also a chance to meet young people from other parishes. At a fair held in a parish near the monastery of Melrose, which was under the supervision of the monks, a priest from the monastery was accustomed to do the rounds trying to persuade the 'handfasts' to marry, and it is quite clear from the records that although the Church may have disapproved of the custom of 'handfasting' they bowed to the old custom. The itinerant monk, who was the 'marriage persuader' carried a copy

71

of the marriage office in the breast pocket of his habit, and on account of this he was known as 'Book i' Bosom'.

By 1562 this custom became unpopular with the Reformers, and in the same year the Kirk Session of Aberdeen issued a decree that all 'persons living together under handfast contracts should forthwith be united in wedlock'. Evidence that this law was not carried out is that, twenty years later, the Reformed Church was still battling against the custom of handfasting.

But in spite of the 'putting down' of handfasting, the laws of marriage in Scotland remained lax. Although many people after the Reformation did get married in church, legally this was not necessary. A mere acknowledgement by the future husband and wife, whether made verbally or in writing, which could be either followed or preceded by their living together, was held to be a true marriage.

It is not difficult to see that such simple marriage laws could lead to a great many abuses, for if it was only the evidence of the lovers themselves which constituted a marriage, one person's denial was as good as another's, and once the ardour had cooled different opinions could easily be advanced.

The Scottish Reformed Church, reasonably, was against all such casual marrying, and banned all secret marriage contracts, declaring that they were invalid, and the contracting parties were soundly condemned as 'breakers of good order'. The Reformers declared that marriage must be declared before 'famous and unsuspect witnesses', who must verify the contract.

If the Catholic Church had been lax over handfasting, at least, when they eventually managed to get bride and groom to church, the ceremony was solemnized at a nuptial mass. But the Reformers found themselves in a dilemma, for once marriage ceased to be a sacrament it came to be looked upon as little more than a civil contract which took place preferably before a bailie or sheriff, who in effect merely witnessed the fact that the bride and groom were marrying each other.

These marriages were perfectly legal in the Scotland of the time, and in effect were a kind of extension of handfasting. It was not even necessary, indeed, to have an official present at the marriage. This was, of course, the reason for the survival of the anvil marriages at Gretna Green. There was no special privilege attached to the blacksmith's parlour at Gretna Green, it was simply that it was near the English border, and that in Scotland marriage laws were different from those in England.

Betrothal ceremonies varied according to the wealth and station of the future bride and groom. Among the peasants they could get engaged privately, but immediately after the betrothal they were expected to inform the 'old folk'.

Among the bourgeoisie and the upper classes, where property was of more consequence, the relatives of the engaged couple assembled, like a committee, to discuss the thorny question of property. This must have provoked some stormy meetings, for in the sixteenth century a women with property could not *at any age* choose a husband not approved by her 'procurators'; and if the procurators were interested relatives, they might easily decide on the protection of property, and perpetual spinsterhood for the girl.

The dowry, or 'tocher', was something which had to be considered, and if a mother disapproved of her daughter's choice she could withhold the daughter's dowry. No doubt many a hopeful young man with a rich bride in view must have found that love and ways and means were not compatible. Even the peasant girl was expected to produce a dowry—the song about Jynny and Jok (quoted in Chapter 3) makes this clear. While Jynny produces the household goods like pots, pans, knives, a sheet, her spinning wheel, a mallet to knock the barley, Jok contributes a plough and all kinds of agricultural implements. Obviously marriage was not regarded with any seriousness amongst any class unless good solid backing could be produced to make the thing an economic possibility.

After the betrothal the couple were known as the bride and groom. The bride was given two 'maids' to attend her, and two male kinsmen were appointed to 'protect' her. This betrothal was known as 'booking'.

Before the Reformation, forty days were supposed to lapse between the 'booking' and the ceremony itself. During this time the future bride was to receive no visitors except her relatives and very old friends.

At the Reformation the custom was started that those who wished to marry must submit their names to the minister or clerk, for the proclamation of the banns on three successive Sundays. But later, in return for a larger fee to the minister, the banns were declared in one public announcement.

In 1575 the General Assembly tried to straighten out the custom

73

of 'booking' and decided that it was enough if the names of the happy pair were written down by a public official. From that time onwards two male friends of the couple paid a fee to the session clerk. This was known as 'laying doon the pawns'—the money being the guarantee that the parties were serious, and that the marriage would take place. Presumably the Reformers were still fighting a rearguard action against handfasting. In 1579, it is recorded in Stirling that James Duncanson, 'Reader and Notary public', certified that Alexander, brother of the Laird of Menstrie, and Elizabeth, daughter of Robert Alexander, had appeared before him, and 'both in one voice granted mutual promise of marriage, whereupon he admonished both not to cohabit till the legal completion of the union, and further that they and their 'companies' abstain from all public dancing and playing in the gaits of the burgh on the day of the marriage under pain of £10 of money'.

Because the reign of Mary Queen of Scots was a time of transition between one set of rules being demolished and another established, there were numbers of discrepancies.

The General Assembly had in 1579 prohibited marriages performed by Popish priests, and the publication of banns was forbidden for those practising the Catholic religion. Catholics were supposed to profess the Protestant faith before marrying. In 1588, the Presbytery of Edinburgh allowed the banns of the Earl of Huntley, provided he subscribed to the current faith.

But even Reform has its disadvantages, and once marriage is regarded as a mere civil contract, then other reforms must be instituted to reform the reforms. The Kirk had become bothered about people who wanted to get married and had no idea of the reasons why they *should* be married. So prospective brides and bridegrooms 'were ordained to be instructed in the true knowledge of the causes of marriage'. In 1579, the Kirk Session in St Andrews decreed that no one could be married unless they could recite to the local reader the Lord's Prayer, the 'Believe', and the Commandments.

The Kirk was not only concerned with spiritual matters, for anyone who was in financial difficulties was not allowed to marry. 'James Annan is in great debt therefore it cannot be ordained Helen Bar to be married upon him'. There could, however, be a good deal of spontaneous generosity such as 'Penny bridals'. These were a means of getting a small amount of money for a poorly endowed couple. A number of self-invited guests appeared at the wedding feast, and the money left over after the celebrations was used to start the young couple in their housekeeping.

The family and the Kirk were not the only parties to interfere in wedding plans. Apprentices could not marry without permission of their craft, and they could be expelled if they married without such permission.

In all ages and all countries, marriages have been surrounded with superstitions, customs, and taboos. Scotland at this time was no exception. Here are some.

January and May were unlucky months to marry in. 'A bride in May is thriftless aye', was an old Scots adage.

It was necessary to avoid a dog passing between the bride and groom.

Between the 'booking' and the marriage ceremony, the friends of the bride would rub shoulders with her, so that they should be able to catch the matrimonial 'infection'.

A day or two before the wedding, some friends might call on the groom, bringing a washing bowl, and volunteer to wash his feet respectfully. But as soon as he had undressed, his legs were covered with grease and soot, scrubbed clean, and the whole 'dirtying up' process restarted. When the groom and his chums were exhausted, the groom was expected to pay for drinks all round.

The wedding feast was usually in the evening. After the party the young couple left for their new home, preceded by the best man and bridesmaid. The duty of the bridesmaid was to break a cake of shortbread over the bride's head as she entered her new home. This was known as the infar-cake and portions of it were given to the friends of the bride and groom. The bride completed the ceremony by sweeping the hearth presumably to show that she would make a good and efficient housewife.

Another custom was that the wife kept her maiden name after her marriage. This was presumably because once a women was born into a clan she remained part of the clan—once a Campbell, always a Campbell. But it cannot have helped the general pacification of the country, for an insult done to the daughter of a clan would be taken up as a cause by the rest of the clan.

Sometimes old customs were made into binding contracts. The moistening with the tongue of the lovers' right thumbs and their subsequent pressing together was considered a betrothal which could not be broken under pain of perjury. In the same way, a promise made across a stream of running water was also a firm betrothal which probably had some old pagan significance.

Putting Down the Fun

The Reformers, although they were on the side of wedded bliss, and against extra-marital activities, were exercised by the fun and celebrations which took place at the weddings.

In 1570 they tried to stop weddings on Sundays, on account of what they termed 'great abuse' which disturbed the town with 'minstrelsy and harlotry'. They decided that if they allowed marriages on any other day of the week, they might in this way be able to keep the Sabbath sacrosanct.

But they seem to have had an uphill task in their fight against fun and games, because some years later they passed a statute to keep the cost of the wedding feast down to eighteenpence. But later on the price had risen to four pounds. Obviously these attempts to curb the expense of wedding feasting could not be successful, and indeed the good people of Stirling began to hold their wedding parties in tents outside the town.

At the beginning of the new century the Kirk fathers were still battling against wedding feasts, and in addition trying to fine people for holding the weddings outside the town.

One David Wemyss was pretty forthright with the Kirk Session at St Andrews. When brought up before the church fathers for illicit dancing, he said that 'the custom was kept before any of the Session were born'. Presumably the Kirk fathers took exception, for they imprisoned this plain-speaker in the church steeple.

Although the Kirk was against dancing and piping at weddings their efforts did not bear fruit, for more than a century after the beginning of the Reforms they were still passing decrees trying to suppress the fun.

The Fun the Reformers Did Not Like

Bridal feasts very often could consist of up to a hundred people, especially in the Highlands. The bride and her party walked in first, accompanied by pipers, then the groom and his friends and more piping. The bridal pair sat at the head of the 'board'. Some guests sat round the trestle table but others sat on logs, or pieces of timber resting on stones.

76

The Blithesome Bridal, by Sir Robert Sempill, written towards the end of the sixteenth century, describes the kind of fare at simple wedding feasts to which the Reformers were taking exception:

'Long kail and pottage, bannocks of barley meal, good salt herring, a cup of good ale, onions, radishes, pease—boiled and raw, abundance of mouthfuls of skate, sheep's head broth, fresh ox feet, crabs, winkles, speldies [dried fish], haddocks, and broth with barley to sup till ye're fou.'

Sir Robert goes on to describe with enthusiasm

'sour milk cheese, flummery, oatcakes, baps with new ale, tripe [weel strappit with paunches], brandy in stoups, and in coups, meal kail custocks, skink to sup till you rive [burst] and flounders which were taken alive roasted over the fire, scraped haddocks, whelks, Tulse and Tangle [seaweed] and a mill of good snuff to taste; when wearied with eating and drinking, We'll up and dance till we die.'

Obviously this kind of drinking, stuffing, and prancing could not be to the taste of the Kirk fathers, and occasionally there were other complications, for even the local wedding feasts were not proof against the reavers, not even amongst the aristocratic ones. Here is an account of one.

'Lord Maxwell being contracted in marriage to a sister of the Earl of Angus, the lady's relation, the Earl of Morton [the Regent] proposes to give a banquet on the occasion at Dalkeith Castle.' The necessary good cheer including the wine, the venison, and the silver plate to serve it on were being brought up from Leith, when 'Kirkcaldy and his friends in the castle hearing of this sent out a party of horse, which surprised Morton's servants', and took the materials of the proposed banquet as spoil. Morton who, it was said, smarted more from the loss of the plate than the killing of a few of his servants in the struggle, immediately sent a party to requite Kirkcaldy's attack by laying waste his estate in Fife. Kirkcaldy, again, repaid these attentions by sending a party a few nights after to set fire to the town of Dalkeith. On this occasion he killed ten of Morton's people and took nine prisoners. On their return they 'perceived fifty-six horses from Dalkeith to Leith, passing laden with ale; they brake the barrels, and made prey of the horses, and brought into Edinburgh many kye [cows] and oxen of that lordship

77

for supply of their skant and hunger' [*History of King James*]. 'These three scuffles went all under one name, and were ever after called Lord Maxwell's Handfasting.'

The Wedding Day

On her wedding morning the bride was dressed with great ceremony. It was the custom of ladies of rank to give a present of a wedding dress to those who had served them. There is a record of Mary Queen of Scots doing this when one of her four Marys married. Many of these dresses were extremely costly—a bride's dress could cost 100 merks—and even the most humble bride was expected to have new clothes for the occasion.

There was a custom that the wedding dress must not be put on before the wedding day, nor could it be altered if it did not fit. This seems an odd way to make a bride happy, for the average girl is not likely to treasure a wedding dress which fitted where it touched. But possibly in those days, with so much padding and bolstering, a court gown did not actually need any particular person in it. In the Highlands the plaid would fit almost anyone, so no doubt the superstition could be followed without much sartorial danger.

Another superstition connected with the wedding day was that it was good luck if all the knots in the happy pair's clothing were untied. In country districts the bride had her head uncovered on her wedding day, but after that she wore a cap.

Even the Queen herself had to publish her banns on her marriage with Darnley:

'The 21st of July, anno Domini 1565, the which day John Brand, minister, presented to the kirk a writing, written by the Justice Clerk's hand, desiring the Kirk of the Canongate and the minister therefore to proclame Henry, Duke of Albany, Earl of Ross etc. on the one part, and Marie, by the grace of God, queen Sovereign of this realm on the other part. The which the Kirk ordains the minister so to do with the invocation of the name of God.'

There follows an entry of the banns being published: 'Henry, Duke of Albany, Earl of Ross; Marie, by the grace of God Queen Sovereign of this realm. Married in the chapel.'

The marriage is then reaffirmed by another entry: 'The 29th day of July anno 1565 Henry and Marie, King and Queen of Scots.'

But after all this the royal marriage ceremony was fairly simple.

'Upon Sunday in the morning, between five and six, she was conveyed by divers of her nobles to the Chapel. She had upon her back the great mourning gown of black with the great wide mourning hood, not unlike unto that she wore the doleful day of the burial of her husband.

'The words were spoken, the rings which were three—the middle one a rich diamond—were put upon her finger, they knelt together and many prayers were said over them he taketh a kiss and leaveth her there.'

Darnley was taking precautions not to hear Mass—for fear of the Protestants.

After the Mass, the English Ambassador to Scotland, Randolph went on to describe the fun and frolics.

'According to the solemnity to cast off her care, and lay aside those sorrowful garments, and give herself to a pleasanter life, she suffereth them that stood by, every man that could approach her to take out a pin, and so being committed unto her ladies, changed her garments, but went not to bed to signify unto the world that it was not lust moved them to marry, but only the necessity of her country, not if she will to leave it destitute of an heir.'

Possibly this taking out of pins had something to do with the old superstitions of Scotland about leaving all the clothing untied. If this were the case, it did not bring much luck to the Queen of Scots. Although the Reformers had sanctioned Mary's marriage with Darnley, by the following year, possibly more sure of their strength in the country, they had thought better of anything which smacked of popery. In September 1566 the Kirk Session of the Canongate resolved 'that they would no ways authorize anything that is done in that idolatry chapel contrary to God and his word'. They had happily wiped the marriage from their minds at that time, and the following year, when Mary wanted to marry Bothwell *en secondes noces*, they were back on form. Mr Craig, publishing the banns, 'took heaven and earth to witness that he abhorred and detested the marriage because it was odious and slanderous to the world'.

Even Mr Knox himself could not escape a certain unpopularity caused by his second marriage at the age of fifty-eight to a girl of sixteen. He married Margaret Stewart, daughter of Lord Ochiltree. The circumstance of a young woman of rank, with royal blood in her veins, for such was the case, accepting an elderly husband so far below her degree, did not fail to excite remark; and John Knox's papist enemies could not account for it otherwise than by a supposition of the black art having been employed. The affair is thus adverted to by the Reformer's shameless enemy, Nicol Burne:

'A little after he did pursue to have an alliance with the honourable house of Ochiltree, of the king's majesty's awn bluid. Riding with a great cortege on a trim gelding, not like a prophet or an old decrepit priest, as he was, but like as he had been one of the bluid royal, with his bands of taffeta fastened with golden rings and precious stones: and as is plainly reported by the country, by sorcery and witchcraft, he did so allure that poor gentlewoman, that she could not live without him: which appears to be of great probability, she being a damsel of noble blood, and he one old decrepit creature of most base degree, so that such a noble house could not have degenerated so far, except John Knox had interposed the power of his master the devil, who, as he transfigures himself sometimes appears as an angel of light, so he caused John Knox to appear one of the noble and lusty men that could be found in the world.'

John Knox may not have been noble, but he managed to leave children by his second wife, so possibly he did not lack lust after all.

Another wedding which is recorded sounds like a very social occasion: 'The Lord Fleming married the Lord Ross's eldest daughter, who was heretrix both of Ross and Halket.'

Obviously the Lord Fleming was not unaware of the value of the Lord Ross's daughter.

'The banquet was made in the park of Holyroodhouse, under Arthur's Seat, at the end of the loch, where great triumphs was made, the queen's grace being present, and the king of Swethland's ambassador being then in Scotland, with many other nobles.'

These triumphs to celebrate marriages were not to last long, for three years later the Queen's Grace had fled, and the Reformers had won. But, in spite of their efforts, fun at weddings kept on breaking through the sad grey and brown of the Reformers' minds.

Birth and Baptism
As with all fundamental threads of life, birth and the christening of the child were interwoven in Scotland with old pagan practices and celebrations.

Before the birth the women of the family 'prepared a large and rich cheese called the kenno'. This large cheese was supposed to be kept a secret from the males of the family. Afterwards it was cut up and served to all the matrons who were looking after the mother-to-be. Presumably the linking of cheese with milk, and so with fertility, had something to do with the choice of such a curious dish.

As soon as the child was born he was put into a big vessel into which a burning coal had been dipped. Obviously this was merely a way of bathing the child in warm water, but coal and water were thought to have some magical significance. The new-born baby was then wrapped in a woman's petticoat if it were a boy, and a man's shirt if a girl.

It was considered to be unlucky if the child was praised for this might cause it to be 'forespoken' (i.e. unlucky). When the mother had sufficiently recovered, friends and relations assembled, and drank to the child. This party was known as the 'gossip's wake' or 'cummer-fialls', and it was an occasion for no heel taps, for it was thought that if anything should be left in the glass this might affect the prosperity of the child.

It was not long before the Reformers got around to taking the population to task about this too.

'Taking to their consideration the abuse of mixed meetings of men and women merely for the drinking of cummer-fialls as they call it—and the inconveniences arising therefore, as mainly the loss and abusing of so much time, which may be better employed in attending to business at home, by such as frequent the occasion thereof, the prejudice which persons lying in child-bed receive both in health and means, being forced not only to bear company to such as come to visit, but also to provide for their coming, more than is either necessary or their estate may bear. Considering also that persons of the better sort carry a secret dislike to it, and would be gladly content of an act of this kind that there might be to them some warrant against exceptions, which might be taken by friends and neighbours if the ancient custom were not kept by such, . . .'

the church fathers made an order for pains and penalties against cummer-fialls in their usual way.

Another obviously ancient custom connected with birth was that the mother and child were 'sained' after the birth. This was a ceremony in which a fir-candle was whirled round the bed three times. There could possibly have been a Norse influence in this idea, fir-trees having such significance for northern peoples.

At the time of the baptism the child was put into a basket over which was spread a white cloth on which were placed bread and cheese. The basket was then hung on a hook over the fireplace, and moved round three times. This was supposed to counteract the evil influences of fairies and any other malignant ill-wishing spirits who might be lurking about.

If the child was to be christened in church, the godmother who took it to church also took portions of bread and cheese, which were offered to the first person she met on the way. If the bread and cheese were not accepted by the passer-by, this was considered to be bad luck. Should there be a baptism at which a number of children were to be christened, then the males must be baptised first. It was thought that if a girl were handed up to the font before the boys, then she risked growing a beard.

Naturally, at the change-over from being a Catholic to a Protestant country, Scotland suffered a certain disruption of her old customs. Although the old custom of having two godparents was still followed, once the Reform had taken place these were called witnesses, the name godfather possibly smacking too much of papistry. The Scottish Reformed Clergy did not recognize a Catholic baptism. In 1564, there is a record of the Kirk Session of the Canongate:

'William Smibert being called before the Kirk why he suffered his bairn to be unbaptised, answers: "No, I have my bairn baptised, and that in the queen's chapel" because as he alleged the Kirk refused him; and being required who was witness unto the child, answers: "I will show no man at this time." For the which, James Wilkie, bailie, assistant with the Kirk, commands the said William to be holden in ward [imprisoned] until he declare who was his witness that the Kirk may be assured the bairn to be baptised and by whome.'

It seems fairly likely that the indicted William was a Catholic who did not want to divulge the name of his witness. It did not seem to matter to the church fathers whether the people attending heretical baptisms were lowly born or among the nobility for, on December 31, 1567, the Countess of Argyll was indicted 'for assisting at the baptism of James VI in a papistical manner'. She was made to 'submit herself to the Assembly who ordained her to make public repentance in the Chapel Royal of Stirling one Sunday in the time of preaching'.

Obviously the baptism of James VI and I had been a great social occasion, but between the christening on December 17, 1566, and the following year the Queen's party was in rout and it had become judicious to toe the official line. The christening had been conducted with great splendour. There were representatives from the king of France, the Queen of England, and the Duke of Savoy. The baby had been dressed in cloth of gold and all the nobles were present wearing the rich velvets and gold chains which were the status symbols of the age. Queen Elizabeth was godmother, and sent a gold font. This, alas—like so many other treasures—was dissipated, for it was melted down to pay Mary Stuart's soldiers when she was fighting with Bothwell against the Reforming lords. The sequel is recorded by a contemporary: 'One has told me that he saw the font broken, and also upon Wednesday the Queen bitterly wept.'

In her happier days, the Queen took baptisms more lightly. There was an old Scottish writer called Abacuck Bisset, who wrote a legal book called *The Rolment of Courtis*. This was written in the reign of Mary's grandson, Charles I. How he came by his baptismal name seems to show that looking in the Bible for names is a custom which has existed for many hundreds of years. The father who adopted this oddly named baby was apparently the Queen's caterer.

'One day, as she was passing to mass, he acquainted her with his having a child to be baptised, and desired her to give the infant its name. She said she would open the Bible in the chapel, and whatever name she cast up, that should be given to the child. The name cast up was that of the prophet Habakkuk, which in the form of Abacuck, was accordingly conferred on the future writer.'

In a similar fashion foundlings were often given names according to the whim of those who found them. A child picked up in a garden could be given the surname of Garden, or if in a Park, Park.

There are no proper baptismal registers before the middle of the seventeenth century, either because of the illiteracy of the people, or else perhaps because many of the records were destroyed with the monasteries' documents. The Baptismal Register of Errol commences in 1553, but the entries seem to have been copied from a former record which was destroyed.

Some parish clerks in the sixteenth century did record events which they thought to be worthy of preservation. The parish clerk of Aberdeen wrote down in his register the birth of James VI at Edinburgh. From the entry it is obvious that the record was made after the abdication of Queen Mary on July 27, 1567:

'On Wednesday the nineteenth day of June, this year of God 1566 years, our King's grace, James the Sixth King of Scotland was born in the Castle of Edinburgh, who reigns now above us, whom God might preserve in good health and in the fear of God, to do justice in punishing of wrong, and in maintaining the truth all the days of his life. So be it.'

Deaths

As with the other fundamentals, marriages and births, funeral practices varied in early Scotland according to the rank of the person being buried.

A Highland chief, attended in his lifetime by his retinue of status-giving followers, was no less well attended when he went on his last journey. Sometimes a Highland chief would be accompanied by thousands of his followers and the funeral procession of a chief could be over two miles long. 'At these processions were chanted, at intervals, the coronach or lamentation. Poured forth by an hundred voices it awakened the echoes,' as one writer says, 'and as an expression of tragic grief, was singularly effective.' With a good bout of misty Scottish weather, the wailing of the pipes, and the lamentations of the clan followers a Highland funeral procession must have been an occasion which would touch any but the stoniest heart.

As in Ireland, the Scots held a wake, and though there are no early descriptions of one of these, they apparently included a great deal of drinking. An eighteenth-century writer says:

'After the death of anyone not in the lowest circumstances, the friends and acquaintances of the deceased assemble to keep the relations company . . . they dance as if it were at a wedding, though all the time the corpse lies before them in the same room. If the deceased be a woman, the widower leads up the first dance; if a man, the widow. But this Highland custom I knew to my disturbance within less than a quarter of a mile of Edinburgh, before I had been among the mountains. It was upon the death of a smith, next door to my lodgings, who was a Highlander.'

The bodies of the poor were buried quickly to avoid the expense of a 'latewake', but richer persons were expected to remain unburied for at least a week, so that the vigils and wake could be kept up.

Late wakes sometimes ended with a banquet on the evening before the funeral, and the festivities ended with a funeral dance and bagpipe music.

Even the most humble people were expected to offer whisky to the people who attended the funeral. The amounts of whisky and ale consumed at funerals were considerable. At a later date it was recorded that a gallon of whisky and ten gallons of ale had been drunk at one funeral and presumably earlier generations had not been more abstemious, for in the sixteenth century there was passed an Act of Parliament 'restraining the exorbitant expenses of marriages, baptisms, and funerals'.

If the old Roll in the Museum of Antiquities in Edinburgh, giving the order for a funeral procession of a nobleman at the beginning of the new century, is anything to go by, the organization not to mention the entertainment must have been considerable.

Here is the procession considered to be suitable for a nobleman of rank.

The procession starts off with twenty-four hooded men, rather like the penitents in a Spanish Easter procession; these walked two by two, carrying the coats-of-arms of the dead nobleman and members of his family.

There follows two stewards, and behind them four trumpeters dressed in mourning with black crape hanging from their hats, and embroidered coats-of-arms attached to the trumpets. Then comes a gentleman bearing a funeral banner of taffeta, the skull and crossbones with two flanking spades, and the words *Memento Mori*. Two more men follow carrying the dead man's pennant (in mourning) and his standard (in mourning).

His horse follows, clad like a horse in a medieval tournament, so that only the horse's hooves are showing; but sombrely with black trappings.

Another posse of men with different pennants, and banners of a symbolical nature follow. Yet another horse is shown, this time with

85

a lackey, both horse and leader clad in colours. All these banners, pennants, and horse trappings have red and white edgings as opposed to the black and white carried by the other gentlemen in the procession.

There follow five men in file bearing the dead man's helmet, gauntlets, arming sword, spurs, corselet and an antique shield. All of these pieces of armour are carried on poles, except the shield.

After the procession of the armour comes a man riding in full medieval armour on a caparisoned horse, followed by five men carrying the quarterings of the dead man's arms. The Horse of Parliament, riderless and caparisoned in heavy black is then followed by eight men in file carrying the various quarterings of the family—the dead man's father, mother, father-in-law, mother-in-law, grandmother, and grandfather on the father's side; and grandmother and grandfather on the mother's side.

It is obvious from this display of ancestry that when anyone claimed to be of 'noble blood', from time to time he had to produce banners to prove it.

Following the family display come two macebearers, and another man carrying yet another coat of arms; then comes the master of ceremonies—very necessary with so long and complicated a procession—who carries a black wand and wears a hat much bedecked with black crape.

The rear of the procession consists of three men carrying firstly his coat of arms with supporters, and then, the final gloomy touch, another skull and crossbones again with the words *Memento Mori*. The final banner shows the Roman fasces with wings on them and the words *Fugit Hora*.

If this was the kind of funeral procession expected for a nobleman it was no wonder that Parliament was concerned about the expense of funerals.

From this grandeur to the wretched peasants in the fields is a long step indeed—from the processional way in Edinburgh to the northern Highlands. In a book called *Sports and Pastimes of Scotland* by Robert Fittis it is recorded, rather oddly, that the danger which the dead had to contend with in the northern regions was not the expense of entertaining their friends—that was the family's worry. It was that of being dug up by wolves.

'The wolves ransacked, when hungry, even churchyards for new-buried corpses.' Along the tract of Eddrachillis, in north-west

Sutherland, the inhabitants took to burying their dead on the adjacent Isle of Handa. Indeed, the book of Highland minstrelsy collected by Mrs D. Ogilvy, quotes a ballad about this:

Thus every grave we dig
The hungry wolf uptore,
And every morn the sod
Was strewn with bones and gore;
Our mother earth had denied us rest
On Ederachillis' shore.
To Handa's isle we go
Encircled by the sea,
A swimmer stout and strong
The grey wolf needs to be
And cragsman to scale the rocks
If he follow where we flee.

One of the reasons for these gruesome epilogues to a funeral may have been the fact that the method of burial in the north of Scotland was very primitive. The bodies were placed in graveclothes, but only at a depth of one or two feet. In Caithness the bodies were placed with the heads northwards; in the eastern lowlands the graves were all similar with the feet resting towards the east. In some districts it was thought that the body in the grave was only safe from evil influences if it was carried three times round the churchyard in the direction of the sun. This custom may have been, like other old practices, of pagan origin.

As in so many Roman Catholic countries, the normal practice before the Reformation was to have a requiem mass. This was very often held annually on the day of the person's death or on the day of their burial, and money was given by relatives to the Church to have a mass said on that day for the repose of the dead person's soul. On the eve of this mass there was a gathering in the house of the survivors and they observed a ceremony of the 'dergen' or 'dirgie' (dirge) when they lamented the dead. The following day the requiem mass was said.

Unbaptised babies were not buried in the same plot of ground as that of people who had been baptised. Suicides were also buried apart. They were buried between two counties, either on the mountain tops or on the sea beach at low tide. A lonely burial for a lonely deed.

The earliest registrations of death are to be found in Aberdeen. These begin in 1561, and in Edinburgh, at the Canongate, in 1565. In the Death Register of the Canongate can be found the record of the murder of David Riccio. The record is succinct: 'Monsr. David ves slane in Halrydhouse the IX day of Merche anno 1565.'

The entries about Darnley's murder show certain discrepancies. The record in the Canongate states: 'The King's Grace blown up with buder in the Kirk of Field the X of February 1566,' but in the Register of Aberdeen it is equally firmly stated:

'The ninth day of February the year of God 1566, Henry Stewart, Lord Darly, King of Scotland, who married Mary Stewart, Queen of Scotland, daughter to King James the Fifth, was cruelly murdered under night in Edinburgh in the Cowgate at the Kirk of Fydall by James Hepburn, Earl of Bothwell, and others, his assisters, whose deed God to Revenge. So be it.'

Scottish history having been, in the sixteenth century, bloody and sudden, the killing of the Earl of Moray is also recorded, sometimes inaccurately, in the registers. The Register at Perth records it as follows: 'The 18th day of January 1569 was the Regent slain in Linlithgow at ten hours afore noon.' But the clerk at Aberdeen goes into more detail about the melancholy event:

'The 23rd day of January the year of God 1569 years James Earl of Moray, Lord Abernethy Regent to the King and the realm of Scotland was cruelly murdered and shot in the town of Linlithgow by a false traitor James Hamilton of Bothwellhaugh by the conspiracy and treason of his own servant William Kirkcaldy and John Hamilton, bloody bishop of St Andrews, whose deed we pray God to revenge. So be it.'

The spelling, in the original, of the Registrar of Aberdeen somehow gives the record added force: 'bludy bischoip of Sanctandrois'.

He also records the massacre of St Bartholomew, and the murder of Admiral Coligny on August 24, 1572, and prays God to revenge these murders, too. Revenge was a quality which was much cherished and fostered at the time, but especially in Scotland where it was a political and social force.

While the simple poor were buried in shallow graves on the hillsides and in the countryside, the grander folk found their resting places mostly in the church or graveyards. In early times it was the custom to bury priests in or outside the churches where they had preached, which was natural and proper. The lord abbot and the princes of the church were buried in their abbeys and cathedrals, up to the time of the Reformation.

But the General Assembly of October 1576 rules that 'burials should not be made in the Kirk'. Those who transgressed this regulation rendered themselves liable to excommunication. In spite of this rule, lairds and lords, who replaced the Church princes, were often buried in the local churches attached to their land, even after the Reformation.

As with many other practices, the customs which had been usual before the Reformers came on the scene were found hard to break.

CHAPTER FIVE

EARNING A LIVING: ON THE LAND

It is easy to give a totally depressing picture of Scottish agriculture in the sixteenth century, with stunted children peering out of smoky hovels with only a hole in the roof for ventilation, keen north-easterly winds whistling through the sides of the stone and turf-made cottages put together without any form of lime, and with only an ox-hide hanging down over the entrance instead of a door.

All this could be true, because Scotland at this time was mostly a treeless country, poor and with a very primitive notion of farming and farming practices.

But Mary Queen of Scots' father, who, like his daughter, wrote poetry, describes a different picture of girls and young men at the fairs, the sound of songs and smacking kisses, the cheerful paying of reckoning at the alehouse, and the fair thronged with pedlars selling their wares. And courtships, quarrels, men brawling and their wives scolding them until, beaten in their turn, the wives decided to keep the peace by keeping silent.

> Was never in Scotland heard nor seen
> Such dancing or bouncy mirth,
> Neither at Falkland on the green,
> Nor Peebles at the Play,
> As was of fun and jollity,
> When I was at Christ Kirk on a day
> There came our kitties, washed clean, full gay,
> At Christ Kirk on the Green.

The 'kitties' was the contemporary phrase for girls. It presents a cheerful picture of simple fun and happiness. Another anonymous writer describes the shepherds eating their lunch or disjune, 'making great cheer of every sort of milk'—milk, because their meal consisted of butter, cheese, and curds, which they eat with rye bread and 'fustean skones'. After the disjune they began to talk 'with great merriness that right pleasant to be heard'. They danced and told one another tales.

James was constantly wandering about the country, on his missions to administer justice or perhaps simply, as we have seen, to allow his followers to consume the dues which were owed to him, and on these occasions there are many instances of his paying for singers and musicians. He was obviously a man who enjoyed jollity and liked to enliven his official duties with a little song and dance.

The Labour Force

It has already been mentioned that in the thirteenth century Coldingham priory paid three merks for Turkil Hog and his sons and daughter. This was not an unusual kind of sale. The abbey of Dunfermline kept a kind of stud book which contained the pedigrees of all the serfs on its estate. This included the names of the persons whom the daughters had married and the tax paid by the bondmen when the married daughter's services were denied to the abbey in this way. These bondmen or 'neyfs' are mentioned in abbey accounts to the end of the fifteenth century. But by the sixteenth century the practice of near-slavery had almost ceased, although the peasants still had to give services, as well as rent, for their patches of land which they cultivated for the Church or for the local lord or laird.

Agriculture was much promoted in Scotland by the various orders of monks. The Cistercians, who owned the abbeys of Melrose, Newbattle, Dundrennan, Kinloss, Cupar, Deer, and Balmerino, worked enormous estates where they cultivated the land in an orderly fashion. Other orders of monks raised wheat, vegetables, and fruit trees, and their employees lived in cottages clustered round the granges or barns.

There is scanty direct evidence of descriptions of the countryside or of the state of agriculture in Scotland in the sixteenth century. But it is generally agreed that very little progress was made from the feudal days until the more scientific methods which were brought in during the eighteenth-century expansion of agriculture all over the British Isles.

One description of the state of the land in the fifteenth century was given by Aeneas Silvius Piccolomini, the envoy of the Pope who visited Scotland. He says that the country was bleak and wild, with few trees and very little corn. A 'sulphurous stone dug out of the ground' (coal) was used as fuel. The towns were without walls, the houses built without mortar, with doors of ox-hide. The diet of the common people was fish and flesh—and bread was a luxury or sweetmeat. The men were

'short in stature, but of daring enterprise; the women were fair, and saluted with their lips as freely as did Italian women with the hand. The horses were small, and were used without bridles. Trading with Flanders the people exported hides, wool, salt fish, and pearls. They hated the English, who in turn disliked the Scots and dreaded their incursions.'

Apart from this vivid description of Piccolomini, who afterwards became Pope Pius II, most of the evidence about Scottish land and its cultivation comes from the rent books of the old abbeys. These show that the monks, even when their tenants were no longer bound to them as 'slaves', exacted certain standards of cultivation and fostered the fertility of the soil as much as they could. The land must be planted with trees, hedges, and broom. Both trees and hedgerows were protected, and broom was used to enclose cottages, gardens, and rabbit warrens.

The Cistercians at Cupar Abbey exacted certain duties before they would even grant a lease. The prospective tenant of Carsgrange, for example, must 'preserve trees, keep open ditches, and watch the orchards'. David Howieson, who leased three gardens from the monastery, was bound in 1542 to cultivate onions, colewort, parsley, beet, and lettuce. He also agreed to nourish the fruit trees, prune the hedges, repair the stone fences, preserve the alleys, and keep clear the watercourses. The final duty which was exacted from him was that he should not let one single crow build a nest 'within the bounds'.

Other work exacted from a tenant might be ploughing or digging, supplying fishing tackle to the monks when they went fishing, providing the abbot's carriage with horses, furnishing fuel, digging peat and driving it to the monastery 'along with bent, roots, and branches of fallen trees'.

They also had to provide what was known as 'carriage service'. This was divided into two kinds, common or short carriage and the 'great draught'. The great draught was a yearly chore when two horses and four oxen had to be provided to drag the monastery goods from Cupar to Dundee where they were exported or sold.

Rent in kind could include oxen, calves, sheep, lambs, hogs, and kids; from their granaries the tenants provided oats, barley, straw and corn for the horses as well as pullets, hens, capons, eggs, and butter.

It was compulsory for the tenants to cultivate their 'yairds' or gardens. Other clauses in various leases dealt with the moral aspects of the tenants, for the monks were obviously realists as well as excellent cultivators. One lease would be null and void if the tenant 'not prove sober and temperate, preserving more strictly a kindly intercourse with his neighbours and relatives'. Trouble with the neighbours is no new problem.

Some leases were to be forfeited if the tenant was guilty of theft or the retaining of stolen goods, or the destruction of young trees or the removal of ancient ones. Other forfeitures would follow 'unchaste behaviour', and 'sorning' or sponging. There were strict rules for the cutting of turf: a 'vegetable' layer must be preserved so that the topsoil could be replaced to provide fair pasture, and the pastures must be irrigated from the neighbouring burns.

Apart from providing hedges, broom was planted to counteract bogs, and to try to prevent malaria. There were also laws against allowing 'guld', or marigolds, to grow on the land. The penalty for allowing marigolds to grow was the forfeiting of a sheep for every marigold plant. This seems a stiff punishment.

The fertility of the soil was safeguarded by the use of peat ash, stable manure, the refuse from the brewhouses, and bakeries. Another method of keeping the soil fertile was to graze the sheep, hogs, and calves where the corn grew, but if cattle were found in the corn after the Feast of the Nativity of St John the Baptist (June 24th) they would be forfeit.

After the fifteenth century many leases were granted for nineteen years. Robert Forsyth writing in 1805 says,

'It is probable that this term was fixed upon the golden number, or cycle of the moon, in astronomical calculations. Our ancestors had much faith in the influence of the moon, and appear to have believed that a farmer did not obtain a fair chance of success in his employment, if he was not allowed to occupy his lands for nineteen years, because a complete revolution of good and bad seasons did not occur in a shorter time. During the first half of the term, he might have wet summers and bad crops; but during the remainder of the period, it was in this case supposed that he would be compensated by seasons of a contrary description.'

The leases seem to have been granted to husbands and wives jointly, and could be passed on to the eldest son, if he was named by his parents. If the tenant died with no sons, then his daughter could take on the lease through her husband, who was known as the 'gude son'. At other times a tenant could name the people to whom he wished the lease to be assigned on his death.

Although widows could take on their husband's leases, they had to have permission to marry, otherwise their leases became forfeit. Should the second husband be approved, then a fee for the transfer of the lease was exacted.

As with other kinds of work, second-hand clothes were often given as part of the wages because cloth was expensive. A mason of one of the monasteries was promised one of the abbot's old albs, 'reaching to the ancles', every year. The picture of sub-tenants working around in old abbots' albs is somewhat comical, although no doubt they were not the elaborate fine linen and lace albs which were afterwards worn by the grandees of the Church. In this case they were probably his second-best albs, made of coarse linen which could be used as a labourer's smock.

Although tenants were expected to give some form of military service to the monks, owing to the state of the country with reavers and wild Highlanders likely to carry off cattle and sheep, this was certainly necessary as much for the benefit of the tenants as the the monks. In the tenants' leases it was stated that they 'must keep in readiness leathern coats, bows, arrows, swords, bucklers, and axes, also plated armour for the head and legs'.

The Lochaber battle-axe was an ancient weapon which consisted of a shaft of ash to which was attached a double-sided weapon—on one side a crescent shaped axe, and on the other a hook for dragging attacking horsemen from their saddles.

The handlers of spears and lances were supplied by the tenants themselves who grew in their enclosures 'ash trees, sauchs, and osiers'. Sauchs were willow trees, and presumably, like the modern cricket bat, the lance handles had to have a certain elasticity and spring to them, especially if they were designed for hooking attackers from their horses.

One monastery due which led to many abuses was the taking of the best beast of the herd on the death of a tenant. Although many monasteries did not insist on this right, the smaller ones did. At the break-up of the monastery estates, the lords and lairds, who took over the abbey estates, used this right as a means of despoiling bereaved tenants. This iniquitous tax on inheritance was called 'caupe or herezeld', and was not finally repealed until the eighteenth century.

There seem to have been two or three classes of tenants of the old abbeys: firstly, the freeholders; then the abbey administrators, known as 'kindly tenants of the Church'; and finally the labourers. Some of the administrators eventually became the owners of the land after the Reformation. John Porter, formerly porter of the abbey at Cupar, became overseer of a large part of the lands. By the end of the sixteenth century this office had become hereditary and was transferred by the heirs to the family of Ogilvie and the earls of Airlie.

Methods of Farming

Farming was extremely primitive in the Scotland of the period, partly because of the lack of knowledge of scientific methods and partly because of the rugged nature of the land. Agriculture in Scotland was indeed a system which had been evolved over the centuries, and there was no break in the simple methods until the eighteenth century.

The land was divided into ploughgates. This was a portion of land which eight oxen could bring into cultivation in one year and was between 104 and 120 acres. The larger measurement of land was called a davoch, from the Celtic *damh* (pronounced *dav*), an ox, and *ach*, a field. This was about 400 acres.

Although very little has been written about the methods of farming until the eighteenth century, there was apparently a fairly uniform method over the country. This was called 'infield' and 'outfield'. The infield was the most fertile land and was very often held by one tenant—although it could be held in common—and farmed in strips. Sometimes it could be the land nearest to the farm; at other times it would be the land which was the easiest to work. The infield would receive all the farm manure, and the crops grown on it would be barley or oats, with occasional crops of wheat, or peas and beans.

The outfield was mostly pasture but occasionally some of it was

95

ploughed up for crops. Manuring was done by letting the farm animals graze there. Owing to the infertility of the outfield, such land as was cultivated was allowed to go out of cultivation from time to time, or strips would be allowed to go fallow, or the areas of cultivation were moved from place to place as they became less likely to produce good crops. The outfield was usually held in common by several tenants.

As a rule, an area of a hundred or so acres (or a ploughgate) was held in common by a number of tenants, who each contributed an ox to the common plough, plus, of course, their own labour. This commonly-held land was a useful way of cultivation with the primitive methods used, because it was hard to drain the boggy patches or to sweeten the sour ones, and the farmers, living from their land, and dependent upon it for their daily bread, could not risk having a bad crop on a very wet or very dry piece of land.

The method of moving the cultivation of the land from place to place is an early German process described by Tacitus: 'Arable allotments are shifted yearly, and there is unallotted land to spare.'

Adam Smith quotes from a Swede, in the eighteenth century, on the same subject:

'They make scarce any manure for their cornfields but when one piece of ground has been exhausted by continued cropping, they clear and cultivate another fresh piece of land, and when that is exhausted proceed to a third. Their cattle are allowed to wander through the woods and other uncultivated grounds where they are half starved.'

Adam Smith remarks, 'It is a system of husbandry not unlike that which still continued to take place in so many parts of Scotland'.

The system of infield and outfield is possibly derived from the Anglian influence which had great weight in the Lothians, and like their language spread to other parts of Scotland. It is unlikely that these farming methods could have been handed down by the Gaels, who did very little farming.

With the decay of the feudal system there had been many beneficial changes in the leasehold system, but much letting and sub-letting was building up a number of landless people without obvious places in the agricultural scheme, and is probably one reason for the number of beggars who roamed the land. Another cause of

6. *Top:* Glamis Castle

left: Cawdor Castle

7. *Top:* Borthwick Castle   *bottom:* Craigmillar Castle

disruption was a gradual turning away from the keeping of flocks and herds to the growing of various kinds of crops.

It is not correct to see the towns and the country as two separate entities at this time. For the burghs were extremely small and the merchant classes all had their own strips of farmland outside the town limits so that, in one sense, almost everyone was engaged in some form of subsistence farming.

There is an early law which orders 'all rustics living in the burghs to begin to plough fifteen days before the Feast of the Purification'. Should any of them have more than one team of oxen they are to sell to those who have none, and other rustics 'shall dig with their hands and feet to maintain themselves'. This could mean that they were ordered to use their foot-ploughs.

The foot-plough was a shaft, 6 feet long, fastened to a 'sole' about a yard or more long, shod with a piece of iron like a one-sided blade. When the foot was applied to the pin which stuck out of the shaft, the iron shoe was driven into the soil, and the shaft acted as a lever which turned the sods. It is quite possible that when leases exacted so much digging from the tenants, the digging would have been done by this kind of foot-plough.

These foot-ploughs were still in use in remote parts of Scotland and the Isles in the nineteenth century, and there are photographs of men using them.

Most of the information about early methods of agriculture has been built up by the careful study of abbey records and leases. Some writers say that the ploughgate, or 100 acres, was worked in common by four husbandmen holding leases from the abbey or the laird, assisted by their cottars or 'hinds'. This necessity of working land in common was again brought about by the difficult soil and the heavy and primitive implements used to cultivate it. The heavy plough was drawn by eight oxen, and needed four to six men to use it. Two led the oxen, one or two held the stilts, and one cleared the 'mould board'. Another man was needed to regulate the breadth of the furrow by means of a long pole attached to the plough by an iron hook.

Another type of large plough consisted of a crooked piece of wood with a pliable piece of oak fastened to a yoke laid across the necks of the oxen. The man who guided the plough used a handle, and the driver went in front dragging the oxen by the horns. This was done by the men leading the teams, singing or calling to them

D

as they urged them forward. The hired hands or 'hinds' followed, levelling the furrow, and breaking up the earth. The method of ploughing was to plough down the slopes. This did not serve to conserve the moisture in the land.

Other agricultural methods were equally primitive and biblical. Grain was separated by using a flail, while the chaff was blown away in the wind. The same kind of primitive flail was also used in other lands which were connected to Scotland either by invasions or emigrations, such as Norway, Ireland, and the Orkneys.

Methods of preparing the corn for eating were equally simple and these continued to be used for several centuries. Here is one description:

'The ancient way of dressing corn which is yet used in several isles is called graddan from the Irish word *grad* which signified quick. A woman sitting down takes a handful of corn holding it by the stalks in her left hand, and then sets fire to the ears which are presently in a flame. She has a stick in her right hand which she manages very dextrously beating off the grain at the very instant when the husk is quite burned, for if she miss of that she must use the kiln but experience has taught them this art to perfection. The corn so dressed, is winnowed, ground and baked within an hour after reaping from the ground. The oat cake dressed as above is loosening, and that dressed in the kiln astringent, and of greater strength for the labourers.'

Sometimes the corn was pounded in a hollowed stone with a wooden mallet. Another method was the use of the quern or hand-mill. The quern was formed by two flat circular stones, one above the other. The top stone had a hole in it with a narrow funnel, and revolved on a wooden pin controlled by a handle. The person grinding the corn dropped it into the funnel with one hand, while revolving the upper stone with a wooden handle. The majority of these querns were made of stone, although a quern made of solid oak has been discovered. The meal fell from the grinding stones on to a wide tray, and the coarseness or fineness of the grain could be regulated.

An old song equates the noise of the 'quernie' with a good meal.

The lament stills the sad heart
The lullaby stills the bairnie,
The music for a hungry stomach
Is the grinding of the quernie.

Some of the monasteries owned water-mills, and in this case their tenants had to take their corn to the mill to be ground, giving in return every twenty-first sheaf to the monks, or about five per cent of their corn. They also had to keep the mill ponds in good condition, and were sometimes required to supply their own millstones.

The crops which were grown were wheat, oats, bear (a kind of coarse barley), peas and beans. In the sixteenth century, farming was done for subsistence, and such wheat as was grown was considered a luxury. It was taken to the abbey landlords to be exchanged for oats. All over Scotland at this period the monetary rents were very small, sometimes a mere token rent, and the real bulk of the rent was paid in kind. The landlord would receive grain, meal, meat, poultry, cheese, butter, and eggs. Small wonder the sovereigns and nobility moved about to allow their considerable following to consume their 'rents' *in situ*.

Services by Tenants

A few of the services exacted from the tenants as rent have already been mentioned. Among other terms of old leases are the following:

Supply reapers at harvest time.

Winter the landlord's cattle.

Sow 'parks'. A park was a grazing ground.

Maintain fences, carry sand, maintain the sheepcotes, drain the marshes, supply 16 wagon loads of divots.

The tenant of an orchard had a 'life lease', but in return he had to 'build houses, dykes, plant hedges and the best possible fruit trees, and keep the pastures in good condition', as well as keeping the 'stanks' (ponds) for fish and eels clean and clear, and looking after the dovecote.

In exchange, the abbey gave the tenant his meal for bread, but the tenant had to supply the abbey with fruit at current prices, and the fowler supplied the abbey with game, and the fishermen with fish.

The abbots and their minions seem to have been very good businessmen.

Four tenants of the abbey of Cupar were in charge of its woods and fishing grounds. The abbey supplied the fishermen with boats and nets, but the abbey was to receive £10 towards the cost. In exchange, the fishermen were to supply the abbey with three dozen salmon, either fresh or kippered, during the year 'according to their fortunes'. They must not sell, eat, or give any fish away before their quota to the abbey had been made up. If they did not catch enough salmon, they were allowed to make up the total with inferior fish.

The craftsmen such as masons, carpenters, and others were engaged by the year—there is one record of a mason and his son being engaged by the abbey for life. These men received a cottage, money, and a daily allowance of fish and meat, as well as 'two short white cakes and a half gallon of convent ale'. Their craft names became their surnames—Mason would be the hereditary descendant of the monastery or convent mason, and Porter the monastery or convent porter. Monastery and convent in those days had a similar connotation.

Condition of the People

As with so many other accounts of life in Scotland at this period, the reports of travellers and others present different views of the general life of the people and their food.

Some writers wax lyrical about moors and forest abounding with game and 'herds of kine with flesh of a marvellous sweetness, wonderful tenderness, and excellent delicateness of taste'. Pictures are painted of rivers, lochs, and seas teeming with fish.

But Don Pedro de Ayala, travelling in Scotland at the beginning of the sixteenth century, remarks coolly that the land was not adequately cultivated but the corn was good. Estienne Perlin, writing in 1551, says that the arable land was indifferent and 'most of the country a desert'. Both were impressed by the numbers of sheep and cattle.

The tales of the large herds of cattle and flocks of sheep are corroborated by the lists of exports of wool and hides which were Scotland's main trading commodity at this time. The diet of the general run of the people was meat and fish, eked out by small quantities of coarse barley bread or oatcakes.

A bad harvest was a great disaster and led to what was called 'dearth'. The 'dearths' easily led to famine conditions owing to the lack of transport and the difficulty of helping those living in remote districts. A parish priest keeping a journal in the last half of the sixteenth century records:

1554—Stormy winter.
1563—Year of Scarcity—1 boll of meal £3 6s 8d.

This compared with 18s the following year, when the weather presumably was better.

The priest's district was in fact lucky, for the 1563 conditions were worse elsewhere, where it is recorded: 'This was a year of dearth throughout Scotland. Wheat being six pounds the boll [about six bushels], oats fifty shillings, a draught ox twenty merks.'

John Knox, in his usual way, draws some religious comfort from the famine: 'All things appertaining to the sustentation of man in triple and more exceeded their accustomed prices.' He goes on to say that the famine was most severe in the north, where the Queen had travelled the preceding autumn and that many died there.

'So did God, according to the threatening of his law, punish the idolatry of our wicked queen, and our ingratitude that suffer her to defile the land with that abomination, the mass. The riotous feasting used in court and country wherever that wicked woman repaired, provoked God to strike the staff of bread and to give his malediction upon the fruits of the earth.'

Unfortunately for Mr Knox, as was noted by the parish priest, there was another 'dearth' in 1571, after the Queen's flight.

It is recorded:

'On Feb. 22nd there came a great storm and snow and hail and wind, that nae man nor beast might take up their heads, nor gang nor ride, and many beasts, and many men and women were perished in sundry parts, and all kind of vituals right dear, and that because nae mills might grind for the frost' [*Chronicle of Fortingall*].

There are constant records of different methods of rationing owing to the fear of famine. In 1526 it was forbidden to export tallow, and again in 1540. In 1551, wine and other produce were to be sold at fixed prices 'owing to dearth'. In 1567 and 1578 'no victuals were to be taken out of the country', and in 1592 it was again forbidden to take cattle or sheep out of the country. There were also acts making it illegal to eat meat, in Lent, on Wednesdays, Fridays and Saturdays.

In the West Highland Museum at Fort William there is preserved, 'A permit to eat Flesh', signed by James VI:

'We understanding that our loved James Menzes off the Weyme is subject to seiknes and dyveries diseases of the body therefore we be the tennour hereof gives licences to the said *James* and his *spous and five persons* with thame in company to eat fleche alsoft as they please from the 5th day of March instant till the 19th day of April without further exam or danger to be incurred by them therefore in body and in goods notwithstanding any by our acts proclamations or inhibitions made in the contrary presents given under our signet and subscribed with our hand at our castell of Stirling the day of Marche and of our Regnne the 12th year 1578.'

The words 'James' and 'spous and five persons' are written in a different hand. Possibly they were added by other members of the family anxious to join in the dispensation caused by the head of the family's delicate stomach.

Lent would have been the obvious time to compel people to eat fish because of the shortage of winter pasture for the cattle, and the fact that many had had to be killed off and salted down. Like the Jewish dietary laws, it is possible that the Roman Catholic 'fish-eating' laws had a basis of common sense, although some writers allege that the 'fish on Fridays and in Lent' rule was originally brought in to help give employment to fishermen.

According to Privy Council Records: 'Seeing that in the spring of the year all kinds of flesh decays and grows out of season, and that it is convenient for the commonweal that they be sparit during that time, to the end that they may be mair plenteous and better cheap the rest of the year,' the Council expressly forbade the use of flesh of any kind during Lentern. Fleshers, hostellers, cooks, and taverners were forbidden to slay any animals for use during that season under pain of confiscation of their moveable goods.

One commentator says: 'This order was kept up in the same terms for many years, a forced economy preserving a rule formerly based on a religious principle.' It is, therefore, anybody's guess which came first, the fishing and fasting, or the Order in Council.

Naturally, as the Highlands were a more primitive and less cultivated land than the rest of Scotland, they lived more from their flocks and herds than the people living in the more fertile Lowlands. Laws were promulgated ordering the barons and

102

freeholders 'not to keep great herds of sheep to the wasting of other men's land, and they were ordered to live upon their own lands, rents and farms'. The way they lived on their 'lands and farms' comes vividly to life from a description in the *History of the Family of Mackenzie*. From the context it is obvious that Mary Queen of Scots was making one of her royal progresses round the countryside.

'John Mackenzie of Kintail was a great courtier with Queen Mary. He feued [leased] much of the lands of Brae Ross. When the Queen sent her servants to know the condition of the gentry of Ross, they came to his house of Killin; but before their coming he had gotten intelligence that it was to find out the conditions of the gentry of Ross that they were coming, which made him cause his servants to put a great fire of fresh alder wood, when they came, to make a great reek; also he caused to kill a great bull in their presence; which was put altogether into one kettle to their supper. When the supper came, there were half a dozen great dogs present, to sup the broth of the bull which put all the house throughother [upside down] with their tulyie [fighting]. When they ended the supper, each one lay where they were. The gentlemen thought they had gotten purgatory on earth, and came away as soon as it was day; but when they came to the houses of Balnagowan and Foulis and Milton, they were feasted like Princes.

'When they went back to the queen, she asked who were the ablest men they saw in Ross. They answered: "They were all able men, except that man that was her majesty's great courtier, Mackenzie—that he did both eat and lie with his dogs." "Truly," said the Queen, "it were a pity of his poverty—for he is the best man of them all." Then the Queen did call for all the gentry of Ross to take their land in feu [take up their leases] when Mackenzie got the cheap feu, and more for his thousand merks than any of the rest got for five.'

A story which seems to prove that being oneself and not keeping up with the neighbours sometimes produces financial advantages.

At this time there were apparently still wild cattle in some parts of the Highlands, for it is recorded as one of the horrors committed by the Earl of Lennox on Lord Fleming's land that

'They have slain and destroyed the deer of his Forest of Cumbernauld, and the white kye [cows] and bulls of the said forest, to the great destruction of policy and hinder of the commonweal. For that kind of kye and bulls has been kept these many years in the said forest, and the like was not maintained in any other parts of the isle of Albion as is well-known.'

They are, however, supposed at this date, to have also been found in the 'parks' of Stirling and Kincardine.

These cattle are believed to have been survivors of the original wild cattle of the Caledonian forest.

Hector Boece describes them as white, with lion-like manes, fierce, untameable, and shunning society so much that they would 'eat nothing which the hand of man had touched'.

From these old descriptions they sound like strange heraldic animals.

Like any hill-people, the Highlanders certainly sent their beasts to the uplands in the summer; but by the sixteenth century this custom had ceased in the Lowlands. The word 'shealing' reflects this custom and can be found in place names like Luckysheal, Popelsheal, and Outsheal. A 'shealing' was a shelter for sheep and men.

Another curious custom was the division of land or rights, or duties in the land by the casting of lots. The share of a piece of turf-cutting, or the duty of mending a road, could be allotted in this way. Even the burgh agricultural holdings in Glasgow and Edinburgh were divided by the casting of lots. So normal was this custom considered that the Privy Council of Scotland suggested that the 'debatable land'—the land in dispute on the borders of England and Scotland—should be settled by the two countries by drawing lots.

The general picture which is built up from the records of the period, from the rent books, and the rent disputes, is of an agricultural and fishing community eking out a precarious living from their toil, and eating the products produced in their own districts.

There were the other usual hazards.

'In all this time frae the Queen's grace putting into captivity [October 1567] the thieves of Liddesdale made great hardship on the poor labourers of the ground, and that through wanting of justice; for the realm was sae divided in sundry conspirations, that there was nae authority obeyed, nor nae justice executed' [*Diurnal of Occurents*].

Men were not the only predators. In the reign of Queen Mary the wolf plague spread unexampled devastation. 'The ravages were such that the extensive forests in Rannoch and Lochaber and other places were burned down to prevent the harbouring of these ravagers', writes one historian.

The reality of the wolf menace is made plain by the fact that many tenancy agreements contained wolf-hunting stipulations, and requirements to keep hounds to hunt the wolves.

In 1552 'the tenants of Nether Illrik are to maintain a hound for tod (fox) and wolf', and about the same time the lease of land in Glenisla to the Countess of Crawford and her son, Lord Ogilvy, contained the stipulation that they 'sustain and feed ane leash of hounds for tod and wolf'.

Boece, in his history, describes how the inhabitants of Glenmore protected their fowls against wolves:

'The wolves are right noisome to the tame bestial in all parts of Scotland except one part therefore named Glenmore in which the tame bestial get little damage of wild bestials, especially of tods; for each house nourishes a young tod certain days, and mixes the flesh thereof, after it be slain, with such meat as they give to their fowls and other small beasts, and so many as eat of this meat are preserved two months after from any damage by the tods, for tods will taste no flesh that tastes of their own kind; and be there but one beast or fowl that has not tasted of this meat, the tod will chase it out among a thousand.'

But in spite of their harsh lives, the Scottish seem to have been a people with plenty of resilience. Froissart says that although the country seemed totally devastated after an English raid, the country folk 'made light of it, they had driven their cattle into the woods, and with six or eight stakes would soon have new houses'.

If they lacked amenities, they also lacked the character which is easily cast down by disasters. Therein, lay their sturdy, unbreakable strength.

It has endured to this day.

CHAPTER SIX

EARNING A LIVING:
IN THE TOWNS AND ON THE SEA

It might be thought that in the small compact towns the citizens, being free from raids and clan feuds, would have lived in affection, harmony, and happy industry. This was not always the case. Class privileges rather than sweetness and light could prevail. As with the rest of the country, fracas and what were locally known as 'tulzies' were the order of the day. A tulzie could mean anything from an ordinary dispute between citizens to an all-out riot and manslaughter or murder.

Many of the troubles of the citizens arose from the fact that there were several classes of citizen, all insisting on their rights. The 'top people' in the burghs were the merchants. It had been the custom for the kings of Scotland from an early date to create royal burghs, and in these enclaves the merchants were given the monopolies of trading, both in exports and imports.

Under the merchants came the craftsmen, but this class, in order to qualify, had to employ at least two hired hands. A lower class of tradesmen were those who worked for themselves. The lowest of all were the journeymen, working by the day for other people, and the apprentices who were kept under strict surveillance for seven years.

It can easily be seen, given the Scottish character, that these disparate elements could from time to time boil up into a good tulzie or two.

The burghs in Scotland were still partially farming communities, because the burgesses, whether merchants or craftsmen engaged in trade, had grants of land which they worked on the basis of feeding themselves and their families. The lands were small holdings of six or ten acres and had certain duties connected with them. Burgesses were expected to keep them clear of 'underwood with a view to making their profit from them'.

Right up to the end of the sixteenth century, the burgesses in the burghs combined their trading with their agricultural pursuits. One writer has traced the old ploughlands of the burgh in the ground plans of the city of Glasgow.

It is very difficult, in the modern context, where agriculture and manufacture are carried on separately, and, in most cases, divorced from one another, to understand a primitive economy where a merchant would keep farm machinery in his town office.

In modern European conditions there is a tendency to think that the industrial community is the most important factor in the country's economy. But in the Scotland of the period under review the main exports were the primary products: hides; wool; salted fish; the skins of rabbits, deer, foxes and marten. Other exports were a simple woollen cloth of a coarse weave. By the beginning of the seventeenth century the products were the same, but they included salt, coarse linen cloth, linen yarn, and knitted 'hose', as well as leather.

Although some of the goods, like salted fish in barrels, and the coarse linen and woollen cloths, could be considered to be 'manufactured' in the sense of being finally prepared, or made by hand, these were simple industries, sometimes cottage industries, which took place mainly in the rural areas outside the burghs, and the towns were small. They were theoretically highly organized, and each type of citizen had his especial rights or, in some cases, lack of rights.

The only people who had any really strong and effective rights in law were the burgesses and the freemen of the burghs. The merchants were the especially privileged class. Next came the craftsmen, who were also freemen, although with less privileges. They included weavers, butchers (fleshers), hammermen (these included smiths), masons, coopers, slaters, goldsmiths and armourers, tailors, furriers, glovers and saddlers.

In the fifteenth century, anyone who held public office in the town as a provost or bailie had to be a merchant. This led to many abuses because, as the members of the old town council were empowered to elect the new town council, they had a natural tendency to elect their trading friends and colleagues to take their places. As a result of this, by the sixteenth century there were constant disputes between the merchants who were engaged in the happy task of protecting their privileges, and the craftsmen equally intent on extending theirs.

These quarrels were widened into the general disputes extending over the whole country. For example, the craftsmen seized the opportunity of supporting the Regent, Queen Mary of Guise Lorraine, against the merchants and the Reformers. In this way the burgh quarrels between merchants and craftsmen were welded into general disorder in the country, to the benefit of neither.

That the craftsmen had a certain case for their discontents is undeniable. The merchants were the only people allowed to trade in skins, in hides, in wool, and in fish. As these basic commodities formed the bulk of the exports, it was virtually a blanket monopoly which included most of the trade of the country, except local trading. Not only did the merchants hold the whole of the export trade in their hands, but they also had the exclusive rights of importing the luxuries from abroad which were craved by the nobility and by other rich merchants.

In some cases the craftsmen won certain rights, but in many burghs the merchants managed to cling to their privileges. Certain agreements were, however, worked out in order to define the areas of trade in which the merchants should deal exclusively.

An agreement in Dundee pinpointed the goods which the merchants considered it 'dignified' to handle. They would deal in 'smalls', which included wine, wax, woad, and spices, except the coarse varieties. 'Grosswares' they eschewed, and these covered oil, soap, butter, fruit, dried figs, raisins, prunes, eggs, vinegar and fish. There is a certain discrepancy in this agreement because in other burghs the burgesses seem to have retained a monopoly of fish exports. Possibly their dignity rose and fell according to the state of the markets.

According to this Dundee agreement, although the merchants were prepared to forgo their interest in 'grosswares', the craftsmen on the other hand had to pay more taxes and dues to the burgh. So although the dignity of the merchants of Dundee was offended by the idea of dealing in soaps and oils, it seems to have pursued a forward course when it came to their monopolies of the bulk of the country's exports, like wool and hides. No dignity seems to have been affected by handling these.

Not only did the merchants jealously guard their trading privileges with the outside world, but they also strictly enforced their rights to the handling of the local products of the craft trades in the surrounding districts, the villages, and the countryside beyond. A number of acts were passed protecting the rights of the merchant.

At the beginning of the century no man of craft could trade unless he renounced his craft. Like the Victorian traders who made a great distinction between the man who traded wholesale, and the man who lived above the shop, the sixteenth-century merchant insisted that no merchant should be a manufacturer of goods. Should he be found carrying on a little shoemaking in the back of his office he would be considered unfit to be a merchant.

The laws protecting the merchants' monopolies were indeed strict. In 1503, an act was passed protecting 'the freedoms and privileges of the burghs', which confirmed that anyone who lived outside the Royal Burghs was forbidden to trade, use merchandise, sell wine, wax, silk, or spices, and, as an additional protection, there were to be no 'packmen' trading in the burgh of Leith, or any other place in the king's burghs. As the burgh organizations tended to be uniform all over the country, a law passed in one burgh could soon apply to burghs in other districts. In the sixteenth century, thirty or more Acts were passed confirming these monopolies.

An Act in the early part of the sixteenth century, which was renewed in 1535 and 1555, further protected their privileges because it stated that provosts, bailies and others 'having jurisdiction within the burghs were to be changed yearly and that none have jurisdiction within the burgh but if they merchandise within the said burgh'.

The burgesses were encouraged by the crown to enforce their privileges. This was partly because it was easier to collect dues from a body of merchants, intent on enforcing their own rights, than it would have been to collect taxes in a more indiscriminate way. There was, however, a distinct difference between the taxes paid by the merchants and those paid by the craftsmen. In 1550, the taxation levied on the property of the merchants was double that paid by the craftsmen. The method of collection was also different, for the merchants were assessed as individuals but the craftsmen were assessed as a 'craft', that is on a collective basis.

The merchants, exercising their monopolies in inward and outward trade, nevertheless had certain duties, apart from special taxation. They had to keep a good horse, and be prepared to muster in defence of the burgh when called to that duty.

Occasionally the names of one or two craftsmen are found on the town councils, but these are the exception rather than the rule, as is proved by the constant quarrels between the burgesses and the craftsmen.

It is, of course, a mistake to assume that the burgh organizations were of a rigid nature, but in the sixteenth century the organizations of the burghs did become less fluid. The Dean of Guild gradually became more and more identified with the organization of the burgh. In Edinburgh, for example, his duties were extensive and included responsibility for the loading of ships. This, possibly, included the supervision of 'cockets' or bills of lading showing that taxes had been paid on outgoing goods.

The Dean of Guild's Court was another official body which held sway over burgh business. The members were chosen from the town council, and they took over the settling of disputes about boundaries and buildings, as well as supervising weights and measures at the 'Tron', the official town weighing place. They regulated the loading of ships, and upheld the town's laws in cases of ships' captains, merchants, and any disputes which concerned them.

This court also taxed the guild brethren in order to provide for merchants who had fallen on evil days and their dependants.

It can be seen that, although the merchants had the burgh organizations fairly and squarely in their own pockets, they also had certain duties to perform, and although some of these may have been in their own protection, they formed in fact a responsible and necessary element in the burghs. While their monopolies and privileges may seem to modern eyes to indicate great disparities, yet the burghs were small enclaves or trading posts carrying on their trade in primitive conditions in a primitive country, and often at considerable risk to their foreign cargoes from pirates, storms, and foreign depredations. If and when their 'ships came in', their tenacity had won them a reasonably fair reward.

Some of the merchants' trading was transacted on a community sharing basis. In the early part of the century the bailies and Town Council of Edinburgh held that any freeman of the burgh could demand a share of any bargain if made by one of his fellow burgesses in his presence. The only condition was that he should be able to put up his share of the stake. It was also the custom that when a merchant lost his goods 'by storm or pillage' his fellow merchants must share in the losses so incurred. This seems to have been an organization operating rather like Lloyds today.

Merchants were expected, apart from being liable for general military duties when called up by the sovereign, to keep order in the burghs. This was no mean task when the disorderly state of the nation is taken into account. To this end, merchants and craftsmen were expected to keep handy various weapons such as axes, swords, and whingers, as well as armour, so that when trouble brewed in the burgh they could come to the aid of the provost and bailies.

They were not always as quick on the draw as the town authorities would have liked, as is proved by the fact that the Privy Council in 1597 commented on the 'great slowness' of the citizens in coming to the aid of various parties. It seems that they were not as eager to don armour, swords and bucklers 'for ridding and stopping parties which commonly enter in sudden tulzies, quarreling and pursuite of others by way of deed upon the public streets of the burghs', even though, when aroused by the wakestaff, they were supposed to 'come forth armed with 2 weapons and watch wisely and busily'.

The powers of the burgh authorities were considerable and included all punishments of criminals, including flogging, branding, ducking, banishment, and even the death penalty. They also, inevitably, brooded over the morals of the town.

The Craftsmen
Bearing in mind that the bulk of the trade was in the hands of the merchants, it was probably natural that the Government should incline to the side of the merchants. Most of the manufactured goods needed by the country were imported; therefore the craftsmen had much less importance in the general economy than the merchant class. And apart from being richer, the merchants, like many people who have achieved a certain standing in the world, were anxious to protect their status.

In 1587, Robert Vernour, a skinner, was admitted to being a 'guild brother'. But only on certain conditions. He was solemnly exhorted

'to observe and keep the laws and consuetudes of burgh concerning the Guild brethren therefore, and to desist and cease from all trade and occupation in his own person that is not comely and decent for the rank and honesty of a Guild brother, and that his wife and servants shall use and exercise no point of common cookery outwith his own home, and namely that they shall not sell nor carry meat dishes or courses through the town to private chambers, hostelries, or other parts outwith his own house under whatsoever colour or pretence, nor pass to bridals nor banquets within or without this burgh to the occupation of common cookery, or yet to be seen in the streets with their aprons and serviettes as common cooks and their servants use to do.'

This warning is given out 'under pain of losing the freedom of the city and of the Guild brotherhood for ever'. Clearly it was no good Mr Vernour thinking he could become a guild brother and carry on a cookshop on the side.

But not all craftsmen were prepared to give up their perks, and in fact by 1560 it had to become law that anyone dealing in staple wares was to become a burgess and a guild brother. In 1579, a certain guild brother, having suffered a series of trade losses, tried to get out of belonging to his guild. In spite of his plea that he was 'so extraordinarily extended in all extents bygone . . .' he was not let off his taxes, and he remained an unwilling member of the guild.

Owing to the nature of the trade, which was in the primary products, at first the craftsmen were marginally smaller in numbers than the merchants. Men called up to defend Edinburgh in 1558 numbered 736 merchants to 717 craftsmen. But by the beginning of the seventeenth century the craftsmen were beginning to outnumber the merchants.

The numbers of people engaged in the various crafts gives some indication of their relative importance. In Edinburgh in 1558 there were 178 tailors, 151 'hammermen', and 100 bakers. The total quota of men engaged in making cloth, both weavers and fullers, was only 69. There were 25 barbers and 9 furriers. Goldsmiths, in spite of their glittering trade, were not a prosperous craft in Scotland at this time.

Although the merchants handled all the imports and exports of the country, the craftsmen were allowed to do their own selling from booths or stalls in the burghs. Presumably, as the trade was on a very small scale, the merchants had no objections to this.

There were fourteen main crafts, although many of these, as for example the hammermen, were divided into various areas of specialization. There was a distinctly religious aspect to a craft's activities. Each craft had its own altar at the local church. During civic processions or on solemn state occasions they each carried their craft banner, and like the merchants they supported their own poor and indigent members, as well as the dependants.

If the merchants had their trade monopolies, so did the craftsmen. They had the right to forbid 'unfreemen' from selling their goods in the burghs, except on the rare market days. Because the craftsmen were under the necessity, like the merchants, of paying taxes and bearing arms, so they had the sole right of trading in the burgh, and the pages of the statute books are filled with appeals from craftsmen against the unfairness of strangers daring to come into the burghs and sell their goods.

There were also complaints about unfreemen 'dwelling in the landward and in the suburbs of the burgh to the great damage of the craftsmen who are utterly decayed and depauperated on account of these unfreemen at their very doors eating their bread out of their mouths'. This complaint came from the weavers, who had the sole monopoly of weaving in the burgh of Edinburgh. Sometimes interlopers who had been sneaking in to sell hats, or meat, were cornered and ordered to join the appropriate crafts of hatmakers and fleshers.

The position taken up by the craftsmen were based on the argument that they considered it unfair that men who had not to shoulder the duties and taxes of craft members should be allowed to trade freely in the burgh.

Another of the rights of the crafts was that their deacons had the power to enforce a certain standard of work both from the craft members themselves, and from the 'unfreemen' who were allowed to sell their goods on market days.

The organization of the crafts in the burghs was built upon the supervision of the quality of goods and the regulation of prices. It was inevitable that there were many accusations of craftsmen taking advantage of their privileged position in the trading situation, especially in times of 'dearth', to put up their prices.

Many of the disputes by craftsmen have the ring of the modern trade-union 'demarcation' quarrels. In Edinburgh the magistrates often took a hand in the various craft quarrels—they settled a threatened bakers' strike, and they made peace between some tailors and furriers in a 'who does what' quarrel. In 1577 the masons and 'wrights' were overcharging, and they had forbidden unfreemen from coming in to finish the work they had already started. The magistrates overruled the masons and their fellow workers, until such time as the masons brought down the prices for their work.

The apprenticeship for joining a craft varied from three to seven

years, though most of the crafts demanded the longer apprenticeship. Whether this was to keep up the standard of workmanship or
to restrict entry into the craft is a moot point.

There were, of course, certain privileges for the sons of the
freeman of the craft. A hatmaker had to serve his seven years, but the
son of a hatmaker only needed to serve three years. Another way of
restricting entries was that the sons of freemen paid less as an
entrance fee to join the craft than did outsiders.

James VI did not take a good view of craftsmen or of their
privileges. Writing to his son, Prince Henry, the King remarked:

'The craftsmen think we should be content with their work, how
bad and dear soever it be, and if they in anything be controlled, up
goeth the blue blanket [the banner of the Edinburgh craftsmen].
But for their part take example of England how it hath flourished
both in wealth and policy since the stranger craftsmen came in
among them. Therefore not only permit, but allure, strangers to
come here also; taking as straight order for repressing the mutining
of ours at them, as was done in England at their first in-bringing.'

Craftsmen vs. Merchants, and the Burgh Authorities
The struggles between the craftsmen and the merchants had been
going on for more than a hundred years. The main heads of their
quarrels were the eagerness of the craftsmen to have a share in the
government of the burghs, and their natural anxiety to join in
foreign trading. On the other hand, Parliament and the Government
authorities, for their part, were trying to counteract the restrictive
practices and price-raising activities of the crafts.

It was in this sphere that the struggles merged into the more
general struggles of the country. All the Acts which tried to restrict
the powers of the craftsmen were passed by Parliament, while those
favouring the craftsmen were promulgated by the sovereign.

From the end of the fifteenth century, and for the next hundred
years, the struggles in the burghs went on. Nor did the craftsmen
react peacefully to their troubles. In 1543, when some deacons of
the craft were complaining to the provost about their wrongs, they
did not rely on mere words, but drew their swords on him and as a
result were sent to Edinburgh Castle. Fortunately for them the
English attack on Edinburgh intervened, and the Regent Arran had
them released.

By the middle of the century the craftsmen had managed to advance their cause with the Queen Regent, and in 1556 Mary of Guise Lorraine desired that the privileges of the craftsmen should not be curtailed. The excuse given was that 'everything is done more carelessly among those craftsmen at this day than formerly'. As a result of this decree, the craftsmen were allowed to trade in the kingdom and 'beyond as would seem most advantageous to them'. The Queen's sole proviso was that the craftsmen should pay their back taxes. Despite this sting in the tail, 'the Queen's decree was solemnly proclaimed with sound of trumpets and heralds with her coat of arms. The market cross all hanging about with fine tapestry which was right honest and pleasant to all craftsmen.' And no wonder.

Whether the merchants felt so happy about it does not seem to have been recorded. Moreover an echo from Stirling seems to prove that the craftsmen's newly won rights were sometimes illusory. For the craftsmen at Stirling complained that although they were allowed by royal decree to 'use merchandise', the town authorities and the merchants prevented them from trading. It was one thing to get a decree passed, and another to see it enforced, especially in sixteenth-century Scotland.

Although the craftsmen and merchants, each in their own way, were attempting to keep trade in their own hands, market days were days of real 'free trade'. These fairs were occasions not only of trading opportunities, but also of a good deal of fun and games. Once the 'peace of the fair' had been proclaimed, then all the unfreemen and the travelling traders were able to please themselves from whom they bought and to whom they sold.

The fixing of prices of certain staple goods by the burgh authorities was a very necessary part of town life in the sixteenth century. The ever-present threat of starvation made this vital to the well-being of the community. Not only were prices fixed, but the quality of the goods was examined by the burgh authorities. Sometimes when famine threatened, as in 1587, exports of foodstuffs were forbidden.

The crime which the burgh authorities attempted again and again to stamp out was 're-grating'. This was buying up foodstuffs in time of dearth, and re-selling them at a higher price. In a country whose economy was on a subsistence level it was natural that this habit should have incurred the censure of the burgh authorities, but although the intentions of the burgh authorities were good, and many of their laws were equally good, the carrying out of them provided a contrast of intent. One example of this was the 'Common Good', a fund which included fishing rights, mills, tolls, and certain general land about the burgh which was farmed in common. The money derived from these different enterprises was supposed to be used for the benefit of the town. But as the years went by and the 'Common Good' was let out on leases to different parties, less and less of the revenues seemed to flow into the town, and more and more into the pockets of the burgh authorities.

In 1535 it was stated that the burghs 'were becoming wasted and destroyed in their goods and policy and almost ruinous', and although a run of bad trading years was said to be partly to blame, it was also said that 'outland men were becoming provosts and bailies for their own weal in consuming the common goods of the burghs', activities not confined to the sixteenth century.

The adopted remedy was that only merchants were to be elected to be officials of the burghs. But whether this proved a remedy may be doubted.

In spite of their sweeping powers the authorities do not seem to have been able to keep the burghs either quiet or peaceful. 'Leagues and bands' were common. 'Tumults and tulzies' were everyday occurrences. And at the end of the century, in Edinburgh,

'certain craftsmen and other wicked persons under silence of night convened themselves together in arms, and in a most treasonable, barbarous, and shameful manner broke into the house of one of the bailies by means of forehammers, and with awful countenances and boasting words forced him to liberate a malefactor who was imprisoned in the Tolbooth.'

Foreign Trade

During the fifteenth and sixteenth centuries the Low Countries were the centre for the exchange of goods of all kinds. In many cases, when the Scots traded, it was on a barter basis. A merchant could order the captain of a ship to exchange his wool either for English currency, or for silks from Flanders. Many Scottish merchants traded in common, and a curious custom had grown up that the bulk of their trade should be conducted with a specified 'staple port' in the Low Countries.

Dues were collected at the port of export, so the staple port was merely a centre for actual trade, and for the mutual protection of

Scottish merchants abroad. In 1541, the staple port was fixed at Campveere, sometimes called Veere, in the Netherlands. This agreement was made between James V, father of Mary Queen of Scots, and the Emperor Charles V who owned the port.

In return for fixing the staple port in his territory the Emperor gave the Scots merchants certain privileges and rights: a commodious and convenient house furnished with a garden, and a cistern for rain-water with leaden pipes, to be provided rent free.

Shipping was protected. If Scottish ships in harbour were robbed or spoiled, they could obtain restitution from the Emperor. Reasonable rates were to be charged for those who were shipwrecked, and free pilots, buoys, and beacons were to be provided at the expense of the Emperor, and Scottish ships must be found moorings in the harbour. 'Workmen, porters and suchlike' were also to be provided at reasonable fixed rates, and storage space was provided at equally fixed rates. Protection against overcharging by the customs was also promised.

A Scottish Conservator was established to oversee this trade at Campveere, and he was to decide any disputes between Scot and Scot. This seems to have been a very sensible precaution on the part of the Emperor, in view of the character of the Scots at this time.

The Scottish merchants were also to be provided with a chapel in one of the local churches and a chaplain to attend to their spiritual welfare.

In return for the privileges granted by the Emperor the Scottish merchants agreed not to trade with any other port. But unfortunately, shortly after this agreement, the troubles in Flanders which involved them in their struggle against their Spanish overlords broke out, and the Scottish merchants were temporarily driven away from Campveere. The port was re-established in 1578 and it was then said that the 'staple being vagrant and removed to sundry places this time bypast through the occasion of the civil tumults wherewith the most part of Flanders has been these divers years occupied to the hurt of many'.

The 'Conservator of the Privileges of the Scots Merchants' acted as a kind of combination of commercial attaché and ambassador in the Netherlands. He had to regulate all the laws concerning the merchants' presence at the staple port, and he was also the representative of the Convention of the Scottish Burghs.

The idea behind the establishment of this staple port was to have a central trading post in the Low Countries, the great cloth-making district of their world; and as wool was the major export of Scotland it was necessary to have some organization abroad to handle this vital part of the Scottish economy. The importance of the Scottish wool trade in the international marts of the period, is shown by the fact that at the beginning of the sixteenth century the English sovereign was obliged to reduce tariffs on the export of wool from England, so that English wool could compete in the markets of the Low Countries with Scottish wool. Otherwise English wool could not be sent to the Low Countries 'from the great plenty of Spanish and Scottish wools in the Flemish market'.

The general shortage of manufactured goods of all kinds is made clear by Froissart, who comments, 'There is neither iron to shoe horses nor leather to make harness, saddles or bridles; all these things come ready made from Flanders by sea; should these fail, there is none to be had in the country'.

But in spite of an Act passed in 1587, which declaims about useless imports, 'costly, superfluous and unnecessary merchandise . . . commonly brought within this realm', the rich seemed to have managed to evade the needs of the common weal and to have done themselves moderately proud. Imports of 'incarnate' silk, mantles of Roman satin, fine woollens from England and Flanders, as well as gold cups still came in on favourable tides.

In the ledger of one Andrew Haliburton, the process of barter is clear: wool, salmon, and hides—in exchange for books, a tombstone, vessels for the church, an altar frontal, wine, spices, cloth, clothing, hats, napery, thread for embroidery, a case for a clock, and tiles for the floor.

Timber was another necessary import owing to the shortage of Scottish forests. This came mostly from Scandinavia, but also from Germany. From Germany likewise came the swords which were such a necessary part of the equipment of the sixteenth-century Scots.

The chief exports to England were linen cloth, yarn and salt; and the imports were wheat, oats, and beans. France took cloth, wool, skins, and salt fish, and in exchange the Scots imported wine, prunes, walnuts, and chestnuts. To the Baltic ports went cloths and skins, and the imports were flax, hemp, iron, pitch and tar.

Ships and Shipping
The writer of the *Complaint of Scotland* gives a poetic and carefree impression of a ship setting sail from a Scottish port:

'The mariners began to wind the cable with many a loud cry and as one cried all the crew cried in that same tune as if it had been an echo ... and as it appeared to me they cried their words as follows "veyra, veyra, gentle gallants. Wind I see him wind, I see him ... haul all and one, haul all and one. Haul him up to us, haul him up to us".'

The charming picture of the different jingles for each operation of the ship hauling the anchor, hauling up the sails and the sheets, gives a picture of jolly tars singing sea-shanties.

The reality was somewhat different, for the seas around Scotland swarmed with pirates. Even as late as 1581, the Firth of Forth had become a 'receptacle of pirates'. In fact, after his defeat, the Earl of Bothwell set off to the north of Scotland to become a pirate, and sometimes the burgh magistrates themselves joined in the general spoliation of the ships of others.

Nor were the Scots the only pirates; the English and the Dutch joined in the general fray. Between 1569 and 1587 goods worth more than £20,000 were taken from Scottish ships.

James Melville says,

'At my first coming to Anstruther there fell out a heavy accident which vexed my mind ... and drew me nearer to my God. ... One of our ships returning from England was beset by an English pirate, pillaged, and a very good honest man of Anstruther slain therein.'

The upshot of this incident was that the men of the town fitted out two ships and set out in hot pursuit, making

'every ship they foregathered with, of whatsomever nation to strike and do homage to the King of Scotland showing them for what cause they were rigged forth, and inquiring of knaves and pirates. At last, they meet with a proud, stiff Englishman who refuses to do reverence.'

With one shot the Scottish hit the Englishman's mainsail—which was said to be the merciful providence of God, as the Englishman had a large gun on board which he had not had time to discharge. The Scots then approached the coast of Suffolk and found some English pirates who had taken one of the Scottish ships and were in the act of despoiling it.

The English left their prize and the Scots pursued them on to the land. 'The gentlemen of the country and the towns beside hearing the noise of shooting, gathered with haste supposing the Spaniards to have landed', for this was in 1588, the year of the Armada. The Scots were then questioned about their prisoners, and the justices of the peace, when they had been told of the Scottish wrongs, and when

'they saw the King of Scotland's arms with two gallant ships in warlike manner, yielded and gave reverence thereto, suffering our folks to take with them their prisoner's ship and the pirate's ship which they brought with them and half a dozen of the loons [rascals]; whereof two were hanged on our pier end, the rest in St Andrews, with no hurt at all to any of our folks who ever since then have been free from English pirates. All praise to God forever. Amen.'

This story gives a different slant to the usual stories of the gallant Elizabethan seamen, although quite possibly the English and the Dutch could tell equally stirring tales of the depredations of the Scottish pirates.

The Convention of the Royal Burghs made great complaints about pirates to James VI, saying that the ships putting out of Dundee were despoiled 'as if there were neither God in Heaven, nor we had a King on earth to complain to'.

Sometimes the merchants took reprisals into their own hands. The Lords of the Council were asked to stop two men from disposing of the goods in a Dutch ship which they had captured because

'through taking of the Hollanders in times by past there has been great trouble and hurt because all merchants in time of peace shall put their gear to the sea and under truce of peace shall be taken up by Hollanders which ligh in their highway passing to France and Flanders'.

Piracy and near piracy, legitimate trading, and reprisals for injuries done, caused many international complications. The Scots seized Dutch ships in Danish waters; the authorities in Copenhagen then tried to arrest the Scots, who promptly set sail for Scotland. The Dutch then took possession of a Scottish ship in a Danish port, killed one of the crew, and sold the cargo of silks, velvets, and spices. The dispute was then carried merrily on in various countries.

Apart from piracy on the high seas, storms and shipwreck accounted for sending many cargoes to the bottom. Because of the risks of foreign trading, there were many co-operative ventures in the sale of cargoes. Sometimes twenty or more people would take shares in a cargo, and in one case no less than forty-three owners were concerned in a dispute over the cargo of an Edinburgh ship.

Allied to shipping was the trade in fish. Scotland was a large exporter of salted fish (herrings and haddocks) as well as salmon. In an age when fish was regularly eaten in Lent and on other days of abstinence, Scottish salted fish was used all over the Continent. Although in some cases the barrelled and salted herrings were referred to as 'Flanders herrings' throughout Europe, in fact they were re-exports which had originally come from Scotland to the flourishing markets of the Low Countries.

Salt, so necessary in this trade, was both imported and exported. The native salt was made by the evaporation of salt water with the aid of coal fires, but this salt was not suitable for the effective curing of fish, and on this account foreign salt had to be imported. As was usual in the Scotland of the period there were many regulations and disputes about salt.

The 'masters of the salt-pans' alleged that they could not make a living unless they were allowed to export some of their salt. There was the usual price fixing, and export by licence (there being nothing new under the sun) and, as is also usual, there were ways found of counteracting the rules. Sometimes salt was allowed to be exported only in exchange for timber or silver. The fish trade was very important to Scotland, as is proved by the disputes about fishing rights. In 1580 the burgh of Aberdeen complained to the Privy Council that their rights had been infringed 'seeing that without the industry and commodity of salmon no burgh nor inhabitant of burgh could well be but desert solitude'. They added a rider that in that case the burgh could not meet its taxes.

The Dutch and the Germans were fishing in the waters of the Outer Hebrides and the Shetland Isles, and in the early part of the century a fishery war was waged with the Dutch, the Scots alleging that they were being driven from their own fishing grounds by the Dutch. It was said bitterly that the city of Amsterdam had been 'built on Scots' herring bones'.

Quality of Life in the Towns

The tron, or public weighing place, and the market cross formed the centre of the official life of the trading community. The market crosses which were built in most towns had a gallery running round them and it was from here that the official proclamations were made, a very necessary act in a century when most people were illiterate.

The market cross was also the centre for the dissemination of news, the summoning of burgesses for military duties, and many other official acts. It was from the market cross in Edinburgh that Darnley attempted to whitewash his own deeds after the murder of Riccio—although this particular proclamation was received 'not without laughter' by the local citizens.

The streets were, of course, filthy, and constant Acts were passed ordering the citizens to get their middens off the main streets. Their pigs were to be either kept in sties or to be 'herded in the fields'. Swine were not to be allowed to wander loose in the streets. But more than a century later it was recorded that children had great fun riding on the backs of pigs in town streets.

The picture built up, then, of the towns and ports at the time is of small huddled streets round the central castle, of small ships setting sail for England and the Low Countries, of merchants doing business in their own houses which were a combination of shop, office, and farmhouse. Much of the shipping was coastal for, in spite of the constant trouble with England, a great bulk of Scottish trade was with England and was carried on in the teeth of wars, insurrections and revolutions.

Goods were carried from the ports by the chapmen ('cheapmen'). They often travelled in convoys of pack horses, presumably armed, for once outside the burghs they were subject to the same depredations as the small farmers, from the 'wild Scots' who preferred to live by feats of arms rather than soil their good right hands with trade. It was at one time the custom in Scotland for the 'good right hand' not to be christened with the holy oil at a baptism for this hand could be used for killing, and so was not blessed by Holy Mother Church.

The pedlars carried their goods in packs on their backs, and no doubt their trading was either restricted or dangerous. The roads were little more than moorland tracks between the hills and peat bogs. There were no carts used, even in agriculture, but simply a kind of primitive sledge, which was dragged. Even as late as the eighteenth century many agricultural carts had no wheels. The Scots knew about the wheel, of course, but because of the lack of roads the application of this useful invention was a near impossibility.

Rivers were crossed by fords, and the means of crossing them consisted of women who pulled up their skirts and waded across with a man or other burden on their backs. James VI is said to have facetiously remarked that one of the rivers in his kingdom of Scotland had 500 bridges. He was referring to a small town which had 500 fordwomen.

International trade, then, away from the ports, was carried on against odds which included lack of communications, physical hazards from river, mountain, wild animals, and winter snows, and death from raiding parties. It was no wonder that packmen and pedlars tried to ply their trades in the burghs. There were many chills in the air of the open country and mountainsides.

An added difficulty was money.

Owing to the troubled state of the country, the value of money continually declined. By the time James VI and I joined the crowns of Scotland and England, the value of the Scottish shilling had declined to a penny. It is odd, in the modern context of currency restrictions and attempts to regulate the flow of money, to see the Privy Council trying to do the same things in the sixteenth century when it was forbidden to take currency out of Scotland.

Other measures adopted were the barter of wool for foreign money, and the forbidding of the export of gold and silver. Some attempts were made to mine gold and silver in Scotland; leases were granted for the exploitation of gold mining both in the reign of Mary Stuart and her father, but with little results. After a while the mines were abandoned as uncommercial.

When the crowns of England and Scotland were joined, James VI brought the Scottish currency into line with English currency, and with the loosening of trade restrictions and the mutual exchange of ideas trade gradually increased.

At the beginning of the century, Aberdeen and St Andrews were more important trading towns than Edinburgh. This was partly because the sovereign moved his court from place to place. But when the court became settled in Edinburgh and its surroundings, the trade in Edinburgh and the port of Leith increased.

By the end of the century Edinburgh had become the capital of Scotland both for administration as well as trade.

CHAPTER SEVEN

RELIGION

Like all revolutionary movements the Reformation began slowly. The Renaissance opened the mind of man to the plastic arts, to painting, and to new forms of literature. At the same time the invention of easier forms of printing enabled that literature to spread. The coming of the Bible in the vernacular tongues made it possible for literate man to read, judge for himself and be no longer dependent upon the interpretations of the learned priests and monks. Again like all popular revolutionary movements, the Reformation had two points of departure—moral indignation and economic reform.

The Reformation came over more slowly into Scotland, partly because of the illiterate nature of the bulk of the inhabitants, and partly because Scotland in the sixteenth century was a remote country attached to the continent of Europe only by its sea-ports. Although the influence of France upon Scotland was, on the whole, limited to the large towns, the court, and the fighting men, once communications started to improve, and Bibles began to be imported, the Scots, like all the other nations of Europe, began to feel the subtle influences of the new doctrine.

Mary Stuart was born in 1542, but already before her birth the tentacles of the Reformers were stretching towards Scotland. Mary's father, James V, was quite aware of the abuses of the Church, but he never considered forsaking the Old Religion any more than did his daughter in her turn. On the other hand, James V did encourage Buchanan to attack the friars in his *Satire of the Franciscans*, and attended a performance of Sir David Lindsay's *Satire of the Three Estates* at Linlithgow in 1540. This play attacked the corruption of the clergy in coarse and rumbustious terms.

Nineteenth-century writers, secure in their morality and their Protestantism, condemn the Roman Catholic Church in rounded terms:

'The history of clerical celibacy is indeed tender ground. The

124

benefits which it is supposed to secure are the personal purity of the individual, his separation from secular ways, and interests . . . but the results were very different. Instead of personal purity, there is a long story of licensed and unlicensed concubinage, and appendant to it, much miscellaneous profligacy.'

But, even if the moral Anglo-Saxon indignation of the Protestant writers is left aside, the facts of the state of the Church speak for themselves.

In the years immediately before the Reformation it could reasonably be said that a great many churchmen, especially in the higher rungs of the bishoprics and monasteries, had numbers of children, and they made it their business to see that these children were well provided for.

Cardinal Beaton had produced five children; his successor, Archbishop Hamilton, three. The Bishop of Aberdeen had a number of children and married them off well. Bishop Chisholm of Dunblane also had children. When one of his daughters married Sir James Stirling of Keir, in 1542, she was presented with a dowry of £1,000 a year, and the good Bishop even contracted to keep Sir James and his wife for five years. Possibly the daughters of bishops were thought to have matrimonial disadvantages and extra cash was needed to marry them off.

The Prior of St Andrews had ten children altogether; three sons while still Prior, five sons when Bishop of Moray, and two daughters. This makes the lines in the *Satire of the Three Estates* very easy to understand:

How beit I dare not plainlie spouse a wife,
Yet concubines I have had four or five,
And to my sons I have given rich rewards,
And all my daughter married upon lairds.

In 1549 the Provincial Council of the Clergy, held at Edinburgh, condemned the clergy in round terms which left little to the imagination:

The clergy, therefore, were enjoined to put away their concubines, under pain of deprivation of their benefices; to dismiss from their houses the children born to them in concubinage; not to promote such children to benefices, nor to enrich them, the daughters with doweries, the sons with baronies from the patrimonies of the Church. Prelates were admonished not to keep in their households manifest drunkards, gamblers, whoremongers, brawlers, night-walkers, buffoons, blasphemers and profane swearers. The clergy in general were exhorted to amend their lives and manners; to dress modestly and gravely; to keep their faces shaven and their heads tonsured; to live soberly and frugally so as to have more to spare to the poor; to abstain from secular pursuits, and especially trading.

'Provision was to be made for preaching to the people; for teaching grammar, divinity, and canon law in cathedrals and abbeys; for visiting and reforming monasteries, nunneries and hospitals; for sending from every monastery one or more monks to the university for preventing unqualified persons from receiving Orders and from holding cure of souls; for silencing pardoners or itinerant hawkers of indulgences and relics; for compelling parish clerks to do their duty in person or to find sufficient substitutes; for registering testaments and inventories of persons deceased, and for securing faithful administration of their estates by bringing their executors to yearly account and reckoning; for suspending unfit notaries, and for preserving the protocols of notaries deceased; for reforming the abuses of consistorial courts.'

Every line of this indictment paints a picture of a church which has long ceased to fulfil its duties. Parallel with the moral abuses, the mistresses, the selling of indulgences, the parishes neglected, and the widows robbed, went the economic aggrandisement of the princes of the Church.

As we have seen, the Church not only owned great stretches of land attached to its monasteries and foundations, but also exacted tithes and many other dues. The right of the Church to tithes had long been accepted in Scotland as elsewhere. This meant that, however long and hard a man worked, the Church creamed off a tenth of his industry. And this not only applied to obvious wealth, but was extended to include farm produce, livestock, poultry, and even the produce of gardens, fruit and vegetables, and embraced flax, hay, products of mills and fishing, and wool from the backs of the sheep. As well as all his other perks the priest could demand rights of pasture for his cattle anywhere in the parish.

The lengths to which this was taken is illustrated by a quarrel between a man called Straiton and the clergy about a tithe of his fish. His servants were accustomed to go fishing, and the clergy demanded a tenth of the catch. When the collector insisted upon his pound of fish, Straiton told his servants to throw every tenth fish back into the sea and said, 'Let them seek their tithe where I found the stock.' Unfortunately Straiton suffered for his attitude: he was burned at the stake.

Like the modern income tax, the taxes exacted by the Church were an enormous and ever-increasing field of annoyances and disputes, extending as they did into every field of human endeavour.

The Church obtained many additions to her lands and wealth by endowments on the death of pious landowners and nobles. She not only benefited by the death of the rich, but also exacted dues known as 'corse presents' on the death of every one of her parishioners. These moneys were taken from surviving relatives irrespective of the misery of their circumstances. Although many people were pleased to give an offering for the souls of their departed, the difference between what was exacted and what was legitimate led to abuses and disputes.

Other offerings were expected on happier occasions: the Sunday penny, the Christening penny, candles for Candlemas, and paschal offerings. As with many things which start in a small way, these offerings had been voluntary at the beginning, later began to be expected, and then were exacted.

Once a ruling class, like the Church, has so much wealth in its hands, it becomes an investor, and consequently the admonition to 'obstain from secular pursuits, and especially trading' can be readily understood in the context of the riches to be invested. In the same way, when an organization, whether it is ecclesiastical or secular, becomes sufficiently rich or powerful, the kind of people who are attracted to it change in character, and a powerful bureaucracy, well paid and pampered with benefits, will attract less dedicated people than a small bureaucracy with ideals. The kind of people who saw a future for themselves (and for their probable children) in a bishopric changed with the course of time. Many were worldly men, with an eye to the main chance, masquerading in the robes of bishops and cardinals. Church ceremonies became duties which they had to carry out as part of the job, like a lord mayor parading the streets after his election.

Some small attempts were made to reform the Church in Scotland. For example, the dues exacted from the relatives of the dead were

127

lifted from the very poor. But already it was too late; the open abuses had now caused too many voices to be raised against them. Once the economic balance of a country turns too far in one direction, and the riches and power are concentrated in too few hands, whether of bureaucrats or churchmen, there is a counter-swing, and this, combined with the new simplified doctrines preached by the Reformers, began to make its impact.

The first Scotsman to be executed for his adherence to the Reformed Religion was Patrick Hamilton, Abbot of Ferne, who had learned the new doctrines from Luther himself. He was executed on February 29, 1528, being burned at the stake in front of the College of St Andrews. But, as so often with this kind of summary execution, once the first martyr has been burned, the torch of reform is lighted. He died leaving a wife, a daughter, and a treatise in Latin giving a summary of his doctrines. This was translated into English by John Firth, an Englishman, and by 1540 there had already been three editions published.

Naturally, because most of the riches of the Church lay in the hands of the bishops and the abbots, the new doctrines began by permeating the lower orders of the clergy. The friars spread the doctrines up and down the country, raising their voices against the open scandals of the riches of the Church and the licentious lives led by churchmen. In Dundee, a friar named Erth preached a sermon, 'in which he touched upon the licentious lives of the bishops and the evils connected with excommunication and miracles'. The local Bishop of Brechin had his armed followers handle the friar roughly, and he was accused of heresy.

The friar, obviously a sound Scotsman who was sticking to his opinions, journeyed to St Andrews and consulted a well-known doctor from the Sorbonne as to whether what he had said could be counted as heresy. On being assured that it could not, the stalwart friar announced that he proposed to preach the same sermon again in the parish church of St Andrews. He took as his text 'Truth is the strongest of all things', and went on to say that excommunications should not be rashly or wrongly used, but only against real evil.

'But now the avarice of priests, and the ignorance of their office has caused it to be altogether vilified; for the priest whose duty and office it is to pray for the people stands upon Sunday and cries, "There is a flail stolen from them beyond the burn, the goodwife on

3. *Top:* Dunstaffnage Castle   *bottom:* Stirling Castle

9. *Top:* Edinburgh, the Cross
right: Edinburgh, the West
Bow

the other side of the street has tint a horn spoon; God's malison, and mine, I give to them that knows of this gear and returns it not."

The facts that Acts of Parliament, passed about the same date, referring to 'the dishonesty and misrule of churchmen' confirmed the friar's blunt words, mattered little. His outspoken sermon caused offence, and he was obliged to cross the border into England—where he was promptly imprisoned by Henry VIII. This time his offence was on the opposite count—that of defending the Pope. Like many honest men he was cordially disliked by both sides.

A number of outstanding churchmen had tried, in the years immediately preceding the spread of the new doctrines, to reform the Church from the inside. But the rot had spread too far. King James V was locked in conflict with his rebellious nobles, and because of the disturbed state and anarchy in the country, both on the Borders and in the Highlands, the bulk of the government of the country had fallen into the hands of churchmen trying to restore order.

But already the nobles, their hands raised both against the king and against the Church, began to see the beauty of the new doctrines, while at the same time contemplating the broad lands owned by the Church. The reform of abuses and personal advancement were suddenly seen to be blowing concurrently into the same broad attractive river. It is at times like these that moral duties become a positive pleasure.

So the doctrines spread on different levels: the level of the genuine zeal of many of the clergy of the lower orders, who saw the Church being destroyed by corruption; the level of the upper ranks of the clergy, who had studied abroad and brought back the news of the new doctrines on an intellectual level; and finally the level of the nobles, who saw the Church as a power structure which could be taken over to the moral advantage of the country, and to the financial advantage of themselves.

There was another factor, which was the pressure of the Reformed Church in England in general, and the pressure of Henry VIII in particular. Henry VIII, too, like most Renaissance princes, operated on a double standard. While exerting military pressure on the one hand, on the other he was attempting to woo Mary Stuart's father away from the Catholic Church on the grounds of its moral decrepitude. But his blandishments fell on deaf ears.

E

129

Replying to Henry, James V said: 'We may not, of our conscience, but first keep our part towards God, and our Obedience to Holy Kirk as all our forefathers had done these thirteen hundred years by past.' James V, although not averse to fathering illegitimate children, was not disposed to reject the Church as his moral guide, much as he might take a broad view of some of the doctrines in his private life. But although the King of Scotland remained steadfast to the old Church, the doctrines continued to spread, at least partly, by virtue of the persecution suffered by the lower orders of the clergy and the laity.

In 1539, James Beaton, Archbishop of St Andrews, died and was succeeded by his nephew David. In fact, anticipating his inheritance, David Beaton was safely installed in his new office six months before the actual death of his uncle. He had also consolidated his family position by obtaining a grant of land for his own natural son. By 1544 David Beaton had become not only a cardinal, but had also obtained, as well as his cardinal's hat, the post of Papal Legate. This was not bad going, but while the old-time clergy, as represented by the Beaton family, were sailing on to fresh honours and power, the persecution of the lower and reforming clergy continued.

Among those arrested for heresy was George Buchanan, afterwards to be tutor to James VI and I. George Buchanan, luckier than some of the other persecuted reformers, escaped and lived to write *The Tyrannous Reign of Mary Stuart*, a book which calumniated the Queen of Scots. Others of the reforming party were more luckless.

A young friar called Russel was burned for heresy at Glasgow. before he died he said:

'This is your hour, and the power of darkness; ye now sit as judges, whilst we stand before you, wrongfully accused, and more wrongfully condemned. But the day shall come when our innocence shall appear, and then ye shall see your own blindness to your everlasting confusion. Go forward and fulfil the measure of your iniquity.'

Like all repressive measures, the burnings of the heretics did not have the expected bonus. The proscribed doctrines continued to spread; and with each burning of a heretic, the flame of the Reformed Religion itself burned clearer. New laws were passed against heretical opinions. The very questioning of the authority of the Pope became a crime meriting death, and all meetings for the discussion of religious doctrines were banned. The State offered rewards to informers, hoping in this way to increase their knowledge of the way in which the new doctrines were spread.

The Regent Arran, a man of vacillating opinions, attempted like many weak characters to have the best of both worlds. He allowed the reading of the Old and New Testaments in English or Scottish. But, as very few Bibles were being printed at this particular time (1543), the concession made little material difference. A few months after authorizing the printing of the Bible in English, Arran changed his policy again and got rid of two Reformed preachers whom he had in his own household. As a result of the shilly-shallying attitude of the Regent, Cardinal Beaton became more powerful than before.

But in spite of their vacillating rulers, the ordinary people became more and more violent against the abuses of the Church. As so often happens, the lower orders and the peasants were those who had suffered the most acutely from the depredations of the clergy. It was then that the attacks on the monasteries began, symbols as they seemed of all that was rotten in the state of the Church.

John Knox quotes the Earl of Glencairn's verses giving a contemporary view of the monkish fraternity:

The new-made monk, though all his life before,
The name of blockhead or of dunce he bore
Becomes, as soon as shorn, both learned and wise,
Quick from his mind each imperfection flies,
He who but lately tended goats or cows,
When the grim cowl has decked his greasy brows,
Changed and grown learned, at once a face puts on
As grave as Plato or Xenophon.
Though all his early years he drove the plough,
A priest and prophet he commences now.

Cardinal Beaton reacted sharply against the spread of heresy, and in 1544 he struck hard. Numbers of heretics were arrested and brought before a court in Perth. Some were banished, but four were condemned. Among the four was the wife of a burgess Robert Lamb. Before being thrown into a pool, she gave her suckling child to some bystanders. Her hands and feet were then roped together, and she was drowned. This was the only act of violence against a woman for her religious opinions which was recorded in Scotland at this time. But even a solitary act of this cruel nature, and in these circumstances, has an impact far in excess of the circumstances which caused it. It gave added impact to the reformed simplicity of the new doctrine, and piled fresh infamy on the reputations of the clergy of the old Church.

It was about this time that George Wishart and John Knox entered upon the Scottish religious scene. Perhaps the martyrdom of Wishart, followed by the murder of Cardinal Beaton, and the subsequent condemnation of John Knox by the French to serve in their galleys—a melancholy train of events—added the necessary publicity and impetus to the cause of the Reformers.

George Wishart returned to Scotland in 1544. Among his supporters he numbered the Earls of Cassilis and Glencairn, and the Lords of Brunstone, Ormiston, and Calder. These nobles were under the influence, and possibly in the pay, of Henry VIII. Their aim was the destruction of Cardinal Beaton.

Some authorities contend that George Wishart was concerned in the plot against Beaton, but there is only the slim evidence of his name in one letter to link him with it.

Both sides of religious opinion in this age held their views literally to the death—whether it was their own death, or the deaths of others. And no doubt George Wishart was no exception to this stern rule. His co-religionists Knox and Calvin hymned the deaths of Henri II and François II of France as friendly Acts of God, known to be on the side of the 'Saints'. Possibly Wishart would have regarded the death of an opponent such as Cardinal Beaton with satisfaction, but this is not an equivalent of being actively concerned in plotting his murder.

There is no doubt that George Wishart was a man of great sincerity who was prepared to suffer for his opinions. Whether he would have been quick to visit sufferings on others for their opposing views is open to doubt.

At the time he began his preaching in Scotland, the Church was still rich, powerful, and predominant. Therefore Wishart knew that he preached in the teeth of great dangers, just as later the Jesuits, when they landed clandestinely in the England of Elizabeth I, knew that they administered the sacraments to the recusants at the risk of death.

The evidence of Wishart's compassion to his opponents is given by John Knox:

'While he [Wishart] was spending his life to comfort the afflicted, the devil ceased not to stir up his own, the Cardinal again, who corrupted by money a desperate priest, named Sir John Wighton, to slay the said Mr George who looked not in all things so circumspectly as worldly men would have wished. And upon a day, the sermon ended, the people departing, no man suspecting danger, and therefore not heeding the said Mr George, the priest that was corrupted stood waiting at the foot of the steps, his gown loose, and his whinger drawn into his hand under his gown, the said Mr George, as that he was most sharp of eye and judgement, marked him, and as he came near, he said, "My friend, what would ye do?" And therewith he clapped his hand upon the priest's hand wherein the whinger was, which he took from him. The priest, abashed, fell down at his feet, and openly confessed the verity as it was. The noise rising, and coming to the ears of the sick, they cried, "Deliver the traitor to us, or else we will take him by force," and so they thrust in at the gate; but Mr George took him in his arms, and said, "Whosoever trouble him shall trouble me, for he has hurt me nothing, but he had done great comfort both to you and to me, to wit, he has led us to understand what we may fear. In times to come we will watch better." And so he appeased both the one part and the other, and saved the life of him that sought his.'

Although this little story portrays Wishart, the friend of Knox, in Christ-like terms, yet it has the ring of truth, and true reporting. Even allowing for partisanship and exaggeration, it is difficult to equate the man who was prepared to disarm his would-be assassin, and forgive him, with a man who could plot the murder of Beaton.

John Knox retails other plots of Beaton's against Wishart's life, and recalls that on escaping from a trap laid for him Wishart said: 'I know that I shall end my life in that bloodthirsty man's hands, but it will not be of this manner.' This again has an echo of the Gospel story.

Not that Wishart is always portrayed by Knox in terms of gentleness. He also records that when Wishart saw two Grey Friars in the Church during his sermon he addressed them in no complimentary terms.

'Oh serjeants of Satan and deceivers of the souls of men, will ye neither hear God's truth nor suffer others to hear it? Depart and take this for your portion, God shall shortly confound and disclose your hypocrisy within this realm; ye shall be abominable unto men, and your places and habitations shall be desolate.'

133

The Reformers were not letting their opponents off lightly.

Knox records the preachings and the journeyings of Wishart, and gives many instances of the plots against him. But eventually, by a judicious use of bribery and treachery, the Cardinal managed to trap Wishart.

'The manner of his taking was this: departing from the town of Haddington, he took his goodnight, as it were for ever, of all his acquaintance. John Knox pressing to have gone with the said Mr George, he said, "Nay, return to your bairns [pupils] and God bless you, one is sufficient for the sacrifice . . . before midnight the place was beset about.'

According to Knox's account, the Earl Bothwell then promised that Wishart would be safe, and 'that it should pass the power of the Cardinal to do him harm or scathe'.

Knox puts down his opinion of the Earl Bothwell in no uncertain terms.

'But as gold and women have corrupted all worldly and fleshly men from the beginning, so did they him; for the cardinal gave gold, and that largely, and the queen promised favours in all his lawful suits to women if he would deliver the said Mr George to be kept in the Castle of Edinburgh . . . and so was the servant of God transported to Edinburgh Castle, for that bloody wolf, the cardinal, ever thirsting for the blood of the servant of God, so travailed with the abused governor that he was content that God's servant should be delivered to the power of that tyrant.'

A long and complicated trial for heresy ensued in which both sides gave good and forthright accounts of themselves. Like all trials for heresy, it was full of complicated and devious illustrations and refutations, one accusation being 'Thou false heretic didst say, that a priest standing at the altar saying mass, was like a fox wagging his tail in July'.

The answer was, 'I said not so, These were my sayings, the moving of the body outward, without the inward moving of the heart, is nought else but the playing of an ape, and not the true serving of God.'

In spite of all such illustrations taken from the animal world, the result of the trial was a foregone conclusion, and on March 11, 1546 Wishart was executed at St Andrews. The simplicity of John

Knox's account has a dramatic impact which stamps it with some truth:

'Last of all the hangman that was his tormentor sat down upon his knees and said: "Sir, I pray you to forgive me, for I am not guilty of your death." To whom he answered "Come higher to me." When he was come to him, he kissed his cheek and said: "Lo here is a token that I forgive thee; my heart, do thy office." As Wishart was led to his martyrdom, he said, "For the word's sake and the true gospel which was given me by the grace of God, I suffer this day by men, not sorrowfully but with a glad heart and mind. For this cause I was sent, that I should suffer this fire for Christ's sake. Consider and behold my visage, ye shall not see me change my colour. This grim fire I fear not, and so I pray you for to do if that any persecution come to you for the word's sake and not to fear them that slay the body and afterwards have no power to slay the soul." '

Wishart was then hanged and his remains burned. But his opinions lived on. He had produced an English translation of the Swiss Confession of Faith which was printed after his death.

Like so many martyrdoms the burning of Wishart aroused great popular feeling. In Knox's words, 'After the death of this blessed martyr of God, began the people in plain speaking to damn and detest the cruelty that was used; yet men of great birth, estimation and honour at open tables avowed "That the blood of the said Mr George should be revenged, or else they should lose life for life." '

This according to Knox was the reason for the instigation of the plot against Beaton, although other authorities alleged that it was more likely the sweeteners given by Henry VIII which caused the murder. The chief conspirators against the Cardinal were William Kirkcaldy of Grange, Norman Leslie, the Master of Rothes, and James Melville. It was known that these men received pensions from Henry VIII, and indeed were 'lauded by him as his friends and supporters'.

After the execution of Wishart, the Cardinal, feeling perhaps that he had cut off the head of the tallest poppy of the Reformers, went happily to attend the festivities at the wedding of one of his natural daughters at Finhaven Castle. During the celebrations the news came that Henry VIII was preparing to invade Scotland once more.

The Cardinal hurried back to his castle of St Andrews to put his defences in order.

The conspirators got into the castle by a ruse which John Knox narrates in his usual succinct way:

'First, the gates being open, the drawbridge let down for the receiving of lime and stones, and other things necessary for building, for Babylon was almost finished; first William Kirkcaldy of Grange, younger, and with him six persons, getting entrance, held purpose with the porter "Is my lord Cardinal waking?" Who answered "No" and so it was, indeed for he had been busy with his account with mistress Marion Ogilvy that night, who was espied to depart from him by the private postern that morning; and therefore quietness, after the rules of physic, and a morning sleep were requisite for my lord.'

A Scottish spy of Lord Wharton's sent the good news of the Cardinal's murder to England and described it: 'Syr, to advertise you, this satterday [May 29, 1546] betwixt five hours and six in the morning the Cardynal is slane in the castle of St Andrews by Norman Leslie.'

The spy goes on to recount the killing of the porter and continues: 'The Cardynal heard the dyn in his chamber and came forth to hear what it was, Norman Leslie met him in the turnpike and slew him.' The alarm bell was rung and the citizens of the town rushed to the castle calling for the Cardinal.

Ye provost and town to the number of three or four hundred men came to the castle while Norman Leslie and his company came to the wall head, and asked did they desire to see one dead man. Incontinent they brought the cardinal dead to the wall head in a pair of sheets and hang him over the wall by the arm and foot, and so bade the people see their God. Hugh Douglas, and Master John Douglas which was in St Andrews saw the same with their eyes.

Written this Satterday at midnight,
your servant,
James Lyndsay.

After the death of Cardinal Beaton the conspirators seized the castle of St Andrews and were soon joined by a number of their fellow Protestants. In 1547, John Knox also joined them and began

136

his preachings in the castle. For some time, services of both the Catholic and the Reformed persuasions were heard in the castle. But this mood of mutual tolerance did not last. In 1547 the bishops and clergy demanded that the Regent Arran should take firm action against the Reformers. Unfortunately, owing to the fact that the Regent had no great forces at his disposal, he was not able to attack the strong point of the castle.

By June 1547 a French force had arrived, and the castle was reduced by cannon fire. The defenders of the castle then decided to surrender, imagining that they might be able to obtain more merciful terms from the French than they would from their fellow countrymen.

This turned out to be a mistaken impression, for the principal offenders were taken to France. Most of the gentlemen prisoners were clapped into gaol, while others, including John Knox, were put to practical work for the Catholic cause in that they were chained in the French galleys.

After suffering forced labour in the galleys for a year and a half, Knox was subsequently released, possibly owing to the influence of the English government, and he recommenced preaching in Berwick and Newcastle. By 1551, Knox had become one of Edward VI's chaplains, and after this went abroad to Germany and Geneva to pursue his studies and wait for a more favourable opportunity to resume his labours of reform in Scotland.

In the interim, Henry VIII died, but his successors carried on the war against Scotland. The struggle between the English and the Scottish on the one hand, and the French and the Scottish on the other continued. But in 1548 the young Mary Stuart was sent to France, and in April 1550 peace returned.

This left the Scots to continue their religious and fratricidal feuds unmolested by foreign enemies. The crunch of the real revolution was approaching. It was at this time that the popular and scurrilous ballads played a great part in the discrediting of the clergy, and attempts were made to seek out the ballad mongers.

The policy of burning and harrassing the Reformers had proved to be a failure, and now the Church had decided on reforming itself coupled with a policy of attacking the Reformers by burning their heretical books.

The Provincial Council of 1552 took note of the real state of the Church and clergy. 'Even in the most populous parishes very few of the parishioners came to mass or to sermon, that in time of service, jesting and irreverence go on within the church, and sports and secular business in the porch and the churchyard.'

The ignorance of the clergy was also admitted. 'The inferior clergy and the prelates for the most part are not in the meanwhile sufficiently learned to instruct the people rightly in the Catholic faith, in things necessary to salvation.'

The proclamation went on to say that the laity must be instructed in the catechism which was to be

'read from the Pulpit every Sunday and holiday with a loud voice, clearly, distinctly, impressively, and solemnly by the rector, vicar, or curate in his surplice and stole. The clergy were enjoined to exercise daily in reading it, lest their stammering or breaking down might move the jeers of the people.'

These small homely facts paint a picture of congregations which were certainly not impressed with their pastors. It was not surprising that the stern, hard doctrines of the Reformers had the impact not only of something new, but of something cleaner and more uplifting.

By 1554, when Mary of Guise Lorraine, Mary Stuart's mother, had become Queen Regent, large numbers of her subjects had already joined the Reformed Religion. The persecutions of Protestants under Mary Tudor caused many Scotsmen to return to Scotland, for Mary of Lorraine was a sensible ruler of tolerant views, unlikely to persecute them. Like her daughter she had to contend with the religious revolution, and a country divided by factions. A year after the Queen Regent had taken power into her hands, John Knox returned from his travels and took up his preaching in Scotland again.

This was a time of transition for Scottish religion. The Reformers were not, as yet, sufficiently strong to impose their will on the vast bulk of the populace. Some people still hoped for a reform of the Old Church, and while prepared to listen to Knox's sermons they would also attend mass. Knox, as always uncompromising, was opposed to this attitude. But as he was mostly preaching to the nobility and gentry, their cautious attitude was understandable. They were waiting to see which way the tide of fortune would run and at present it did not seem that the Reformers were sufficiently strong.

Shortly after this John Knox was called to answer charges of holding heretical opinions in the Church of the Black Friars in Edinburgh. Curiously enough, a number of nobles of the Reformed Religion were called together in the same city at the same time. Whether this was a show of force on the side of the Reformers is questionable. The charges against Knox were dropped and on the day he should have been indicted he was preaching to a larger congregation than usual. But by July 1556 he had again prudently left Scotland, and shortly after his effigy was burned at the Market Cross in Edinburgh.

By the following year the nobles had begun to see that the tide was running truly and strongly in the direction of Reform. Possibly further thoughts about the tempting broad church lands had something to do with their conversion, and their decision now to take firm action on behalf of the new religion. The Earls of Argyll, Glencairn, and Morton, Lord Lorne, and John Erskine of Dun, drew up a bond which stated their religious beliefs and bound themselves to uphold them:

'Unto the which holy words the congregation we do join us and also do renounce and forsake the congregation of Satan with all the superstitions, abominations, and idolatry thereof.'

The new self-styled Lords of the Congregation then wrote to John Knox asking him to return to Scotland to resume the feeding of the minds of his flock. Whether or not it was because he was unsure of the outcome of the tide of battle, he did not in fact return to feed his sheep in Scotland until the spring of 1559.

Although the Queen Regent tried to moderate opinions on both sides, her tolerant attitude did not fit in with the surge of religious revolution. The Reformers were growing in fervour, and in so doing were rousing the people to fury against the Church.

The destruction of Church property was beginning.

A proclamation warned against these actions:

'In these troublous times it is dreaded and feared that evil disposed persons will invade, destroy, cast down, and withhold abbeys, abbey places, parish kirks, friars' houses, nunneries . . . all and sundry were charged not to spoil the jewels and ornaments of the church, ordained for God's services, and dedicated to it under the penalty of forfeiture of life, lands and goods.'

Knox records the beginning of the destruction, no doubt with satisfaction:

139

'The images were stolen away in all parts of the country, and in Edinburgh was that great idol, called St Giles, first drowned in the North Loch, and after burnt, which raised no small trouble in the town; for the friars ran croaking like ravens upon the bishops, the bishops ran upon the queen, who to them was favourable enough, but that she thought it could not stand with her advantage to offend such a multitude as then took upon them the defence of the evangel and the name of the Protestants.'

The Queen Regent, at this time, unlike the Reformers, continued to show tolerance in trying to rule her subjects of both religious persuasions. Her attitude is revealed in the Reformers complaint:

'We avow to God we shall make a day of it. They [the priests] oppress us and our tenants for feeding of their idle bellies; they trouble our preachers and would murder them and us: Shall we suffer this any longer? Nay, Madam, it shall not be. And therewith every man put on his steel bonnet. There was heard nothing of the Queen's part but, "My boys, my hearts, what aileth you? Me means no evil to you, nor to your preachers; the bishops shall do you no wrong—ye are all my loving subjects. Me will hear the controversy that is betwixt the bishops and you; they shall do you no wrong. O my hearts, should ye not love the Lord your God with all your hearts, with all your mind, and should ye not love your neighbours as yourselves?" '

But the Reformers were in no mood for tolerance any more than were their opponents. The battle was becoming sharper. In April 1558 an old man of over eighty, Walter Mill, was burned at St Andrews. He was a former priest who had left the Church because of the open abuses under Cardinal Beaton, and had joined the Reformers.

Like the execution of Wishart this act of cruelty strengthened the hands of the Reformers. They sent a protest to the Queen Regent against the cruelty of the Church. Not only that, they demanded an end of abuses, and the establishment of their own form of religion.

The Queen Regent managed to remain tolerant in spite of the fact that, according to the laws of the time, the Lords of the Congregation were in rebellion against their sovereign. Ignoring this, she agreed to allow freedom to their preachers provided that they did not hold public meetings in Leith and Edinburgh. Possibly her tolerance was in advance of her times, or possibly she realized that she was already negotiating from a position of weakness.

By November 1558 the Lords of the Congregation were already beginning to threaten force to obtain the reforms they demanded.

But behind the ebb and flow of doctrine, ran the realities of politics and of power. Elizabeth I had come to the throne of England, and France was putting pressure on the Queen Regent to oppose the Lords of the Congregation with more vigour. France saw Scotland as a lever against her enemy England.

The Queen Regent reversed her tolerant policies, and four of the chief Protestant preachers were summoned to appear at Stirling before the Court of the Judiciary for the preaching of heresy. The Lords of the Congregation determined on action, and called their clans together to protect the preachers.

To add fuel to a fire which was already burning merrily, John Knox landed at Leith on May 2nd.

The preachers did not appear before the tribunal, and by May 11th Knox was at Perth, preaching a vehement sermon against the 'abomination of the mass and all the accompanying trumpery of the Roman Catholic form of worship'.

While the congregation were still worked up by his harangue, a priest, obviously a man of little foresight, uncovered the richly carved altar to say mass. A young boy called out, 'This is intolerable that when God by his word hath plainly damned idolatry we shall stand and see it used in despite.'

John Knox records that the priest hit the child, who threw a stone, missing the priest, but breaking the carved tabernacle. Immediately the whole church congregation 'put hands to the said tabernacle and to all other monuments of idolatry which they despatched'.

But John Knox is disposed to be fair. He records that although the 'first invasion' was against idolatry,

'the common people began to seek some spoil. Indeed the Grey Friars was a place well-provided, that unless honest men had seen the same, we would have feared to report what provision they had; their sheets, blankets, beds and coverlets were such that no earl in Scotland had the better. Their napery was fine and they were but eight persons in convent and yet had eight puncheons of salt beef, consider the time of the year, the the 11th of May [i.e. normally by this time of the year they would have run out of meat] wine, beer, and ale, besides stores of victuals corresponding thereto.'

Unfortunately the populace did not do so well at the Black Friars where the 'like abundance' was not found.

Knox then records that the Charterhouse was also destroyed, a building 'of wondrous cost and greatness, that only the walls did remain of all these great edifications'.

He attempts to whitewash the sack of the monasteries by saying that the poor benefited by them, and points out that the Prior of the Charterhouse was allowed to take with him 'as much gold and silver as he was able to carry'—a statement which, considering the poverty of the people, and their excited state of mind, is open to doubt.

The sack of the Charterhouse caused a change of heart in the mind of the Queen Regent. She now saw that so far from dealing with men intent on reasonable reforms she was faced with a complete breakdown in law and order and with destruction on a large scale. It is easy to say that few reforms can be carried out without violence, but in addition to reforms the appetite of the Lords of the Congregation towards power and plunder had also been whetted.

Although the Queen Regent threatened vengeance against her rebellious subjects, her forces were not sufficient to carry out her threats. The Lords took possession of Perth. However, a compromise was reached, and the Earl of Argyll and the Prior of St Andrews managed to arrange a truce. If the Reformers were not molested in Perth they agreed that the armies would be disbanded.

But the Queen Regent, once the town was evacuated, rode into Perth accompanied by a French bodyguard. As this action was regarded as treachery, the Earl of Argyll and the Prior of St Andrews immediately left the Queen's party and joined the Lords. In view of the weak state of the Queen's forces, and the plunder that was to be gained on the other side, it may well have been that their consciences were the more easily directed into the channels of self-interest.

By June 1559, John Knox was back in St Andrews, preaching about casting the buyers and sellers out of the temple—a sermon which was quickly followed by action on the part of the populace who then destroyed all the altars, images, and monuments in all the churches in the city.

The struggle between the Queen Regent, supported by the French and the Lords, washed to and fro across the country. Several attempts were made to reach a truce which each time was broken as soon as it was concluded. In the beginning there might have been a possibility of tolerance between the religious factions, but once the sword had been drawn it was difficult to go back.

The Lords demolished all the monasteries in Edinburgh, and even seized the Mint. If the Catholics had acted foolishly in their initial persecution of the Reformers, the Reformers were not less intolerant in their attitude towards the Old Religion once the tide started to flow to their advantage.

Eventually another truce was concluded and the Queen Regent returned to her palace of Holyrood. Meanwhile both sides were issuing exhortations and appeals to the country. On the one hand, the Queen Regent offered liberty of worship for the Protestants, so long as, wherever she was living, the mass should be celebrated, and that preaching against the Old Religion should cease during her stay.

John Knox, on his side, was not disposed to give any quarter to the 'idolators'. His aim was to 'establish God's eternal verity within the realm'. But as one historian has remarked, there was always a tendency on the part of John Knox to confuse God's revelation with his own opinions.

International politics impinged on the private war between the religious factions in Scotland. In July 1559, Henri II of France was killed while jousting, and the Queen of Scots, Mary Stuart, became Queen both of Scotland and France. This altered the situation of the Lords of the Congregation. Now, instead of their own private war against the Queen Regent, they found themselves also locked in conflict with the more formidable forces of Catholic France.

The Lords of the Congregation left Edinburgh.

John Knox puts up a good case for the Lords, ascribing their retreat to various acts of treachery by the Earl Bothwell and others. But all armies which are not paid are inclined to melt away. This was the case with the army of the Lords. An attempt was made to manufacture their own money. It failed. According to Knox this was again due to treachery. 'To pacify the men of war, a collection was devised; but because some were poor, and some were niggards and avaricious, there could no sufficient sum be obtained.' Money, or the lack of it, even among the 'Saints', could be the root of all evils.

The Lords then retired to Glasgow to 'reform' that city. By the late summer a French army of over a thousand strong had landed at Leith, and by the end of September another two thousand soldiers joined them, and fortified Leith for the crown. But the Lords of the Congregation, although not able to take Leith, were sufficiently sure of their ground to go back to Edinburgh. Here they met at the Tolbooth, and calmly debated whether they owed any allegiance to the Queen Regent, still ruling in the absence of Mary Stuart.

John Willcock stated,

'The Queen Regent was an open and obstinate idolatress, and that she utterly despised the Council and requirements of the nobility, and that he could see no reason why they, the born councillors, nobility and barons of the realm, might not justly deprive her of regime and authority amongst them.'

Knox added a rider to this, that if the Queen Regent repented she might be restored to her former place and honour.

But if the Lords were forthright in the expression of their religious opinions, their followers were not as doughty on the field, and the disciplined troops of the French defeated them in many skirmishes. They were forced to retire from Edinburgh and retreated to Stirling.

Knox, as usual, puts many of the defeats of the 'Saints' down to treachery.

'At least we might have saved the ordnance, and have kept the Canongate from danger; for we were once marched forwards with bold courage, but then, we say, was a shout raised amongst ourselves—God will disclose the traitors one day—affirming that the whole French company were entered in at Leith Wynd upon our backs. What clamour and disorder did then suddenly arise. The horsemen, and some of those that should have put order to others, over-rode their poor brethren, at the entrance of the Netherbow.'

Defeated or not, the voice of Knox continued to encourage the brethren, promising them that the Lord of Hosts was on their side. The Lords of the Congregation adopted a more practical attitude and made approaches to that other reformed country, England.

William Maitland of Lethington was sent to London with a request to Queen Elizabeth for help. Although Queen Elizabeth was reluctant to show her hand on the side of subjects rebelling against their lawful Queen Regent, her advisers were quick to see that a Scotland occupied by French troops was not to the advantage of England.

By the beginning of 1560 an English fleet had appeared off the coast of Fife to help the Lords. In February 1560 the Treaty of Berwick was concluded between the Lords of the Congregation and the English government. After the conclusion of the treaty, an English army of 6,000 crossed the border and was joined by the forces of the Lords. They invested Leith, but in spite of losses on both sides the result was a stalemate.

In July 1560 the Treaty of Edinburgh was ratified. This treaty was to be a source of contention stretching far into the distance, and it could be said that it was the rock on which Mary Stuart's future foundered.

The main points of the treaty were that French troops should return to their own country, that foreign armies should not be invited into the country without the agreement of Parliament, and that an 'act of oblivion' would blot out all the punishable deeds committed by both sides.

The immediate result of the conclusion of this treaty meant that the English and French forces both left Scotland. But many of the clauses of the treaty were never ratified, and this was often pointed out by Mary Stuart in her negotiations with the English Queen.

The Queen Regent had laboured and fought too long with her rebellious subjects. On July 10th she died, worn out with religious factions, with foreign entanglements, and with attempts to pacify her tough Scottish nobles.

As later with her daughter, her dying occasioned a gathering of preachers attempting to convert her. There was something about a deathbed which seemed to appeal to the religious factions of the period. It was probably felt that if someone on the point of death could be induced in their last agony to recant, then a good propaganda point could be made. The people of the Renaissance were not 'nice' in their reactions to death.

It is generally admitted that, even on her deathbed, the Queen Regent showed great tolerance and magnanimity. She even suffered Willock, one of the chief Reformed preachers, to exhort her in her last lingering illness.

In his reporting of the Queen Regent's illness, Knox showed his usual lack of charity. One story which he tells, of the Queen Regent sending a message for some drugs, has a very unattractive ring to it:

'The letter being presented to the Lord Grey, he espied the craft, for few lines written above, and so much white paper left, he said, "Drugs are more abundant and fresher in Edinburgh than they can be in Leith, there lurketh here some other mystery." The paper was burned.'

The preachers were then sent for.

'She did openly confess "that there was no salvation, but in and by the death of Jesus Christ", but of the mass we heard not her confession. Some say she was anointed after the papistical manner, which was a sign of small knowledge of the truth, and of less repentance for her former superstition; and yet howsoever it was, Christ Jesus got no small victory over such an enemy . . . but also she was constrained to hear one of the principal ministers of the realm, and shortly thereafter she finished her unhappy life.'

Knox concludes his account of the Queen Regent's death:

'God for his great mercy's sake, rid us from the rest of the Guysan blood in her, that for our unthankfulness, now reigneth above us, we have had sufficient experience; but of any virtue that ever was espied in King James V whose daughter she is called to this hour we have never seen any sparkle to appear.'

The Reformers were out to make a clean sweep of their opponents and were not disposed to give them the benefit of any doubts, religious or otherwise.

With the death of the Queen Regent the bastions had fallen to the Reformers. Like many people who complain about the suppression of their opinions, as soon as they had obtained power the first thing they did was to suppress this freedom for their opponents.

In 1560, Parliament met in Edinburgh, and issued a Confession of Faith. This long document was produced in four days. It went into points of doctrine about God, the creation of man, original sin, the incarnation of Christ, faith, good works, the immortality of the soul, the authority of scripture, and also took in such small details as the right way to administer the sacraments, the organization of the Reformed Kirk, and even touched upon more tricky subjects, such as 'The gifts freely given to the Kirk'.

A natural rider to this Confession was the abolition of the authority of the Pope:

'The Bishop of Rome to have no jurisdiction nor authority in this realm in times coming, and that none of our said sovereign's subjects suit or desire, in any time thereafter title or right by the said Bishop of Rome of his sect, to anything within this realm, under pain of baratry, that is to say proscription and banishment.'

The Reformers were giving no quarter to papists: 'The contraveners hereof to be called before the justice or his deputies, or before the lords of the session, and punished therefore conform to the laws of this realm.'

With the Pope and the mass abolished, the Reformers had indeed shaken the dust of Rome from their feet. It now became illegal to say or attend mass. For the first offence, mass-attenders had their goods confiscated; for the second, they were banished; and for the third they merited death. The tables had been completely turned.

Since destruction by revolution is easy, and reconstruction more difficult, the Reformers found themselves in difficulties on several heads. Having abolished the priesthood and laid the monasteries and friaries low, they now found themselves short of 'Saints' to preach the new gospel. They got over this difficulty in the short term by having three different categories of people in the church: firstly, the ministers; secondly, the exhorters who could explain and interpret the Scriptures in the correct manner: and thirdly, lay readers who could read the Scriptures.

Having settled the point of the spread of the Gospels, the Reformers, lords and ministers, then came to the more knotty point of what to do with the rich patrimony of the Church which had fallen into their hands. Long accustomed to fight against the crown, the fiercely independent Scottish nobles were not letting the riches and lands of the Church be taken from them by mere churchmen, even the Reformers. There is no doubt that the preachers of Reform, like John Knox, had acted from burning sincerity, and a real desire to clean out the Augean stables of the Roman Church. The Lords of the Congregation were often less dedicated, and in many cases used the cause of Reform for their own aggrandizement.

In December 1560, François II, husband of Mary Stuart died, and in August of the following year Mary returned, somewhat reluctantly, to her Scottish inheritance.

She returned as a Catholic to a country which was now largely given over to the doctrines of Calvin, and his disciple John Knox.

Although over large stretches of the country, especially in the north, where the Earl of Huntley ruled, there were still many adherents to Catholicism, the Reformers' position was becoming impregnable.

The religious clash between Mary Stuart and her nobles was apparent almost as soon as she had reached the capital.

On Sunday, four days after her arrival, preparations were being made to celebrate mass in her private chapel, when Lord Lindsay cried out, 'The idolater priest should die the death!' and there was an ominous surge of angry nobles.

Lord James, afterwards Earl of Moray, prevented the nobles getting into the chapel by holding the door. Knox comments on this action: 'His best excuse was, that he would stop all Scotsmen to enter the mass; but it was, and is sufficiently known, that the door was kept that none should have entrance to trouble the priest.'

Barely a week after her arrival the Queen, following the tolerant policies of her mother, tried to pacify her uncompromising subjects by issuing a proclamation of religious liberty:

'Foreasmuch as the queen's majesty has understood the great inconvenience that may come, through the division presently standing in this realm, for the difference in matters of religion, that her majesty is most desirous to see it pacified by a good order to the honour of God and the tranquillity of her realm.'

In her proclamation Mary Stuart promised not to make any change in the religion of the country and demanded in return that her servants and followers from France should not be molested.

The Earl of Arran protested loudly, and mouthed threats against the committing of idolatry, which for him meant the simple saying and hearing of mass. John Knox was no less uncompromising. The following Sunday he preached a sermon which included the sentiment that 'one mass was more fearful unto him than if ten thousand armed enemies were landed in any part of the realm of purpose to suppress the holy Religion'.

The climate of opinion had gone beyond any form of religious coexistence.

But while the preachers and the Queen were debating liberty of conscience and forms of doctrine, the Lords of the Congregation were engaged on work which in some cases was of more interest: the distribution of Church property. Knox and his fellow preachers had much mistaken certain of the motives of the nobility. It was when they began to get down to practicalities that the real motives of many of the nobles became apparent, and Knox's disillusionment with their alleged religious fervour was made apparent.

In 1560, he and his co-reformers drew up and 'presented to the nobility', the First Book of Discipline, or the Policy and Discipline of the Church.

This is an admirably idealistic document which treats not only of doctrine but of social reform. It goes into great detail about the organization of the new Kirk. It accepts that the new preachers and their families must be provided for, and lists in some detail the provisions to be made for them, for the education of their children, and the support of their widows. On education, it stresses the importance of schools, the payment of preachers who teach in schools attached to their parishes, and suggests the founding of new universities as well as the support to be given to 'those attending them'.

The First Book of Discipline may have been 'presented' to the nobility and 'subscribed by the Kirk and Lords', but some asked how many of the lords who signed the document were going to abide by its provisions. Maitland of Lethington said that, while they may have signed the document, they signed it more as a child at baptism accepts the promises made for him by his godparents.

John Knox was not unaware of the character of the people with whom he was dealing. For under the sixth head of the Book of Discipline, it is stated,

'with the grief of our hearts we hear that some gentlemen are now as cruel over their tenants as ever were the papists, requiring of them whatsoever they paid to the kirk, so that the papistical tyranny shall only be changed into the tyranny of lord and laird'.

Knox and his fellows, forthright in rooting out Catholicism and attacking the Queen, were equally forthright in their opinions of the conduct of the nobles:

'We dare not flatter your honours, neither, nor is it profitable for you that we do so. . . . The gentlemen, barons, earls, lords and others must be content to live upon their just rents, and suffer the Kirk to be restored to her rights and liberty; that by her restitution the poor, who heretofore, by the cruel papists have been spoiled and oppressed may now receive some comfort and relaxation.'

149

But nobility of sentiment and statement, while often expressed by original reformers, is seldom carried into action by those who have helped them to power.

By December 22, 1561 proposals were made that a third of all the revenue of the Church should be turned over to the crown. Those Catholic bishops and clergy who were still carrying on their duties should be allowed to keep their rents. Reasonable provision was to be made for the Protestant clergy.

Naturally the rents were not forthcoming. John Knox put the facts straight:

'I see two parts freely given to the devil, and the third part must be divided between God and the devil. Well, be witness to me that this day, I say it, ere it be long the devil shall have three parts of the third; and judge you then what God's portion shall be.'

An opinion on the other side said, 'After the Ministers were sustained, the Queen will not get at the end of the year as much as to buy her a new pair of shoes.'

Fortunately for the Queen, she had certain revenues from her dowry in France, but a sovereign who does not have sufficient funds is in a weak position, both with regard to government and to the payment of forces to sustain that government.

In the event, Knox's opinion proved to be right.

The rich revenues of the Church disappeared by devious means into the pockets of the reforming lords and their followers. This was done in various ways, by grants of land, by the extension of leases, by pensions, and many other legal wangles, and where these were not sufficient the lands and property of the Church were seized by force.

As usual, the payment for the clergy proved very meagre, and even that was paid irregularly. The clergy were constantly complaining about their poor treatment in their General Assembly, and did not mince their words about their opponents.

'For to the servants of the devil, to your dumb dogs, and horned bishops, to one of these idle bellies, ten thousand a year was not enough, but to the servants of Christ who laboriously preach the Gospel a thousand pounds—how can that be sustained? . . . the Catholics have the two parts, and some have gotten abbacies and feus [leases]. . . .'

150

But in spite of the injustices, everyday life in Scotland went on. As elsewhere, events in the higher strata meant much to a few, and little to many. The bastions of the Church had fallen, but the spoil had evaded the 'Saints'. Nor was the lot of the peasants improved.

They had seen the abbeys burned, the idols cast down. They had listened to the fire and brimstone sermons, but neither they nor the preachers of the sermons had benefited. At least, under the old rotten corruption of the Catholic Church, they had been allowed to cock a snook at the bishop, or carve a rude caricature of a friar on a church stall. Under the Reformers, they would be prosecuted for not listening to sermons, and fined for dancing on the green.

Once the fervour has gone out of it, a revolution can turn out to be dull work for the ordinary people.

CHAPTER EIGHT

FEUDS, FACTIONS AND
LAWS IN THE HIGHLANDS

Many of the difficulties which beset the Highlands in early times were due to the fact that their laws were different from the laws prevailing in the Lowlands. The Lowlands fell under the feudal system by conquests, by marriages, and because they were more in contact with the rest of the world than the Highlands. Apart from the ethnic differences between pure Celts and those of different blood, the impenetrability of the Highlands country made more certain that these differences would endure.

The feudal system had spread over all the east and south of Europe, but it did not extend to the mountainous districts of Wales, Ireland, the Western and Middle borders of Scotland, and above all the Highlands where the patriarchial system of government was universal. This meant that wherever the Saxon invaders penetrated in Scotland their feudal system was opposed to the laws prevailing amongst the Celtic Scots.

Under the feudal system it was the right of the next heir to succeed to the property. But in the Highlands, the important thing was the right to succeed to the chieftainship of the clan. Lineal descendants of the first chieftain had the right to succeed, and it was the relation to this common ancestor from which these rights flowed. This meant that the brother of the chieftain was the nearest in succession, as being nearer in blood to the founder of the clan than the son of the dead chieftain. Brothers, therefore, succeeded before the sons as of right.

Should it happen that the person who should lawfully succeed was under age, then the nearest male relative succeeded, and the chieftainship was his for life, even if the proper successor afterwards reached his majority. The law said:

'In cases that the children of the deceased should not have passed the age of 14 years then he of the blood which was nearest being worthy and capable should be elected without prejudice of the righteous heirs when they attained the perfect age.'

But once the uncle, or whichever nearest relative had inherited the chieftainship died, then the right to be head of the clan reverted to the rightful heir.

It can well be seen that such compromises led to ambiguities and what could be termed 'misunderstandings' about the succession.

Highland Law of Succession and Distribution of Property
Under the feudal system the children other than the heir had to make their fortunes as best they could as mercenaries, churchmen, or administrators. But in the Highlands the Law of Gavel prevailed. This law meant that the property of the clan was divided in specified proportions amongst the whole of the male branches of the clan. Women were totally excluded from this division of property, and from the succession to the chieftainship.

The principal 'seat' and some land around it were attached to the chieftainship. This was simply in order to preserve the outward trappings necessary to the clan chief, and also to give him some means of providing the not inconsiderable entertainment for friends and followers which was expected of the chief of the clan.

While this method of inheritance had many advantages in keeping the clan together, in preserving their common property, and giving them a stake in it, the system had manifold disadvantages. Often minor branches of the clan became much more powerful than the clan chief, and sometimes a bastard son could be found in possession of the chieftainship and the property of the clan in general. This inheritance by natural sons did not lead to peace in the clan, and many of the feuds arose from such a cause. Very often the feudal-type heir would have the support of the clan, but this would obviously depend on the power of the heir; and the strength of the support of the bastard son.

Some confusion has arisen from the complications of the succession to the chieftainship. One nineteenth-century writer says:

'This, as might be expected, has hitherto been attributed to loose ideas of succession among the Highlanders, or to the influence of some principles of election, but when we consider how very inflexible the nations of the Highlands were in matters of hereditary right, it would seem . . . that the Highland law of marriage was very different from the feudal.'

In Chapter 4 some facts are given about the custom of hand-fasting as a method of selection for marriage, and it is relevant to refer to this custom in the context of Highland laws of succession and feuds, in order to understand their origin. The custom of handfasting could consist in a contract between two Highland chiefs that the heir of one should live with the daughter of the other as his wife for a year and a day. If during this time the woman became pregnant, the marriage was considered legal, even if no other legal or church ceremony had been performed. But if, on the other hand, the union was unfruitful than the contract was considered to be at an end.

It is considered that this must have been the original law of marriage in the Highlands, and consequently when the feudal law began to penetrate into the Highlands it was in direct opposition to the system prevailing amongst the Celtic population. The result of this was that the heir according to the law of Gavel was not necessarily regarded as the heir by the reigning government in the Lowlands. Men considered by their clans to be the rightful chiefs of their clans were often disregarded by the government and taken to be bastards in law. This led to many complications both with rival clans and with the government, who took the view that these Highland handfast sons should not succeed.

That this is a very ancient law is proved by the fact that the Roman historians reported that Highlanders 'held their wives in common', obviously a misconstruction of the system of handfast unions which could be broken if they proved unfruitful. An obvious reason for the necessity of a fruitful union was the physical need for male heirs to succeed to the chieftainship.

But there was a clear distinction in the Highland clans between handfast children, and ordinary bastards or children born out of wedlock who did not have any rights of succession.

This custom continued into the sixteenth century, when Alexander Sutherland, who claimed he was the issue of a handfast union of the Earl of Sutherland, tried to succeed to the earldom. His claim was that he 'was one lawfully descended from his father, Earl John the third, because his mother was handfasted and fianced to his father'. Sir Adam Gordon, who had married the heiress of the Earl, bought off the claimant.

Owing to the system of inheritance the clan chief usually lived among his people. His castle or 'tower' acted as a centre of justice, of rewards and punishments. He settled the disputes, and the prosperity or poverty of the members of the clan depended upon his good administration. If he had tenants they were bound to follow him in war, help him in his hunting expeditions, legal or illegal, supply him with the product of their crofts, harvest his corn and find fuel for him. In return, as in the feudal system, he was expected to afford them protection and help if they were subjected to cruelties or raids by other clans. The rest of the clan were considered worthy of honour simply in relation to the nearness of their kinship with the clan chief. In effect some of these 'cadets' of the family became sub-chiefs holding their lands and farms under his chieftainship, but exercising a kind of autonomy in small matters, while deferring to him or offering counsel and assistance in emergencies. Rent was not paid in currency, but in kind and was mostly consumed where it was produced.

Prestige was gained among the clan chiefs not by the possession of wealth, outward display of clothes, riches, or even herds, but by the numbers who were willing to follow them in war. Further distinction was gained from the number of retainers, hangers-on, followers, dependants, and guests he was able to entertain in peace time. In effect, the goods of the clan were held in common, gathered in common, and dispensed in common.

At the castle of the clan chief, where he dispensed hospitality, everyone was made welcome and, according to his standing in the clan, was treated with courtesy and on a basis of dignity. The result of this was that each member of the clan felt a pride in his common blood, it raised him in his own estimation, and the chief was able in this way to draw the members closer to him without injuring his status as chief. Each member of the clan, however distantly he might be related to the chief, considered himself noble and well-born.

Although there might be some difference in personal wealth between the lesser members of the clan and the chief, this did not vitiate the loyalty of the followers since they felt themselves to hold the clan's general possessions in common. So long as the clan had dignity, each member participated in it. If a member was called to defend the clan chief in war, it was not the chief he was defending, but the chief in reference to the honour of the clan and the honour of each member of the clan. He was also showing his gratitude to the head of the clan who dispensed his goods for the general good and was thus worthy of respect and help.

'Hence the Highlanders, whom more savage nations called savage, carried in the outward expression of their manners the politeness of courts without their vices and follies and in their bosoms the high point of honour without its follies.'

Although this was the ideal, the working out of these sentiments sometimes turned out differently. The Highlanders, while they may not have been able to enjoy the vices and follies of contemporary courts, had their own vices and follies which were of a fiercer nature.

The clans were self-sufficient societies. They had arms to defend themselves, and their artisans were skilled enough to make and mend the weapons, tools, and huts which they needed. They had pasture for their cattle, a certain amount of wood for building, turf for fuel, and above all large spaces for hunting and 'spoiling' expeditions.

There was no reason for them to venture beyond their own glens and hills, and visit other districts. Communications with the outside world were not necessary for their subsistence. The result was that each clan became insulated in its own world, and the Highland race was broken up into different tribes with their own customs, their own loyalties, and their own lands to defend.

The clan chiefs governed what were, in effect, independent states and each patriarchal sway formed an hereditary monarchy based on the consent of the clan members rather than on the general rule of law whose writ did not effectively run among the clan chiefs and their followers.

The loyalty of the clan to its chief made for harmony, since all its members considered themselves as blood relatives of the chief, but they did not consider other clans to merit the slightest consideration. The advantage of their loyalty had its disadvantage in the violence which broke immediately it was considered there had been some affront, real or imagined, to the honour of the chief, or hence the clan.

In these conditions there was no real rule of law in the Highlands. Naked aggression could be carried out by one tribe against another, and the weakest clans went to the wall, or more accurately took to the hills.

The result of this local and general turbulence meant that the influence of the central government was disregarded, and the complications which ensued from these concepts of leadership were without number. Later, for instance, the Duke of Gordon, feudal superior of the lands and estates held by the Camerons, Macphersons, Macdonnells, and other clans, had no control over these clans. They followed the orders of their own patriarchal chiefs, Locheil, Clunie, Keppoch and others.

The result of the confusion as to who was governing whom was that the central government was confined to those territories which it was possible to control physically. Laws could be passed in Edinburgh to try to control the blood fury of the clans, but it was impossible to stop it. Owing to the tight loyalties, it was impossible to pursue offenders against the general laws into the strongholds of the clan. Once they were in their own territory they were under the protection of their blood relations who would not betray them to a central authority. An additional difficulty was that the laws passed by the crown could not be administered in the territories of the clans without their good will. This was seldom forthcoming.

Over the years the reigning sovereigns frequently tried to divide and rule. They would side with one clan against another or promote the self-interest of one particular tribe. This policy had inherent disadvantages. It added to the general unrest, and made it more certain that the feuds of the various tribes would be carried on in wider and wider spheres.

A clan map of Scotland makes the historical position clear. The western seaboard is divided into many little territories which touch and divide arbitrarily. Without frontiers of rivers, valleys, or mountains, one tribe could invade another according to their current strength.

Among their chiefs the most deadly feuds arose, sometimes because of warring self-interest, and sometimes from imagined insults to the honour of the chief. The feuds between chiefs were taken up by the rest of the tribe, carried on from father to son over the generations, involving all the members of the clan which bore the same name.

The resultant chaos meant that at any one time it was practically impossible for the country to settle down to peaceful pursuits, most of their energies being given to carrying out complicated feuds, and laying waste the territories of neighbours.

The most trivial causes served to start these bloody conflicts. A contemptuous expression taken in bad part, bitter words against the chief, anything of a like nature was enough to be taken as an insult which then inflamed the clan. A few cattle lifted from one member was certainly taken as an act of aggression against the whole clan. As in many wars the words 'reprisals and vengeance' produced more cruelties than they cured.

If it happened that the clan which had been insulted or pillaged found itself temporarily too weak to repel the attack, or to raid in return, the insult was cherished, nourished, and remembered. It was never forgotten. And if the numbers or weapons to redeem their honour were lacking in the smaller tribe, they resorted to treachery. The hand of friendship would be held out in order to find a better opportunity to turn on their enemies and achieve by fraud what they could not carry out by force, tactics which have not perhaps been absent in the twentieth century.

Feuds and depredations were further complicated by a legal system called a bond of 'manrent'. Bonds of manrent were given by the clan to their chief and were an acknowledgement that they held their lands under him and must pay rent called the 'calpe'. This was usually paid in kind. In exchange the chieftain, by the bond of manrent, acknowledged that the tenant was the person legally entitled to cultivate the soil, and his stake in his land was recognized by the chief. So long as the tenant worked the soil and paid his calpe, the lord was not allowed to ask for more labour than was due under the bond, nor could he be asked for a higher rent.

This was a straightforward deal. The tenant had security of tenure in exchange for the protection of the clan, and the lord had a permanent tenant who gave an agreed amount in goods and labour. The issue only became complicated with the extension of the feudal law, when some of the Highland chiefs took over or acquired other lands by feudal inheritance. They then found themselves with land on which were permanent tenants belonging to some other clan.

If the tenants chose to remain on the land, they risked being stigmatised as traitors by their own clan, and in the event of a small feud being pursued they further risked being destroyed by both sides and their lands and goods forfeit.

The third complication was that sometimes land could be occupied by a few wretched peasants who belonged to no particular tribe. In this case they could pay their rent to the lord and follow him as chief of the clan, but in spite of this, they were not considered to be part of the original clan, but only hangers-on.

As a result of such complications the number and extent of the feuds became greater not smaller. Some clans used these bonds of

158

manrent from independent tribes to increase their own power, and the combinations and permutations of larger and smaller clans combining and separating according to the state of the feud market makes Scottish history a story of heroism, treachery, blackmail, and bloodshed on an unprecedented scale.

Although these bonds of friendship, manrent, or treaties between opposing clans were supposed to be binding, they would often be cast aside should self-interest decide on other courses of action. A further complication, added to the already fragmented situation, was that all the clan chiefs were supposed to owe allegiance and fealty to the king. Their bonds were always sworn between themselves 'always excepting my duty to our lord the King, and to our kindred and friends'.

This small clause was usually forgotten in the general turmoil. Kindred and friends were a variable factor. The loyalty to the king was not often adhered to, especially if his power over the clans was weak.

As a rule the smaller clans prudently attached themselves to the larger, and a combination of two or more clans could often outnumber the king's forces, for some clan chiefs had several thousand fighting men under their command from whom they could exact obedience to the death.

To restore order in the Highlands was beyond the power of the kings of Scotland, and certainly beyond the powers of either the Queen Regent or Mary Stuart. It was a vicious circle. The rule of law could not be enforced in the Highlands, or in parts of the Lowlands. As a result the spirit of revenge was fanned and private individuals carried out their own ideas of justice. This led in turn to further acts of violence.

'The spirit of opposition and rivalry between the clans perpetuated a system of hostility, encouraged the cultivation of the military at the expense of the social virtues, and perverted their ideas of both law and morality. Revenge was accounted a duty, the destruction of a neighbour a meritorious exploit and rapine an honourable occupation. Their love of distinction and their conscious reliance on their courage, when under the direction of these perverted notions, only tended to make their feuds more implacable, their condition more agitated, and their depredations more rapacious and desolating. Superstition added its influence in exasperating animosities by teaching the clansmen that to revenge the death of a relation or friend was a sacrifice agreeable to their shades; thus engaging on the side of the most implacable hatred and the darkest vengeance the most amiable and domestic of all our feelings, reverence for the memory of the dead and affections for the virtues of the living.'

Like all fighting men, the Highlanders largely despised the laborious pursuits necessary to raise a living from farming, or from the grazing of cattle. Fighting was an honourable calling, and as a consequence the clansmen were not slow to seize opportunities for following it. Naturally they did not seek death, and if, in adverse circumstances, they could beat an honourable retreat they did so. But if they were forced to stand and fight, then the challenge was not shirked.

Like the Red Indians, their best methods of defence were the rapidity with which they could disappear, and their knowledge of the country. Their sight was supposed to be so sharp that they could trace the passing of cattle by the bending of the heather. One man's word against another's in the tracing of cattle in this way led to further disputes and feuds. Compensation was paid, cattle yielded up, or battle commenced.

Very often a declaration of war was made simply by carrying off the cattle of a rival clan. As most of the possessions of the clans were in the form of flocks and herds, this obviously constituted a reason for immediate reprisals.

But like the Welsh in the old song 'The mountain sheep are sweeter but the valley sheep are fatter, we therefore deemed it meeter to carry off the latter', the Highlanders found it easier to despoil the Lowlands. There were two reasons for this, the Lowlands were a richer and more fertile country, and they were less protected by clan loyalties.

Reprisals were not to be feared because once the cattle had been carried off into the strongholds of the clans, it was difficult to follow them. The Lowlanders regarded the Highlanders as lawless raiders from whom it was impossible to recover their flocks and herds, nor were they strong enough to punish these aggressions. The Highlanders, on the other hand, regarded the rich Lowlands as an open field for their freebooting activities. They owed no loyalty to the Lowlanders, and so their cattle were fair game.

If, as sometimes happened, any resistance was put up in these raids, or clansmen lost their lives as a result of them, then a 'creach'

10. *Top left:* John Knox

above: Knox's Pulpit, formerly in St Giles' Cathedral

bottom left: Knox's Study

11. *Top:* John Knox's House

left: Knox's Bedroom

or spoliation could be decided upon. This was an order for destruction in which houses were burned, the inhabitants killed, and the whole countryside laid to waste. The raids, reprisals, and creachs were carried on systematically. There was no dishonour in killing, or burning, or carrying off the cattle 'which cropped the grass of the enemy'. This was part of the trade of being a loyal clansman.

The number of these reprisals and raids was not diminished by the rules for the acceptance of a new chieftain:

'Every heir or young chieftain was obliged in honour to give a specimen of his valour before he was owned and declared governor or leader of his people who obeyed and followed him on all occasions. This chieftain was attended with a retinue of young men, who had not before given any proof of their valour, and were ambitious of such an opportunity to signalize themselves. It was usual for the chief to make a desperate incursion upon some neighbour or other that they were in feud with, and they were obliged to bring by open force the cattle they found on the land they attacked, or to die in the attempt. After the performance of this achievement the young chieftain was ever after reputed valiant and worthy of government . . . this custom was not reputed robbery, for the damage which one tribe sustained by the inauguration of the chieftain of another, was repaired when their chieftain in his turn came to make his specimen; but I have not heard of an instance of this practice for these sixty years since.'

Although clan chiefs were powerful they could be opposed or deposed. For example, in the early years of the sixteenth century, the head of the Stewarts of Garth, known locally as Fierce Wolf, was deposed by his clan and imprisoned for life in his own castle at Garth. His cruelty and fury was of such a nature that even his own followers could not stomach it.

'Nothing can be more erroneous than the idea that a Highland chief was an ignorant and unprincipled tyrant . . . if ferocious in disposition, or weak in understanding, he was curbed and directed by the elders of his tribe who, by inviolable custom, were his standing counsellors without whose advice no measure of any kind was decided.'

The clan also took a hand in general administration. The clan of the Earl of Seaforth, for example, prevented him from demolishing

F

his own castle. Whether this was a method of economy or a means of defence is not clear. In this same way, the Laird of Glenorchy was prevented by his clan from building a castle on a hill on the side of Loch Tay. His advisers, having decided that they did not like the place he had chosen, made him change his plans.

A Highland Chief and His Followers

The state kept up by these chiefs was considerable. In the Islands, for example, the chief of the Clan Macdonald had a council of sixteen: four thanes, four freemen or sub-thanes, four squires. These accompanied him when he administered justice. In addition, each island had a judge who was appointed to try to settle disputes among the clansmen. These judges received land from the Macdonald and an eleventh part of the value of every action which they decided, a curious form of legal payment.

Apart from his administrators a chief had his personal attendants. These included a bard or poet, the bladier or spokesman, the gillemore or bearer of the broadsword, the gillecasflue—who carried the chief over fords when he was on foot—a guide to lead the chief home in dangerous passes, the baggage man, the piper, the piper's gillie, who carried the bagpipes, besides numbers of relations, and 'a number of the common sort, who have no particular employment but follow him only to partake of the cheer'. Every outstanding man in every century finds it easy to attract these.

It can be understood that well attended and the recipient of fealty from his followers and hangers on, a laird was a considerable personage when among his own people and in his own country.

The first Marquis of Huntley when he was summoned to court to wait on James VI and I

'stood in the presence chamber with his head covered. On being reminded of his want of respect, he humbly asked pardon from the King, saying that as he had just come from a country where all took off their bonnets to him, he had quite forgotten what he owed to his present situation.'

But whether the lairds took off their bonnets to the queen or king, or not, they remained equally unmanageable when among their clansmen. Periodically, however, the reigning sovereign decided on punitive action against the lairds both in the north and on the Borders. In the reign of James V,

'The King went to the south . . . and after this hunting he hanged Johnnie Armstrong, Laird of Kilnocky, over the gate of his castle and his accomplices to the number of 36 persons for which many Scotchmen heartily lamented for he was the most redoubted chieftain that had been for a long time on the borders of Scotland or of England. . . . It is said that from the borders to Newcastle, every man of whatsoever estate paid him tribute to be free of his trouble. This being done the King passed to the Isles and there held justice courts [assizes], and then punished both thief and traitor according to their deserts . . . brought many of the great men of the Isles captive with him such as Macdonnells, Macleod of the Lewis, Macneils, Maclean, Macintosh, John Muidart, Mackay, Mackenzie with many others that I cannot rehearse at this time, some of them to be put in wards, and some had in courts, and some he took in pledges for good rule in time coming, so he brought the Isles in good rule and peace both north and south, whereby he had great profit, service, and obedience of people a long time thereafter, and as long as he had the heads of the country in subjection they lived in great peace and rest, and there was great riches and policy by the King's Justice.'

The Clash of the Clans

While it is impractical to examine in detail all the feuds great and small which took place in the Scotland of the sixteenth century, there are some which give a general idea of the state into which the country had fallen.

The historian Skene, under the heading 'The Rise of the Mackintoshes', admits that two causes 'rendered their progress to power slow and difficult'. These were quite simply feuding between the Mackintoshes themselves, and a further feud which they were carrying on at the same time against the Earl of Huntley because the Mackintoshes were operating under the protection of the Earl of Moray. These complicated small and large feuds among the Mackintoshes began at the beginning of the century when William Mackintosh of Dunachton became clan chief.

His claim was opposed by John Roy Mackintosh, clan chief of another branch of the family. John Roy on various occasions tried to attack the rival clan chief but with no success. Eventually he resorted to a simpler method. He had William Mackintosh murdered at Inverness.

As a result of the murder, the clan followers of William had John

Roy murdered at Glenesk. Lachlan, the brother of the murdered William then became the head of the clan. But this situation did not last long, for 'sum wicked persones being impatient of virtuous living stirred up one of his own kinesmen called James Malcolmson who cruelly and treasonably slew his said chief'.

This produced more complications, for Lachlan's son was under age, and the clan, according to their laws of succession, chose Hector, his bastard brother to be chief. At this point the Earl of Moray decided to take a hand in the succession and he took the young chief under his protection to be brought up by his mother's relatives. Hector the bastard then decided that this was not according to clan practice and decided to get the young heir back under his protection. As a result Hector invaded the lands of the Earl of Moray, besieged and took the castle of Petty, and put to death the Ogilvies, who happened to be the unfortunate possessors of the castle.

The Earl of Moray, with the permission of the King, raised his clans, attacked the Mackintoshes, took 300 of them prisoner—and killed them all.

Hector then flung himself on the King's mercy, and received a free pardon for his misdemeanours. But he was shortly afterwards 'slain at St Andrews'. William, the young heir, about whom the whole imbroglio had taken place, was then put in possession of his castle and lands by the Earl of Moray. This unfortunately was not the happy end to young William's story, because

'fortune did envy his felicities and the wicked practices of the dissolute lives of his own kin suffered him not to remain long among them but the same factious companies that raised against his father was the cause of his destruction.'

This destruction was the cause of the widening of the feud, which then commenced in earnest between the Mackintoshes and the Earl of Huntley. It was started by Lachlan Mackintosh, son of the murderer of the last chief. He was still intent on the destruction of the family of the reigning chief.

Mackintosh commenced hostilities by surprising and burning the castle of Auchindoun. The Earl of Huntley then joined battle with the clan Mackintosh and a short fierce battle took place. The day going against Mackintosh, he could well see that the Earl of Huntley was in no mood to allow him to surrender with honour. Mackintosh decided to try his fate in another direction.

He made his way to the headquarters of Huntley when he knew he was absent from home and threw himself on the mercy of the Countess. The Countess was as inexorable as her husband could have been, and no sooner had Mackintosh within her power than she caused his head to be struck off.

With the death of Mackintosh the feud with Huntley was considered to have come to an end. Some erstwhile friends and followers of Huntley, who were related to Mackintosh, then changed sides in the usual way, and hostilities died down. The murdered Mackintosh's son was put in possession of the whole of his patrimony. The central government also took a hand, finding it an advantage to have the Mackintosh clan on their side in order to counteract the growing power of the Earl of Huntley in the north. (This came in especially useful at Inverness in 1562, when Mary Stuart nearly fell into the hands of the Earl, who had the idea of forcing her to marry his second son, John Gordon of Findlater. With the aid of the Mackintoshes, this plan went awry.)

It might have seemed that the balance of power could then have been preserved, but such was not the case. The feud broke out afresh soon after. The clan of the Macphersons was involved, and Huntley threw his weight on the side of the Macphersons against the Mackintoshes. This caused a division in clan loyalties, and the feud was carried on between Mackintoshes and Macphersons for some hundreds of years, both claiming the chieftainship of the clan Mackintosh.

There were, of course, a few ancillary feuds which included the Camerons and the Macdonalds of Keppoch—helped on sometimes with Huntley's assistance and sometimes without it. But the Macphersons stayed loyal to their clan chief right up to 1745 when, by a remarkable feat of clan loyalty, they hid him in a cave for nearly ten years, evading the most intensive searches of the Goverment troops.

Another clan, the Macgregors, seems to have given the central government a good deal of trouble. Their history, it is said, 'consists of a mere list of acts of privy council by which commissions are granted to pursue the clan with fire and sword'. As a result of the policy of 'fire and sword' the clan were driven by desperation to commit various atrocities against their attackers, and eventually led the Macgregors to an all-out war *à l'outrance* against the central government. Finally the whole of the clan were proscribed and declared outlaws.

The final act of the Government against the Macgregors was in 1603 when the clan were ordered to change their names, and the name of Macgregor was officially abolished.

If the Highlands were rife with feuds, the Islands did not escape. One of the fiercest feuds was carried on between the Macleods and the Clan Ranald.

A daughter of the Clan Macleod had been married to a chief of the Clan Ranald. This alliance was presumably a conciliatory gesture between the two clans, but it had the opposite effect, because the daughter of Macleod of Glenelg was very badly treated by her husband. Word of this getting around, the Macleods waited for a reasonable opportunity to revenge the honour of one of their daughters.

They did not forget, and at the end of the sixteenth century their chance came. A small party of Macleods had landed by mistake on the island of Eigg. They were well received by the Clan Ranald, but apparently became rather too friendly with the local girls on the island. The men took it in bad part that the Macleods should play fast and loose with their women, so they bound them hand-and-foot, put them back in their boat, and set them adrift.

Unhappily for the Clan Ranald, the boat was met by a party of Macleods, who rescued their kinsmen and took them back to Dunvegan where their misadventures were recounted, no doubt with embellishments.

The Macleod was only too happy that he now had a good opportunity for revenge and a real excuse. He filled his galleys with armed men and set out immediately for Eigg. Word having got round that the Macleods were coming, the wretched inhabitants of Eigg, who had done nothing more than try to protect the honour of their women according to their local customs, became very alarmed indeed. They realized that they could not stand and fight the Macleods because they were outnumbered, and so, with their wives and families, they retreated to a cave which was protected by a waterfall. Here they hid, evading the forces of the Macleod for two days.

Unfortunately, they sent out a scout too soon, thinking no doubt that the Macleods had given up the search. As a result their hiding place was discovered.

The revenge of the Macleod was not attractive.

He managed to divert the water which fell over the cave, and then, having laid hands on everything which was burnable in the vicinity, he lit a fire, and kept it going for a number of hours until all the men, women, and children crouching in the cave were suffocated. This effectively got rid of the opposition to the power of the Macleod. It also exterminated the island's population.

These feuds in the Highlands and Islands continued unabated even after the death of Mary Stuart. In his memoirs, Sir James Melville, one of the advisers of James VI and I, writes:

'Concerning the reducing of the Highlands and Islands: three of the principals, as MacLean, MacDonald, and Donald Gorm (MacDonald of Sleat), were subtly drawn to the court by the chancellor, who understood the differences among them, every one of them being by him put in hope to get his hand above his enemy. But at their coming they were all three warded in the castle of Edinburgh, to their great astonishment; for they had committed such foul murders under trust that it would be horrible to rehearse.'

Apparently these 'foul murders' included the murder of MacLean of Duart by his brother-in-law, and the massacre of the brother-in-law's followers. An immediate blood feud was then begun between the MacLeans and the Macdonalds.

Melville goes on to recount the rest of the story which includes the usual tales of bribery and treachery.

'Being therefore apprehensive of their lives, they dealt largely of their ill-won gold to those who had credit. Nevertheless, they were put to an assize, and convicted of treason and for many other foul crimes; which caused them to redouble their gifts to the guiders, but not to the King; in such sort that there was an agreement betwixt his Majesty and them that they should give pledges that they should pay yearly unto his Majesty 20,000 merks for the lands of the property whereof they had no security; of the which they had of yearly rent, as was given unto the exchequer, 250,000 merks. This was all given them for 20,000 merks. And whereas before they had no right nor security, but a forcible possession, they obtained sure conveyances by charter, seisin, and the great seal, and a remission of their foul crimes; and shortly after, their pledges who were kept in the castle of Blackness, were released by giving 5000 merks to one of His Majesty's chambers; and so the 20,000 merks were lost and never paid.'

167

There seems to be no good moral to this story, except that possession is nine points of the law, and that if a king cannot keep his 'good lords' under subjection, they are at liberty to take what they like, with or without his permission.

Melville, ever happy to give instances of the good advice he had rendered to the King, then goes on:

'I had advised His Majesty to go himself to the isles and build a fort and to remain there two years, and promised to go with him; showing His Majesty that the kings of Scotland were never so rich since they left the Highlands to dwell in the Lowlands, but have ever since diminished their rents and increased their superfluous expenses in diet and clothing . . . which His Majesty found to be most true; and His Majesty was resolved to follow the said advice, but all was altered by the former misrule. Matters thus proceeding, many began to lose hope of amendment or to see shortly such a reformation as was promised.'

Considering the general state of the country their despondency is not surprising.

These feuds continued to influence the course of politics in Scotland among the nobility who were at the court of King James, and old murders cast their long shadows from the past. Melville records: 'There was no good liking between the Master of Glamis and my Lord of Spynie, chiefly for the feud between the houses of Crawford and Glamis.'

Alexander Lindsay (Lord Spynie) son of the Earl of Crawford was in feud with the family of the Chancellor Glamis because the brother of the Master of Glamis had been killed by Crawford's clan followers in 1578. These two families had lands which 'marched' together in Angus.

Melville recounts further complicated ramifications in which Spynie was accused of having plotted with the Earl of Bothwell and was banished from court. Others were included in the general plots and counterplots including 'Young Logie who was also thought to have had much dealing with the said earl and was accused, taken and warded for the same. But he escaped out of a window in Dalkeith by the help of a Danish gentlewoman, whom he afterwards married.' At least 'young Logie' managed to gain a bride in exchange for his misfortune. Presumably she must have been one of the ladies attached to James VI's queen, Anne of Denmark.

Apart from the influence which these clan feuds had upon Scottish politics, and the general distress they caused in the whole country, their fury reached such a pitch that sometimes the clashing clans decimated their own followers, and more, by the fury of their revenges against their enemies. An instance is recorded where, after one of the clan battles, four men were left on one side and two on the other, in a conflict which started out with several hundred.

It is, of course, obvious that it was largely the nature of the Highland terrain and the lack of communications which made it possible for the chieftains and their clans to carry on their private wars unimpeded by interference from outside. Skene, in the *Highland Clans*, writing at the beginning of the nineteenth century, says: 'There are perhaps few countries into which the introduction of strangers is received with less favour than the Highlands of Scotland.' That is a remark which, in the sixteenth-century context does not need to be modified. The Highlanders did not like strangers; they persecuted and harried them; and the word 'stranger' could be stretched to include people from neighbouring valleys and hills, or if the occasion for revenge served, members of minor branches of their own clans.

Apparently in Gaelic the toast 'An honourable death!' is regarded as a friendly wish. Considering the deeds perpetrated in those days many of the deaths do not seem to have been either friendly or honourable.

CHAPTER NINE

FOOD AND FUN

Cooking and Cuisine

As in so many other aspects, there seems to be a certain discrepancy in the accounts given of the cooking. On the one hand, John Knox hits out at the great waste which went on at court and says, 'The affairs of the kitchen were so griping that the minister's stipends could not be paid.' But as he was an interested party it is possible that he could have showed a certain prejudice on the subject of cuisine, *haute* or *basse*. Other writers paint a picture of a land filled with lowing herds of succulent cattle, rivers full of splendid salmon, and moors and hillsides thick with game birds and deer. General Wade, writing much later, at the beginning of the eighteenth century, said that in some parts of Scotland there was nothing to eat and in others plentiful grouse, partridge, salmon, trout, honey and the glory of the country, Usky ('usque baugh', living water, or whisky). This remark probably also represents the truth about sixteenth-century Scotland, for all writers agree that very little progress had been made in that time, either in agricultural or the organization of the produce of the country.

As in most countries, the beginnings of cookery in Scotland were based on the availability of various foods. On the coasts much fish and seaweed were eaten. The English 'meat and two veg.' could be replaced in the north of Scotland by fish and two kinds of seaweed, but the diet of the average Scot varied according to the district. Some commentators say that the Scottish lived exclusively on fish and kale, others that they eat a great deal of meat and no bread. Both statements are probably true.

On the western seaboard, fish was not only eaten a great deal by the people but was one of the country's chief exports. Aberdeen was famous for speldings (small haddocks, salted and dried on the rocks), finnan haddock, and smoked haddock. Salmon was so plentiful in Scotland that it was not well regarded as a food by the upper classes. Herrings from Loch Fyne were famous from the earliest times, and were sent abroad in barrels. Other fish which were eaten were oysters, crabs, winkles, limpets, and mussels. These last came from the appropriately named Musselburgh which was famed for mussels from the time of the Roman occupation.

As with clothing, cookery showed a big split between the classes. The court cookery was French, and many of the dishes which can be found in old Scottish cookery books were based on French recipes. Most of these are believed to have been introduced by the Regent, Mary of Guise Lorraine.

There is no doubt that French desserts were common in court circles. James VI and I was given a 'banquet of wet and dry confections with all sorts of wine, whereat His Majesty camped very merrily a good while'. The sentence now seems open to ambiguity in view of the change in the meaning of 'camp' and the King's taste in certain directions.

There seems little doubt that other more delicate dishes were brought from France. The names of the recipes seem to prove it. Soupe à la Reine, an old Scottish white soup, is made from that favourite meat of the French: veal, mixed with fowl and all kinds of delicate herbs. This rich soup is also the basis for a further complication: to make it into Lorraine Soup, the cook should add to his white soup, almonds, eggs, cold roast fowl, breadcrumbs, lemon peel, nutmeg and cream. It certainly sounds a soup invented for a queen.

An old recipe, supposed to have been invented for the delectation of guests at Holyrood Palace by the cook to Mary of Guise Lorraine, includes the instruction to soak a haunch of venison for six hours in claret. That, too, smacks very much of French ways of cooking.

An ancient dish, Veal Flory, which is a veal stew with herbs and mushrooms is another legacy of the 'auld alliance' and is supposed to have come to Scotland via Paris from Florence. Two other recipes include the word Flory—Almond Flory, and Prune Flory— but these are complicated puddings. Most good French cookery came originally from Florence, the home of Renaissance civilization, and the two French queens, Catherine de Médicis, and Mary of Guise Lorraine had a great influence on the cookery of their day.

Megs Dods in the *Annals of the Cleikum Club* says,

'As we are disposed to give the monks full credit for many of the best French dishes, and for our own antiquated preparations, so are the

Fair recluses [nuns] of France and Italy entitled to the merit of much that is elegant in the confectionary of which they long had and still have tasteful exhibitions on festivals. To their leisure and taste we owe caramelled and candied fruits, fruits *en chemise*, chantilly and caramel baskets.'

Many of the French cookery terms have passed into Scots in this way.

The following list gives a few:

ashet—meat dish (from the French *assiette*)
battry—kitchen utensils (*batterie de cuisine*)
bonally—stirrup cup (*bon aller*)
bufe—beef (*bœuf*)
cannel—cinnamon (*cannelle*)
disjune—luncheon (*déjeuner*)
flam—*flan*
gigot—leg of mutton (*gigot d'agneau*)
mange—meal (*manger*)
petticoat tails (*petites galettes*)
purry—*purée* [one of several explanations for this corruption].
pottisea—pastry cook (*patissier*)
tassie—cup (*tasse*)
vivers—victuals (*vivres*)

A crokain is a pudding made from sugar, water and lemon and comes from the French *croque en bouche*. Another pudding, a kind of *beignet soufflé*, is called simply Nuns' Beads. Finally that most famous Scottish dish of all, Haggis, is a corruption of *hachis*, French for mince or chopped up meat.

The monks come in for a certain amount of sly recommendation in the Annals: 'In the days of Popery and good cheer in those days of paternosters and venison pasties, stoups of untaxed clarets, and oral confession, a pullet so streted [boiled in a well washed haggis bag] was according to waggish legends the secret regale for Mass John by his fair penitents'; and quoting old literature, Megs Dods says that this must be true if Allan Ramsay's 'Monk', 'The Miller's Wife', or 'The Friars of Berwick' are anything to go by.

The monks' interest in food is commemorated in various rhymes:

'The monks of Melrose made fat brose
On Fridays when they fasted.'

Another rhyme credits the Friary of Faill,

'who made gude kail
On Fridays when they fasted.
They never wanted gear enough
As long as their neighbours' lasted.'

Whatever their contemporaries may have thought of the monks and friars their taste is commemorated in several recipes. Friars' Chicken was said to be a favourite of James VI and I—it was made with broth from a young and tender fowl and served with slices of the chicken.

Friars' Fish in Sauce sounds a good cheerful heart-warming dish for a lean meatless Friday: 'Take Red (or other trout), carp or perch, salt them and add spices, onions, cloves, mace, black and Jamaica peppercorns, add claret, anchovies, lemon, cayenne pepper, flour and butter, and dilute with stock and rhenish wine.' Other monkish delicacies were kippered salmon, pickled salmon, and spiced salmon.

The reputation of the Church for good living is supported by the contents of the 'capon cave' of the Parson of Stobo, who was obviously given to what one of his contemporaries calls 'large tabling and belly cheer'. This includes eight salted carcases of beef, a pipe of salmon (eight dozen), another pipe of Loch Fyne herring, forty bolls of meat, six stone of butter, a 22-pound cheese, as well as a barn full of wheat, oats, barley, peas and hay. No doubt the parson of Stobo was making sure that any 'dearth' which might arise in the country was not going to affect his own belly cheer.

Shortages of food were constant in sixteenth-century Scotland, often due to bad summers. *The Chronicle of Fortingall* records in 1574, 'the summer right evil weather and dear, the boll of malt five merk and a half'. The following winter, 'there was a great dearth in Scotland of all kinds of victuals'.

The Government tried to counteract the shortage of food by rationing. At the time of an earlier shortage the Parliament of 1551 had such a scheme. Unlike modern rationing it was carried on according to rank. Although this might seem to be a gross denial of equality, the barons and nobles were expected to keep up a good standard of living for their followers and servants, and these last enjoyed the 'tails', or remains of the meals, as part of their perks.

The order runs:

'Item, it is statute and ordained that having respect to the great and exhorbitant dearth risen in this realm of victuals and other stuff for the sustentation of mankind . . . because of the superflous cheer used commonly in this realm as well amongst small as great men . . . and for the remedy hereof and staunching of such dearth and exhorbitant prices aforesaid, it is devised and ordained that no archbishop, bishop, nor earl shall have at his mess but eight dishes of meat, nor baron nor freeholder have but four dishes of meat, nor no burgess or other substantious man, spiritual or temporal, shall have at his mess but three dishes, and but one kind of meat in every dish.'

The penalties were stiff, and graduated like the messing arrangements—£100 for the higher orders, scaling down to 20 merks for the fourth estate of substantial men. It was suggested that this rationing could be over-generous for the substantial men, but exceptions were made for hospitality, Christmas, Easter, the days of patron saints, marriages, and banquets for people from other countries—but banquets were not to be given for fellow Scotsmen, a somewhat similar limitation to that applying to modern expense-account entertaining and tax allowance.

The feasting was of a considerable nature. At the beginning of the century, in the time of James V (Mary Stuart's father), the butcher's bill, recorded in Latin, included 14 fatted oxen, 100 sheep carcases, 3 large calves, 3 stone of suet, 17 ox tongues, 1 boar's head (possibly for decorative purposes), 1,000 ox feet, 1,340 sheep's feet, 98 tame geese, 16 pigs, over 100 assorted cocks, chickens, fowls, and capons as well as assorted other birds such as redshanks, sea-fowl, partridges, plovers (43), woodcock (30), 54 moor-fowls, 42 blackcock, 34 ducks, 15 wild geese, and 59 rabbits. That was just the meat course. The groceries included 560 eggs, 240 apples and pears, and 40 gallons of ale for jellies.

The small numbers of pigs used was possibly due to the Scottish dislike of this meat, shared by James VI and I, who carried this dislike with him into England.

In 1572, a year or two before the great dearth, Lord Lovat's housekeeping was equally generous and included each year 70 fat oxen, as well as venison, fish, poultry, lamb, veal, and vast quantities of game birds, as well as imported wines, sugars, and spices from France.

Further evidence of the French influence in cookery is shown by the fact that *Archangelica officinalis*, the angelica which is used in sweet making, has been in cultivation in Scotland since 1568, and it is not thought to grow anywhere else in the United Kingdom. Until some years ago the French sorrel, which is used to make the delicious sorrel soup, was supposed to grow in the vicinity of Craigmillar. But Hector Boece comments less favourably on French cookery in Scotland, deploring 'so many delicate courses that they provoke the stomach . . . more than it may sufficiently digest' and he blames the nobility who had favoured the new cookery 'after the fashion which they have seen in France'.

George Buchanan comments more favourably, mentioning the entertainment he found at the Duke of Atholl's house, where he was regaled 'with all sich delicious and sumptuous meattis as was to be had in Scotland, for fleschis, fischis, and all kinds of fyne wyne, and spyces requisite for ane prince'. He was not griping about the kitchen like John Knox.

The fare of the peasants and the men who were not 'substantial' was less bothersome to the stomach. Bread was a mixture of barley and oats, and the Scottish mercenaries when going abroad to serve with the French took their taste for oatcakes with them. Froissart says that the equipment of the Scottish soldier included a flat plate of metal, and a wallet of oatmeal for the 'purpose of making oat-cakes'. Among the cottagers this flat plate was placed on a tripod over the embers.

This was the usual bread of the people. But it varied according to the part of the country. There were four sorts of bread: the finest white bread, called manchet; the second quality, trencher; the third, ravelled bread; and the fourth, mashloch. Ravelled bread was of bruised grain as it came from the mill and included the flour and the bran. Many old recipes include the use of kail which was mixed with oatmeal into a sort of cake and cut into slices.

On the farms the dinner hour could be as early as ten o'clock in the morning. Apart from the fish or meat served, there were many different kinds of milk dishes, and skink (soups). From the earliest times the Scottish were famous for their soups. An old proverb gives a culinary warning about them: 'A spoonful of stink will spoil a plateful of skink.'

The soups included the classic cock-a-leekie. Scott introduced this into his Waverley novel, *The Fortunes of Nigel*, where King James VI says, 'And my lords and lieges let us all to dinner for the cock-a-leekie is cooling.' Scott also puts into his books other traditional old recipes of the early periods he is writing about. In *Guy Mannering* he mentioned crappit heads, which are the heads of haddocks stuffed with oatmeal, pepper, and salt, the fish livers being mashed into this stuffing.

In the same book he has his gipsy, Meg Merrilies, say when talking about stew: 'There's what will warm your heart, there's been many a moonlight watch to bring all that trade together, the folks that are to eat that dinner thought little of your game laws.' The laws against the shooting of game were very stringent and often carried the penalty of death or mutilation, so that it could be a choice between improving the stew or keeping your ears.

Most of the old lists of dishes make it clear that an abundance of fish was eaten, fresh or salted, and some of the agreements between the hired 'hinds' and their hirers stipulated that they must not be expected to eat salmon or fresh-water trout more often than three times a week.

One of the Scottish specialities was wind blown fish. This was made in the following way:

'Take fresh fish, clean, take out the eyes. Cover the fish with salt and pass a string through the eyeholes. Then hang to dry in some place where there is a draught. The next morning the fish can be broiled over a slow fire.'

For some kinds of salting down, it was not possible to use the salt which was won from the sea, but a special kind of salt had to be imported. Their ways of salting beef varied but one is quoted as follows:

'The natives are accustomed to salt their beef (which is sweet and tender as the cows live upon seaweed in winter and spring and are fattened by it, nor are they slaughtered before they eat plentifully of it in December) . . . the salt beef is placed in a cow's hide which keeps it close from the air and preserves it as well if not better than in barrels and tastes they say best when this way used.'

Possibly this method of salting meat down was first used because of the shortage of wood.

Vegetables were eaten only in the form of broths and stews, and apart from the ubiquitous kail included seaweed soup, and sea moss jelly. Various seaweeds were used for these soups, such as sea moss, henware, and tangle, which

'is eat raw and then reckoned to be loosening and very good for the sight. If boiled it proves more loosening if the juice be drank with it. The natives eat it boiled with butter and reckon it very wholesome.'

Another health giving dish was a limpet stew or skink. 'The limpet being parboiled in a very little quantity of water, the broth is drank to increase milk in nurses, and likewise the milk proves astringent to the infants', as well it might.

Fynes Morison, after travelling in Scotland at the end of the century, gives what is probably an authentic picture of the average sort of fare in the country:

'Touching their diet they eat much colewort and cabbage but little fresh meat, using to salt their mutton and geese which made me wonder that they use to eat beef without salting. The gentlemen reckon their revenues not by rents of money but by cauldrons of victuals and keep many people in the families yet living most on corne and rootes not spending any great quantity of flesh—myself was at a knight's house who had many servants to attend him that brought in his meat with their heads covered with blue caps. The tables being furnished with great platters of porridge, each having a little piece of sodden [boiled] meat; and when the table was served the servants did sit downe with us but the upper mess instead of porridge had a pullet with some prunes in the broth and I observed no art of cookery or furniture of household stuff, but rather rude neglect of both, though myself and my companions, sent from the Governor of Berwick about bordering affairs, were entertained after their best manner. The Scots living then in factions used to keep many followers and so consumed their revenue of victuals living in some want of money. They vulgarly ate hearth cakes of oats, but in cities have also wheaten bread which for the most part was bought by courtiers, gentlemen and the best sort of citizen. They drink pure wines not with sugar as the English yet at feasts they put Comfits in the wine after the French manner.'

This sounds like the French custom of putting pieces of sugar called *canards* in brandy or wine which is not matured. 'But they had not our vintners fraud to mix their wines. The better sort of citizens brew ale, their usual drink which will distemper a stranger's body.'

Obviously the Scottish ale was much stronger than the English ale. The French ambassador to Scotland complained in equally pained terms about the whisky. There are often traps for the unwary foreigner in strange imbibings.

The truth about eating and drinking in early Scotland is probably best illustrated by the fable of the town and country mouse published at the beginning of the century. 'The country mouse lived on corn as outlaws do.' In the cold winter she was starved so the clever town mouse persuaded her to go home with her where, in the town mouse's town house, could be found cheese, butter, meat, fish—both salted and fresh, meat in sacks, beef (stricken into great pieces) and wine not water. 'A lord's fare thus could the mice counterfeit.' Added to it were cakes and spices, but the country mouse was chased by Gilbert the Cat and decided that life in the town, though luxurious, was too dangerous and returned to her country fare of water, kail, and beans.

Sports and Pastimes
It was axiomatic that with the rise of the Reformers in Scotland restrictions on sport should have been attempted, but thanks to the sturdy character of the Scots this does not seem to have affected the general delight in games. The love of outdoor sport of all kinds was shared by Mary Stuart, who was fond of hunting, golf, and many other sports. During one of her many progresses round the countryside, John Knox, who rarely missed a point, complained that there was a shortage of wild fowl. Whether this was supposed to be due to her hunting them, or eating them, or both is not stated.

From the earliest times game were protected by law. It is stated in a book about the Game Laws of Scotland: 'The protection of wild fowl (apart from the laws about quadrupeds) form by far the greater proportion of the laws which found their way to the Scottish statute books.'

As far back as 1427 the seasons during which wild fowl could be legally taken were regulated. The birds which were protected included partridges, plovers, blackcock, 'grey hennes', moor cocks and 'sik fowles'. A few years later another law against the 'slaying of wild fowl or the destruction of nests or eggs' lays down a general ban on all birds that are 'gainis to eate for the sustentation of man'.

An Act of 1551 forbids the shooting of wild fowl without going into any details of which kind of wild fowl are being protected. In
178

1567, another act prohibits all shooting at 'herron or foule of the river' and adds that this prohibition is 'under pain of forfeiture of the offender's moveable goods.' This was a stiff penalty at a time when a table or a cupboard could be a luxury item. By the end of the century, there is another general prohibition against the shooting of 'wilde foules'.

By 1600 the statutes go into greater detail, and lay down a prohibition not only against the shooting, but the sale or purchase, of partridges, moorfowl, blackcock, 'aith hennes', 'termigrants', 'wyld dukes', 'teilles atteils' (possibly widgeon), 'goldings' (another species of wild fowl), moryms (supposed to be the common martin), 'skail draik' (sheldrake), 'herron', bittern, or any 'sik kynde of fowles commonly used to be chas with halkes (hawks)', with the exception, oddly enough, of woodcock, plovers, and wild geese. The list of birds which were to be protected indicates that the Scottish taste in game birds for the pot was fairly catholic.

Doves, to provide fresh meat in the winter months, were the object of special protective laws. Queen Mary's favourite castle, Craigmillar, has a large dovecote built into its walls. The right to keep a dovecote was tied to the ownership of land. If a man bought land with a legalized dovecote, he could maintain it, but if it fell down he was not allowed to rebuild it. So once a man found himself in possession of a legalized dovecote he made it his business to see that it did not become a ruin.

A law of 1597 confirmed earlier laws against the shooting of pigeons and decreed that the offender could be put in the stocks for forty-eight hours. Earlier penalties were even more severe and included the forfeiture of all moveable goods, half to the crown, a quarter to the judge, and a quarter to the informant or apprehender. This dubious law was doubtless likely to lead to a quick conviction if the judge had an eye on the offender's movable goods. Other laws were enacted against the killing of deer, rabbits, and hares.

Hawking and hunting may have seemed to be the prerogative of the nobility, but no doubt many humbler people managed to join in the sports in a clandestine way. Hunting was a necessary protection against wolves and foxes and often the clauses of a lease contained a condition that the person owning the land must keep hounds for hunting these beasts. A mid-century lease, dated 1552, enjoins the tenants of Nether Illrik to maintain a hound for 'fox and wolf', and about the same time the lease of a place in Glenisla to the

Countess of Crawford and her son, Lord Ogilvy of Airlie, contained a condition that they 'sustain and feed ane leash of hounds for tod and wolf'. It is possible that this kind of clause was the origin of the county kennels. Something which started as a necessity became an esoteric sport.

Golf

Although golf is presumed to be a Scottish invention some people say that the game originally came from the Low Countries. The origins of the word golf are presumed to come from the German *kolbe*, a club, which in Low Dutch was *kolf*. Some writers say that the earliest golf balls were imported, like so many luxuries, from Flanders.

It seems to have had royal approval as a game from an early date. In the Lord High Treasurer's Accounts in the early sixteenth century are found the following entries:

> 1503/4. Feb 3 Item to the King to play at the Golf with the Erle of Bothvile (whether this was a bet on the game is not specified)   13s.
>
> Item to Golf Clubbis and Ballis to the King that he played with   9s.
>
> 1505/6. Item for 12 golf ballis to the King.   4s.
>
> 1506. July 18th item the 28th day of July for 2 Golf Clubbes to the King.   2s.

Side by side with the spread of the game went the disapproval of the authorities. Scotsmen were playing golf and football, the most popular games, when they should have been practising their war games. In the fifteenth century, two Acts were passed about wappenshawing—target practice and military exercises. 'Wapinschawingis be halden by the Lordis and Baronis spirituale and temporale four times in the year and that the Fute-Ball and Golf be utterly cryit doune, and nocht usit; and that the bowe merkis be maid at ilk paroche kirk a pair of buttis and schutting be usit ilk Sunday.' Be that as it may, we see the prejudice against Sunday golf.

Later in the century the authorities were still trying, and passed another Act about 'weapon-showings' for use against the old enemy, England. Each 'seaman that can not deal with the bow, that have a good axe and a target [shield] of leather to resist the shot of England which is no cost but the value of the hide; and that

180

Fute Ball and Golf be abusit in time coming and the butts made up and shooting used'.

When the Reformers came on the scene the reasons for putting down the Royal and Ancient game changed. The Edinburgh town council put out their usual prohibitions about the heinousness of playing golf or any other game on Sunday, and once again people were being punished who preferred to play golf 'in tyme of sermons', for the Reformers were not letting their captive audiences out of their clutches.

One of the allegations against Mary, Queen of Scots was that a few days after the murder of Darnley she 'was seen playing golf and pall mall in the fields beside Seton'. An addiction to golf was obviously regarded as an indication of guilt and lightness of mind.

The early golf balls were covered with leather and stuffed with feathers, which is possibly why the King wore his out so frequently. Or maybe he just lost them.

Football
Football, too, was very well liked, although, as with golf, various Acts were passed trying to stop its popularity. James IV, in 1491, was already denouncing both these pastimes as 'unprofitable sports'. But again the Lord High Treasurer's accounts give the game away, for the April 22nd figures include: 'Item given to James Dog to buy footballs to the King—2s.'

Football was played on Sundays, prior to the Reformation, but it was apparently a church offence as far as the Reformers were concerned. In the Perth Kirk Session in the early 1590s a dozen men confessed 'that on the Sunday of the Fast in time of preaching they had succumbed to play football in the Meadow Inch of the Muirton north of the city'.

Modern disturbances caused by football are only an echo of earlier troubles. 'Football games', Pitcairn records for his *Criminal Trials*, 'were often taken advantage of for the perpetration of deeds of violence. At least they were frequently terminated by violence and bloodshed, through the feuds of neighbouring clans or districts.'

In June 1600, Sir John Carmichael of that Ilk, Warden of the Middle Marches of Scotland, was present at a big match, and on his way home was killed by a party of Armstrongs. Another time, some Border Scots met at Kelso, ostensibly to play a friendly match,

181

which however ended in a marauding expedition across the border into England.

The Maitland MS., of Sir Richard Maitland, contains the following lines about football:

'Brissit brawnis and broken banes,
Strife, discord and waistit wanis (wounds)
Crook in eld, syne halt withal
These are the beauties of the foot-ball'.

And Maitland consoles himself for his old age thus:

'When young men comes frae the green,
What playing at football had been
    Wi broken spauld (shoulder)
I thank my God, I want my ee'n (eyes)
An am sae auld.'

But all the inveighing against football, and all the condemnation of the Reformers did not stop the progress of the game. Before the Reformation the churchmen were more jolly about it, and indeed joined in themselves.

Other sports which were current in the sixteenth century were cockfighting, and a game called stow ball. One commentator says that he presumes this to be the same game as golf because it was played with a similar ball. It could, of course, have some affinity to the game which in Sussex is called stool ball, which is played with a bat in front of a square wicket on a pole.

Mall, or pall mall, was an early form of croquet, which was played with two hoops and mallets—hence its name.

Bowls were also played in Scotland as well as catchpole. Catchpole, or catich-ball, consisted in striking a leather-covered ball against a high wall, with the hand, and hitting back after its rebound and bounce. It sounds like fives.

Tennis was played, the old variety called real tennis, and there still exists the tennis court on which Mary, Queen of Scots and her father, James V, played at Falkland Palace. This is still in use after more than four hundred years.

Another popular game was the Kiles, which resembled what is now called skittles. The Kiles, or Kayles, were placed in one row, whereas ninepins are placed in three rows. A variety of the game called club-kayles involved throwing a stick at them. Playing of the Kyles was also, of course, another cause of Sabbath desecration after the Reformation.

A sport enjoyed by the nobility was 'riding at the ring'. This sounds to have been like the kind of exercises indulged in at gymkhanas in modern times—the riders tried to make off with a suspended ring on their spear. 'Running at the glove' was another version of the same kind of game, but this time the glove had to be picked up from the ground.

The king and government tried to make archery popular, as it was useful in the wars against the English, famous for their archery and marksmanship. But it was in vain, the Scots remained bad at archery, and the butts were neglected in spite of the various penalties enacted against neglecting archery for football and golf.

Curling and Hunting
Curling has been claimed as the national game, 'Scotland's ain game o' curling'. Unfortunately, some people think that like golf the game may well have originated in the Low Countries. There were during the fifteenth and sixteenth centuries many émigrés from Flanders who came to Scotland, some to teach various industries, some to trade, and they are thought to have brought the game of curling with them. It was, and still is, one of the most democratic games, and on the ice everyone is entitled to call everyone else by his Christian name, whatever the relationship between the players may be when they are no longer ice-bound.

'For on the water's face are met,
Wi' mony a merry joke, man,
The tenant and his jolly laird,
The pastor and his clerk, man. . . .

Now rival parish and shievedoms keep
On upland lochs, the long expected tryst
To play their yearly bonspiel, aged men
Smite with the eagerness of youth, are there,
While love of conquest lights the beamless eyes
    New nerves their arms, and makes them young once more.'

The word 'bonspiel' sounds like a mixture of French and Dutch or German which makes one think it may well have had a Dutch origin.

183

But in spite of the traditions which surround the game of curling, it does not seem to have been universally played in Scotland, and the earliest notice about it appears in the *Muses Threnodie* by a Perth Poet, Henry Adamson, published in 1638. None of the writers of the sixteenth century appears to have mentioned curling. The Lord High Treasurer's Accounts, which listed all the sports and pastimes of James IV, seem to make no mention of the sport. Old curling stones have been found dated 1611 and 1613. Allegedly, the earliest one is dated 1551, but the date of this stone is disputed.

In such a warlike people as the Scots, an ability to shine at sports was regarded as worthy of admiration. David Home of Wedderburn is described as 'being swift of foot, and fond of foot-races'. Horse-racing was also one of his amusements.

'He collected a number of the swiftest horses both from the north of Scotland and from England, by the assistance of one Graeme, recommended to him by his brother-in-law, Lochinvar. He generally had eight or more of that kind, so that the prize was seldom won by any but those of his family . . . He was so great a master of the art of riding, that he would often be beat today, and within eight days lay a double wager on the same horses, and come off conqueror . . . He went frequently from home to his diversion, sometimes to Haddington, and sometimes to Peebles, the one of which is eighteen, and the other twenty-four miles distant, and sometimes stayed there for several days with numerous attendants, regardless of expenses, as being too mean and sordid a care, and below the dignity of one of his rank. Being educated in affluence, he delighted in fencing, hunting, riding, throwing the javelin, managing horses, and like-wise in cards and dice.'

He sounds to have been an all-round sporting type very much in the modern vein.

If golf can claim to be called Royal and Ancient, hunting is just as royal and even more ancient. Here is a description of a hunting party given by the Earl of Atholl. The scene of the hunt is supposed to have been Glen Tilt in Perthshire. William Barclay describes it:

'In the year 1563, the Earl of Atholl, a prince of the blood royal, had, with much trouble and vast expenses, a hunting match for the entertainment of our most illustrious and most gracious Queen. Our people call this a royal hunting. I was then a young man, and was present on the occasion. Two thousand Highlanders, or wild Scotch, as you call them here, were employed to drive to the hunting ground all the deer from the woods and hills of Atholl, Badenoch, Mar, Murray, and the Counties about. As these Highlanders use a light dress, and are very swift of foot, they went up and down so nimbly that in less than two months' time they brought together 2,000 red deer, besides roes and fallow deer. The Queen, the great men, and others were in a glen when all the deer were brought before them. Believe me, the whole body of them moved forward in something like battle order. This sight still strikes me, and ever will, for they had a leader whom they followed close wherever he moved. This leader was a very large stag, with a very high head. The sight delighted the Queen very much; but she soon had occasion for fear, upon the Earl's (who had been accustomed to such sights) addressing her thus: "Do you observe that stag who is foremost of the herd? There is danger from that stag; for if either fear or rage should force him from the ridge of that hill, let every one look to himself, for none of us will out of the way of harm; for the rest will follow this one, and having thrown us under foot, they will open a passage to this hill behind us." What happened a moment afterwards confirmed this warning; for the Queen ordered one of the best dogs to be let loose upon a wolf; this the dog pursues, the leading stag was frightened, he flies by the same way he had come there, the rest rush after him, and break out where the thickest body of the Highlanders was. They had nothing for it but to throw themselves flat on the heath, and to allow the deer to pass over them. It was told the Queen that several of the Highlanders had been wounded, and that two or three of them had been killed outright; and the whole body had got off, had not the Highlanders, by their skill in hunting, fallen upon a stratagem to cut off the rear from the main body. It was one of those that had been separated that the Queen's dogs, and those of the nobility, made slaughter. There were killed that day 360 deer, with five wolves, and some roes.'

A royal hunting, or a royal slaughter, it depends which way the taste runs.

Plays and Pageants
In the days of feasting and popery it was the fashion to hold markets and fairs on the Sabbath, and afterwards when the sales were made the villagers sported on the green, or watched the strolling players.

The first plays which are recorded in Scotland are 'mystery plays'. They were used by the Roman Catholic hierarchy for the instruction of their illiterate parishioners.

The themes were always taken from the Scriptures or the Bible. But afterwards these plays degenerated into parody. As with the French *fêtes des foux*, the relaxing of the dignity of the Church led to abuses. One of the most popular of these entertainments was the Feast of Asses, the chief performers being either Balaam's ass, or the donkey on which Christ rode on his entry into Jerusalem. But these performing donkeys were dressed in priests' canonicals, and the mob were encouraged to make fun of the priestly ass, and as a result a great deal of coarse goings-on resulted. The Feast of the Holy Innocents was another occasion when children were encouraged to run wild and 'exercise their talent for mischief amongst the vestments, ornaments and shrines of the Church'.

Other plays of this nature included *The Lord of Misrule*, *The Abbot of Bon Accord*, and *The Abbot of Unreason*.

Oddly enough these bouts of fun at the expense of the clergy do not seem to have been suppressed by the Church. Possibly, feeling secure, the Church thought that a few jokes at their own expense were not unreasonable, and that the population should be allowed to let off steam. In 1547, a representative of the Primate of St Andrews appeared at Borthwick with letters of excommunication against the Lord of Misrule, which the priest was supposed to read out at High Mass in the parish church. But at this precise time the people living in Borthwick Castle were acting their play, which included the character of the Abbot of Unreason. With their mock abbot at the head of their unseemly procession, the men from the castle beat up the bishop's representative, ducked him in the mill dam several times, and then made him eat the document excommunicating the Lord of Misrule, having previously dunked the parchment in wine.

Another character in these parodies of the church was the Boy Bishop, or the President of Fools. The point and climax of the ceremonies was for the procession to go to the Church and parody the rite of the Mass while singing indecent adaptations of the hymns. It is difficult to comprehend the Church latitude in this.

A play which had great popular success in the sixteenth century was *Robin Hood and Little John*. In the Aberdeen revels at the beginning of the century 'it was ordained that all persons that are able within this burgh shall be ready with their arrayment made in green and yellow, bows, arrows and all convenient things according thereto to pass with Robin Hood and Little John all times convenient thereto'.

All defaulters from dressing in green and yellow and joining in the May Day fun were to be fined twenty shillings by the bailies.

Not everyone seems to have been anxious to tread the boards. An order by the Earl of Arran, Provost of Edinburgh, excuses one Francis Bothwell from taking the part of Little John. Gipsy dancers seem to have been a current attraction: 'Item, to the Egyptians that danced before the King in Holyroodhouse 40s.'

The first real Scottish play of the sixteenth century was Sir David Lyndsay's *Pleasant Satire of the Three Estates*. This was a sharp attack on the Church. It is supposed to have been played for the first time at Cupar in 1535. But another account mentions that the *Pleasant Satire* was played in 1544 before the Queen Regent, as is mentioned by Henry Charteris, the bookseller, who sat patiently nine hours on the bank to witness the play: 'It so far surpasses any efforts of contemporary English dramatists that it renders the barrenness of the Scottish muse in this department the more apparent.'

Scott gives totally different dates for the performance of this old and famous play. He points out the political significance of the play which formed the watershed between the old religious life and the new:

'The difference between the Catholic and Reformed religion was fiercely disputed in some of these dramas, and in Scotland a mortal blow was aimed at the superstitions of the Roman Catholic Church by Sir David Lyndsay in a Morality acted in 1539 and entitled the Satire of the Three Estaitis. In a letter to the Lord Privy Seal of England 26th January 1540 Sir William Eure, Envoy from Henry VIII gives the following account of the play "In the feast Epiphane at Linlithgow the King, Queen, and the whole counsel, spiritual and temporal. In the first entrance comes in Solare whose part was but to make merry, sing ballads with his fellows, and drink at the interludes of the play." '

This sounds much like the modern TV actors' idea of a preliminary 'warm up' act for the captive audience.

'Next came in a King, who passed to his throne having no speech to the end of the play, and then to ratify and approve, as in Parliament, all things done by the rest of the players which represented The Three Estates. With him came his courtiers, Placebo, Piethank and Flattery . . .'

Other characters follow a Bishop, a Burgess, and

'Experience, clad like a doctor, who set them all down on the dais under the King. And after them comes a Poor Man, who did go up and down the scaffold making a heavy complaint that he was harrassed by the courtiers taking his rent in one place, and his produce in another, through which he was forced to scatter his household, his wife and children begging their bread, and so was it with many thousands in Scotland.'

The poor man then says that he knew neither Controller or Treasurer and looked at the stage King saying that before that there had been another king in Scotland who had hanged Johnny Armstrong. 'Then he made a long narration of the oppression of the poor.'

Nine hours of this altogether, with expositions and explanations, seems to show that modern audiences do not have the staying power of the old time Scots.

The following year, 'a little farce and play was made by William Lauder' which was produced before the Queen Regent, Marie of Guise. The author was presented with two silver cups. Possibly the Queen preferred laughter to a political message, and who can blame her?

In the early part of the century Aberdeen was famous for its plays and pageants. The most famous spree of all was the feast of the Abbot of Bon Accord. Bon Accord is the city's motto and the pageant was given 'for the honour, consolation and pleasure of the burgh'. The festivities were taken very seriously by the provost, bailies, and council and planned well in advance.

'In honour of God and the Blessed Virgin Mary, the craftsmen of this burgh, in their best array, keep and decorate the Procession on Corpus Christi days and Candlemas as honourably as they can, every craft with their own banner, with the arms of their craft thereon. And they shall pass, all craft by themselves, two by two, in their order, that is to say in the first the Fleshers, and next them the Barbers, next them the Skinners and Farrowers together, next them the Cordwainers, next them the Tailors, after them the

Weavers and Waulkers together, next them the Baxters, and last of all nearest the Sacrament passes all Hammermen, that is to say, smiths, wrights, masons, coopers, slaters, goldsmiths and armourers. And every one of the said crafts in the Candlemas procession shall furnish their Pageant . . .

'The Crafts are charged to furnish the Pageants underwritten:
The Fleshers, Saint Sebastian and his Tormentors.
The Barbours, Saint Lawrence and his Tormentors.
The Skinners, Saint Stephen and his Tormentors.
The Cordwainers, Saint Martin.
The Tailors, the Coronation of Our Lady.
The Dyers, Saint Nicholas.
The Weavers, Waulkers, and Bonnet Makers, Saint John.
The Baxter, Saint George.
The Wrights, Masons, Slaters and Coopers, the Resurrection.
The Smiths and Hammermen to furnish those who bear the Cross.'

It sounds to have been a well organized pageant, and no doubt the performers who had the most fun were those playing the Tormentors. Some of these pageants led to breaches of the peace. In 1542 a woman was fined for shouting rude names at the Abbot of Bon Accord. But some town worthies at one period seem to have twisted the idea of the fun, and instead of getting up a good show for the town started to spend the money on a good blow-out for themselves.

The Town Council put its collective foot down on this. The banqueting had been 'surmount on their predecessors'. The idea of the junketings was firmly explained by the Town Council: 'The cause principle and good institution thereof which was the holding of the Good Town in gladness and blitheness with dances, farces, plays and games in times convenient.' They added that the original purpose had been 'neglected and abused'.

To read about these pageants is to see a view of simplicity and happiness, based on people joining in and making their own fun and far divorced from the modern concept of mass entertainment. In spite of the brutality and cruelty of the times, the holding of the Good Town in gladness and blitheness shows a shining faith in fun and happiness as part of the current of life.

But already the Reformers were at work. In Aberdeen, on Bon Accord Day of 1538, two Reformers, John and Robert Arthur, were sentenced to appear in the church of St Nicholas 'with bare feet and wax candles in their hands, and publicly to beg the pardon of the Provost and Magistrates for having troubled the Lords of Bon Accord by preventing dancing'. The kill-joys were on the march. And by 1555 Parliament had passed an Act turning a grave face on organized jollity.

'Item. It is statute and ordained that in all times coming no manner of person be chosen Robert Hood, nor Little John, Abbot of Un-reason, Queen of May, nor otherwise neither in the burgh, nor to landward in any time to come. And if any Provost, Bailies, Counsell and Community chooses such a personage as Robert Hood, Little John, Abbots of Unreason or Queens of May within the Burgh the ringleaders shall lose their freedom [presumably the honour of being a burgess of the city] for the space of five years and otherwise shall be punished at the Queen's grace will and the acceptor of suchlike office shall be banished forth of the Realm. And if any such person such as Robert Hood, Little John, Abbots of Unreason, Queens of May be chosen outside the Burghs and other landward town the ringleaders shall pay to our Sovereign Lady £10 and their persons put in ward there to remain during the Queen's grace's pleasure, And if any women or others by singing about the summer trees and making perturbation through the burghs and other landward towns, the women pestering others for money shall be taken, handled and put upon the Cuckstools of every Burgh or Town.'

But stopping the fun was not as easy as the Reformers imagined. In May 1561, an Edinburgh mob were so infuriated by the banning of their *Robin Hood* on the Greenside that a major riot took place. This included seizing the city gates, robbing passers-by, and creating general havoc. In revenge the city fathers condemned one of the ringleaders to be hanged. John Dillon's only crime had been that he was chosen as Robin Hood and Lord of Inobedience.

The mob on hearing the news of the proposed hanging, stormed the gaol and broke up the gibbet. They then forced their way into the Council Chamber, and put the City Fathers to flight. The latter took refuge in the Tolbooth, but the crowd returned to the attack, battered down the doors, and threw stones through the windows.

The magistrates appealed to the Deacons of the Corporation to quieten the mob, but they received a dusty answer: 'They will be Magistrates alone, let them rule the multitudes alone.' The magistrates then appealed to one Constable of the Castle, but he refused to help. They were not released by the mob until they had issued a proclamation granting a free pardon to the rioters:

'The said provost and bailies shall remit to the said craft children all action, crime and offence that they had committed against them in any time bygone and they bind themselves under obligation never to pursue them therefor and also command their masters to reserve them again in their services as they did before. And this being proclaimed at the Market Cross they will disperse and the Provost and bailies come forth of the same Tolbooth.'

Presumably this riot caused the City Fathers to think again, because when Mary Stuart made her state entrance into Edinburgh, this was the occasion for the town authorities to organize some gladness and blithe spirits.

'When she had dined at twelve hours, her highness came forth of the Castle . . at which departing the artillery shot vehemently. Thereafter, when she was riding down the Castle Hill, there met her highness a convoy of the young men of the burgh, to the number of fifty or thereby, their bodies and thighs covered with yellow taffetas, their arms and legs from the knee down bare, in the manner of Moors; upon their heads black hats, and on their faces black visors; in their mouths rings garnished with untellable precious stones; about their necks, legs, and arms infinite of chains of gold; together with sixteen of the most honest men of the town, clad in velvet gowns and velvet bonnets, bearing and going about the pall under which her highness rode; which pall was of fine purple velvet, lined with red taffetas, fringed with gold and silk. After them was a cart with certain bairns, together with a coffer where was the cupboard and gift which should be given to her highness. When her grace came forward to the Butter Tron [Town Public Weighing Machine, or possibly in this case Butter Market] the nobility and convoy preceding, there was a gate made of timber in most honourable manner coloured with fine colours, hung with sundry arms; upon which gate was singing certain bairns in the most heavenly wise; under the which gate there was a cloud opening with four leaves, in the which was put a bonnie bairn. When the Queen's Highness was coming through the said gate, the cloud opened and the bairn descended down as it had been an angel and delivered to

191

her highness the keys of the town, together with a Bible and a Psalm Book covered in fine purple velvet.'

John Knox's comment on these gifts was that the Queen frowned. His implication was that the Bible and Psalm Book were intended as an anti-Catholic gesture.

The account continues: 'After the said bairn had spoken some speeches, he delivered also to her highness three writings, the tenour whereof is uncertain.' (There speaks an honest reporter of the scene, not claiming knowledge without justification.) 'That being done the bairn ascended in the cloud, and the said cloud enveloped him.'

'Thereafter the queen's grace came down to the Tolbooth, at the which were two stages, one above and one under that. Upon the under was situate a fair virgin called Fortune under the which were other fair virgins, all clad in most precious attirement called Justice and Policy. And after a little speech made there, the queen's grace came to the Cross where there was standing four fair virgins, clad in the most heavenly clothing, and from the which Cross the wine ran out at the spouts in great abundance. There was the noise of the people casting the glasses with wine.'

This account from the *Diurnal of Occurrents* goes on to describe more speeches, the burning of a dragon, the singing of a psalm, and finally the 'bairn which was in the cart with the present made some speech concerning the putting away of the mass, and thereafter sang a psalm'.

Edinburgh also gave a great banquet for the Queen. The cost was 4,000 merks, a large sum. Masques were given, some of an improving nature such as the doom of Korah, Dathan and Abiram. Possibly these were to show the Queen the way in which the Reformers' minds were running.

But the populace were not so easily to be turned aside from their May Day revels either. In Aberdeen, in 1562, John Kello, the town bellman, and Alexander Burnet, the town drummer, 'called out the brave Town on the first Sunday of May to pass to the wood to bring in summer'.

The jolly drummer and bellman and five of their friends were made to ask pardon on their knees, not only from God, but from the whole congregation. The idea of the bringing in of summer obviously was not to the taste of the City Fathers.

12. *Top:* Hunter in search of game; *bottom:* James I and attendants, hawking

13. *Top:* Elgin Cathedral,
the Choir from the
south

right: Elgin Cathedral,
the Chapter House

But the rich and famous did not seem to suffer from lack of entertainment. When Aberdeen was making preparations for the King's visit:

'The Inhabitants are informed that the King is soon to visit the Burgh, and that, as on such it had been usual to show their joy by farces, plays, histories, antics and other decorations, 3000 merks be granted to make preparations of a similar character.'

Even John Knox was not proof against a good play. James Melville records in 1571:

'This year in the month of July Mr John Davidson made a play at the marriage of Mr John Colvin which I saw played in Mr Knox's presence, wherein according to Mr Knox's doctrine the Castle of Edinburgh was besieged and taken and the Captain with one or two hanged in effigy.'

This was a piece of forward thinking by Mr Knox because at that time the castle was still holding out for the Queen, and did not fall for another two years, when the captain was in fact duly hanged.

The attitude of the Reformers towards the drama ebbed and flowed. In 1574, St Andrews Kirk Session records:

'About the supplication given by Master Patrick Auchinlek for procuring licence to play the comedy mentioned in St Luke's Evangel of the Forlorn Soul upon Sunday the first day of August next to come, the seat has discerned first the play to be revised by my Lord Rector (and others) . . . if they find no fault therein the same to be played upon the said Sunday 1st August, so that the playing thereof be not occasion to withdraw the people from the hearing of the preaching at the hour appointed as well in the afternoon as before noon.'

But the following year the General Assembly had thought better of play acting:

'It was thought meet and concluded that no plays, comedies or tragedies be made of the Canonical Scriptures as well New as Old, on Sabbath nor work day in time coming . . . that for other plays, comedies, or tragedies or other profane plays as are not made upon authentic parts of the Scripture may be considered before they be shown publicly and that they be not played upon the Sabbath days.'

G

The Reformers were also against Christmas. In 1575, the St Andrews Kirk Session were condemning culprits for keeping up the festivities:

'The said day, James Clunie, cutler, and Walter Younger were accused for violating the Sabbath Day by superstitious keeping of Yule Day holy-day and abstaining from their work and labour that day . . . James Thomson, mason, being accused for superstitious keeping of Yule Day last as holy-day, and that he said that "who would or would not, he would not work on Yule Day, and was not in use of the same".'

He sounds to have been a man who at first stuck to his guns, but the Kirk managed to wear him down:

'Being asked again whether he would stand by that or not promised that in time coming during his remaining in this city he would never keep the said Yule Day holy-day but should work on that day.'

Nevertheless, Christmas was not so easy to abolish. Ten years later,

'In spite of the persecution of the Catholics . . . Father Dury [chaplain to Lord Seton, one of Mary Stuart's supporters] resolved to sing the whole of the Office of the Feast of the Nativity of Our Lord together with the three masses, solemnly in a monastery which is outside the town . . . guards being placed on the bridge to make sure that none crossed without a written order.'

The Catholic persecutors were now the persecuted, and the Reformers had become the oppressors.

At the end of the century, in 1593, one Mungo Craig was excommunicated for playing his 'pipes' on the Sabbath, but at the beginning of the new century attempts were made to bring back the spirit of Christmas.

In 1609, David Calderwood, one of the Reformers, records: 'The Session should rise the 25th day of December and not sit down till the 8th of January. This was the first Christmas vacance of the Session kept since the Reformation.' The Ministers threatened 'the men who devised the novelty for their own advancement'. This remark meant that, as the King was less narrowly religious, their attitude might be taken as trying to curry favour with those in power.

The Ministers added darkly that they hoped the people who wanted Christmas back

'might receive at God's hand their reward for their overthrow, for troubling the people of God with beggarly ceremonies long since abolished with Popery. Christmas was not so well kept by feasting and abstinence from work in Edinburgh these thirty years, an evil example to the rest of the country.'

Apart from sport and plays there were other kinds of casual fun. In 1561, a wonder horse came to Edinburgh, a chestnut-coloured horse called Marocco, owned by an Englishman:

'This Englishman made the horse do many rare and uncouth tricks, such as never horse was observed to do the like before in this land. This man would borrow from twenty or thirty of the spectators a piece of gold or silver, put all in a purse, and shuffle them together. Thereafter he would give every gent his own piece of money again. He could cause him [the horse] to tell by so many pats with his foot how many shillings the piece was worth . . . but the report went afterwards that he devoured his master because he was thought to be a spirit.'

King James VI and I was not averse to a little rope walking as entertainment. Melville writes:

'Being in Falkland, I saw a funambilist, a Frenchman, play strange and incredible frolicks upon a stented tackle in the Palace close before the King, Queen, and the whole court.'

The ice began to melt for the strolling players, too, and in 1599 a company of English actors were granted a special licence to act in front of the King. But the Kirk Session were not giving up so easily, and condemned all players as 'unruly and immodest' and their patrons as 'irreligious and indiscreet'. This did not please the King. The Kirk Session were forced to withdraw their denunciations although they had been proclaimed from every pulpit. Under orders from the King, they had to state openly that they authorized 'all men to repair to the said plays without any pain, reproach, censure, or slander to be incurred by them'. There continued to be 'play Sundays' until the end of the sixteenth century. But in 1599 the presbytery of Aberdeen ordered that 'there be nae play-Sundays hereafter under all highest pain'.

In April 1600, the General Assembly at Aberdeen ordered—and the rule was to be followed elsewhere—that

'on Thursday of every week the masters of household, their wives, bairns and servants should repair, each one within their own parish kirk to their own minister to be instructed by them in the grounds of religion and heads of catechism, and to give, as they should be demanded, a proof and trial of their profiting by the said heads.'

Apart from profiting by learning their catechism, the average citizen was expected to be in church twice on Sundays, to make Monday a 'pastime day for eschewing of the profanation of the Sabbath day, to give Tuesday forenoon to a service in the Parish church, and on Thursday church again with catechism in the afternoon'. But in spite of all this church-going the Reformers were not satisfied, and at the beginning of the new century in 1601 they ordered 'a general humiliation for the sins of the land and contempt of the gospel, to be kept the two last Sabbaths of June and all week intervening'.

The curtain was coming down, and stayed down for hundreds of years.

CHAPTER TEN

THE SOCIAL SERVICES

Between the monastery and the modern Ministry, there was a gap of some four hundred years. In the early part of the reign of Mary Stuart, the poor, the needy and the sick were still cared for by the monasteries, although there was certainly a tendency for each monastery to look after its own 'men'. In the same way, the Guild of Merchants and the crafts made provision for their members, and the burghs were prepared to take some responsibility for their own beggars and disabled; but those from outland places were not cared for.

The Poor
A clear distinction was made between 'sornares' (stoutly armed vagrants who insisted on taking up residence at the houses they decided to visit), 'overlayers and masterful beggars', and 'crooked folk, blind folk, impotent folk, and weak folk'.

Masterful beggars were liable to be imprisoned or put into irons if they had any means of subsistence, but if they had no means of support 'their ears are to be nailed to the tron, or to any other tree, and then cut off, and themselves banished the country'. If they decided to come back to a town from which they had been banished, they were to be hanged.

The constant insurrections and minor wars made it difficult for many people to earn a living in a country as poor as Scotland at this time. In 1535, a law was passed for the 'refraining of strange beggars'. This laid down that no beggars were to be allowed to ask for alms in any parish unless they had been born there.

After the destruction of the monasteries during the Reformation, the whole burden of the support of the poor inevitably fell on the burgh authorities. That it was a great burden is proved by the number of laws passed in connexion with these beggars.

The burgh authorities seem to have veered between temporary measures, showing a primitive kind of social justice, and great cruelty. One method adopted was to give the parish beggars a begging

197

badge; they could either wear this, becoming an official beggar in the town, or they could apply to the council for funds, and the town officials would then give alms from the general funds, much in the way as the monks had dispensed charity. For some reason, possibly because of the humiliation of being labelled an official beggar, the numbers of beggars dropped once they needed to be licensed. At the same time as beggars were granted badges they were forbidden to beg in any parish but their own.

Sometimes the almsgiving was not done from kindness but merely in order to get rid of them. From Edinburgh there are examples of this, such as the giving of clothes to a poor Italian, an ex-prisoner of the Spaniards; and £5 given to a French boy to send him 'home-wards', and £10 to George Hay, 'who is out of his right wits for the present', the money being for him and his wife to be 'put over the water'.

In 1579, a new Act was passed for the 'punishment of the strong and idle beggars, and the relief of the poor and impotent', but in effect the authorities seem to have spent more time inveighing against the strong and idle than in helping the poor and impotent. The Act laid down that 'strong and idle beggars' between the ages of fourteen and seventy should be apprehended and tried, and if found guilty they should be 'scourged and burned through the ear with a hot iron'. The only way they could escape from their fate was if 'some honest and responsible man would of his charity take and keep the offender in his service for the whole of the year succeeding'.

As might be expected, they seem to lump entertainers of all kinds into the category of the strong and idle:

'all idle persons going about using subtle craft and unlawful plays, as jugglers, fast and loose and such others; the idle people calling themselves Egyptians [gipsies] or any feigning themselves to have knowledge of prophecy, charming or other abused sciences by which they persuade people that they can tell their fortunes and such other fantastical imaginations . . . and all minstrels, songsters, and tale tellers not in the special service of some Lord of Parliament or great Baron, all common labourers being persons able in body living idly and fleeing; all counterfeiters of licences to beg, or using the same, knowing them to be counterfeit; all vagabond scholars of the Universities of St Andrews, Glasgow, and Aberdeen not licensed by the Dean of Faculty to ask alms, all shipmen and mariners alleging

themselves to be shipbroken without they have sufficient testi-
monials.'

In modern terms this would condemn the whole of the entertainment industry to be branded, from the heads of BBC Television
down to Madame Arcati on the end of the pier.

It was also an offence to give money to unlicensed beggars, and
provisions were made to have someone in the parish see that the
licensed 'vagabonds' were policed and kept in order. After generally
inveighing against all kinds of idle persons whom they held in
instinctive disregard, the authorities then came to the positive side
of their Poor Laws.

The general condition of the hospitals for the aged and helpless
was to be enquired into. Presumably up to that time these had been
run by the monks. Magistrates were ordered to make registers of
'aged, poor, impotent and decayed persons born within the Parish
or having their most common resort therein the last seven years, and
who of necessity must live by alms'. The scheme put forward was
that any other poor persons except lepers or the bedridden, were to
go back to the parishes where they were born, or where they had
lived most of their lives, and the magistrates in their home towns
were then to decide how many poor there were, how much was
needed to keep them, and to levy taxes on the rest of the inhabitants
of the parish 'according to the estimation of their substance (without
exception of persons) to such weekly charge and contribution as shall
be thought expedient and sufficient to sustain the said poor people'.
Obviously this was not felt to be a popular move, for it was also
enacted that people who refused to contribute to the help of the
poor were to be clapped in gaol.

But it was not easy to become 'a poor person' between the ages
of fourteen and seventy, and any of the aged and impotent who
decided not to work did not have it easy. Unless they were physically
incapable of working by reason of being lame, broken, or diseased,
they were to be 'scourged, and put in the stocks' for their first
offence of being without work, and for the second offence they were
to be punished as a vagabond. Should the town vagabonds have to
be imprisoned, the upkeep of the prisoners was also a charge on the
parish. But as the prisoners' diet consisted of a pound of oat bread per
day and only water to drink, it was not likely that many people were
eager to pass their time in gaol at the expense of the parish.

In 1562, the Glasgow Kirk Session asked Queen Mary for 'some public relief to be provided for the poor within the burghs'. Glasgow at that time was a small town consisting of one parish, and the charge for the poor fell on the churchmen. Owing to the fact that the Reformers had not inherited the former wealth of the Church, which in many cases had disappeared into the pockets of the nobles, the poor and indigent was not a charge they could shoulder, as the monks, with their broad lands, had been able to do in the past.

In 1583, a new idea was tried—a Collector for the Poor was appointed to 'stand at the Laigh Kirk door to receive alms of townsfolk that go into the said Kirk to hear the preaching'. Whether the practice of charity was as pleasant or unpleasant to the godly as listening to sermons is open to debate.

In 1586, they were still issuing orders for the branding of beggars: 'All poor be marked with the town's mark that they have been within this town remaining and lodging for five years bypast.' Five years later taxes were proposed to help 'decayed burgesses' with money or else to give them a room. If times were hard for burgesses in general, decayed burgesses became an additional burden.

The Kirk Session in 1595 was again issuing general orders about taxing the population in order to help the poor. They ordered that there should be 'a roll of the people who were able in the town to be stented [taxed] for helping the poor'. This form of poor law rate was called 'buttock mail for poor householders'. At the same time they ordered that beggars should be kept off the streets, and from doorways, and constables were ordered to see that the law was carried out. It seems to have been necessary since Edinburgh was described as 'a nest of beggars who haunted the markets of meal and other victuals and levied blackmail from honest people'.

From the number of Acts issued in the sixteenth century about beggars it is obvious that they were a national problem which was handled piecemeal, parish by parish, and town by town. Although it was not a problem which existed only after the Reformation the collapse of the monasteries and their simple systems of help for the poor had made the situation much worse. It would be untrue to say that the Church had concerned itself unduly with the poor; the riches amassed by many churchmen disprove this, yet there were forms of charity which the monks dispensed which did help to ameliorate the lot of at least the local poor round the monasteries.

Once a system has been abolished, the good often disappears along with the bad.

The Care of the Sick

Before the Reformation the care of the sick and those who were incapacitated or past working usually lay in the care of the monks. Many monasteries had hospitals attached to them. The Order of the Knights of St John was started to provide hospitals for those going to the Crusades. Many early ideas on the necessity of hygiene were started by the Knights Hospitallers: the wards were kept clean, and the sick, being regarded as representatives of Our Lord, often had food served on silver plates. The fact that silver plate could be cleaned in boiling water was an incidental way of keeping their wards free from germs.

The monks were well known for their 'simples', produced from their herb gardens. They managed hospitals, but these as a rule only cared for the chronic sick and the old, although the monasteries, often situated on the main roads, did also care for travellers who might fall ill. In Scotland, the Dominicans, the Carmelites and the Franciscans all looked after the sick in hospitals.

At the time of the Reformation there were half a dozen hospitals run by monks near Edinburgh, as well as others in Glasgow, Aberdeen, Stirling, and in other establishments, run by the Knights Hospitallers of St John, at Glasgow and Linlithgow. Apart from short term casualties, of which there must have been many in the Scotland of the time, these hospitals were frequently more in the nature of almshouses.

When the Reformation came and the monks were disbanded, and their monasteries destroyed, the problem of the sick and the old remained. A few of these hospitals survived the Reformation. In Edinburgh, the Trinity Hospital was still in existence in 1578, when it is recorded that twelve beds should be reserved for 'people sickly and unable to labour for their living'. A Dominican convent, appropriated by the Council of Edinburgh, was turned into a hospital for plague victims in 1575.

Medicine, Health and Hygiene

Neither health nor hygiene were prevalent in sixteenth-century Scotland; plagues and pestilences were common visitations. The lack of knowledge of the most elementary forms of hygiene made the spread of disease a certainty, and the fact that the diseases were regarded as divine visitations did not ameliorate the situation.

From the middle ages, until almost the nineteenth century, leprosy, plague, syphilis, smallpox, typhus, and cholera not only killed off large numbers of the population but were responsible for demoralizing whole towns and districts, causing the ordinary daily life to be paralysed.

Primitive attempts at the isolation of the victims, the boiling of clothes, and the cleansing of the houses of the infected people were tried. But considering the nature of the towns, the fact that middens were to be found in the principal streets, and the lack of sanitation, these attempts inevitably met with little success.

Combined with the lack of knowledge of medicine, the terror produced by disease led to many acts of cruelty. The early way of controlling disease was by the isolation and punishment of its victims. A terrible story from the Edinburgh of the time illustrates this.

It is told in the harsh, simple fashion of a modern police report.

'David Duly, Tailor, has holden his wife sick in the contagious sickness of pestilence 4 days in his house and would not reveal the same to the officers of the town while she was dead of the said sickness. And in the meantime the said David passed to St Giles Church, and there heard mass among the clean people, his wife being *in extremis* of the said sickness that was in him has infected the town, for which cause he was adjudged to be hanged on a gibbet before his own door.

'The which day David Duly was about to be hanged before noon before his house where he dwells, but he escaped because the rope broke and he fell off the gibbet, and as he is a poor man with small children for pity of him the Provost, Bailies, and Counsel banished the said David from this town all the days of his life, and not to come therein in the mean time under pain of death.'

The normal penalty for the concealment of illness was branding on the cheek and banishment, after having submitted to some simple form of disinfection. Outside Edinburgh, at the Borough Muir, there was a place for such people to be 'cleansed'.

From 1550 to the end of the century, at least a third of the time was considered to have been taken up with 'plague years'. Aberdeen enjoyed a certain immunity from the plague because of the drastic measures which were taken by the town authorities to keep the burgh pestilence-free. In the spring of 1585, the Burgh Magistrates put up three gibbets, one at the Market Cross, one at the Brig of Dee, and the third at the Haven mouth,

'that in case any infected person arrive or repair by sea or land to this Burgh, or in case any indweller of this burgh receive house or harbour, or give meat or drink to the infected person or persons the man be hanged and the woman drowned'

—which seems to have been a relatively effective way of preserving the town of Aberdeen free from disease, at the cost of much human suffering.

The outbreaks led not only to cruelty but to panic. It was impossible to accommodate the sufferers in the few hospitals which existed, and very often families infected with the plague were forcibly removed with all their goods and furniture to places outside the town. Their clothes were then boiled in cauldrons, and their houses disinfected.

Outside Edinburgh this disinfecting station was at the Borough Muir. The evicted families were then forced to stay in huts. In one year the plague carried off 2,500 people in Edinburgh alone. Considering the normal insanitary conditions normally prevailing in the towns of the time, the condition of the plague camps must have been far worse, and probably led to further outbreaks of the disease.

During these periods of plague it was the custom of the richer citizens to leave the town. James VI fled the plague of 1585, going first to St Andrews, then to Falkland, to Tullibardine, and then to Stirling Castle. Everywhere he went the plague followed him. He had said, 'The pest always smites such as flies it farthest and apprehends deepliest the peril thereof'. Obviously he did not heed his own theory.

But in the plague of 1568, George Bannantyne fled Edinburgh City and occupied himself for three months copying 372 poems, now known as *The Bannantyne Chronicles*. So if the plague in Florence produced the masterpiece of Boccaccio, the plague in Edinburgh also bore literary fruit of a sort.

Leprosy was another terror which stalked the land. This was treated by isolating the lepers from the towns and villages. Although the peak years for the dissemination of leprosy were in the Middle Ages, it was still prevalent in Scotland in the sixteenth century.

Burgh records in Glasgow give accounts, for example, of the inspection of Patrick Bogle for leprosy, and later say that his son Robert was confined to a lazar house. It is possible that many people with ordinary skin diseases were treated as lepers and isolated from their families.

In Perth, lepers were only allowed to enter the town to buy food, and then only on Mondays, Wednesdays and Fridays, from ten o'clock to two o'clock. If these days should happen to be fair days, when the town was full of people, they had to wait until the next day to buy food.

Near Prestwick where there was a leper hospital, the citizens of the burgh were forbidden to carry on any form of commerce at all with the lepers. Anyone trying to carry on trade with the lepers was banished.

In the early part of the century the magistrates of Perth decreed,

'that no manner of leper person man nor woman from this time forth cum amongst other clean persons, nor be found in the kirk, fish, or flesh market, nor any other market within this burgh under the pain of the burning of their cheek and banishing from the town'.

Towns kept lists of lepers, and in Glasgow they had to be registered and were then excluded from the town. In 1599, a man in Glasgow was forbidden to marry by virtue of the fact that he was a leper. Not only were the lepers excluded from the town, but they were forced to wear a hooded gown with sleeves which enclosed even their hands. They carried clappers to warn the other inhabitants of their malady. Even as late as 1610 the Town Council ordered 'that the leper of the hospital shall go only upon the pavement near the gutter and shall have clappers, and a cloth upon their mouth and face, and shall stand afar off to receive alms or answer under the pain of banishing from the town'.

Most of the leper hospitals in Scotland were small, and were designed to house some dozen or so people. They were places of isolation, for the protection of the rest of the population. Their standard of subsistence can be gauged by the fact that the early Game Laws laid down that any game found dead or wounded were to be sent to the leper hospital. Pork or salmon found to be bad in the markets and condemned was also sent to the leper hospital.

The rules of the leper hospitals were strict, and lepers found infringing them were hanged. Only one leper was allowed to go

204

to the town to purchase food. Not only were the lepers forbidden to go outside the hospital, except for the purchase of food, but anyone found in the hospital had to stay there. Their only way of begging was by making use of their clappers.

Their immortal souls were cured by appointing a reader to attend them every Sunday, and he was to have a commodious place to do his reading. Presumably this meant he must be kept strictly away from the inmates, who were adjured to 'live quietly, give no slander by swearing, filthy speaking, or vicious living, or any other way, under the pains to be enjoined by the Council'.

The constant wars between England and Scotland helped the spread of the plague. The invasion of Scotland by the Earl of Hertford in 1545 brought the plague to the borders. From there it spread to Edinburgh and Perth. In Aberdeen, the city fathers burned one David Spilzelaucht on the cheek for not reporting the sickness of his child. The Protestant preacher, George Wishart, was driven from Dundee by the Catholics and shortly afterwards the town was struck with the plague. The whole town was infected. The sick were carried out of the town to hear him preach, and then the gates were locked.

Frantic attempts were made to prevent the infection spreading. In 1574 the magistrates in Glasgow tried to cut off trade with Leith, Kirkcaldy, and Edinburgh by a system of passes. In Edinburgh a week's fast was instituted as the plague was considered a major threat to the kingdom. On the Borders the Wardens were ordered to prevent Englishmen crossing into Scotland.

The worst epidemic took place between 1584 and 1588. Again they tried to stop trade between the towns, even the sails being taken from the boats. The Mint transferred to Dundee, the plague followed it, and it then moved to Perth. The Court of Session was forced to move to Stirling, and the university at St Andrews was shut. In Edinburgh, a little late, a decree was made that all dirt, beasts and carrion were to be cleared from the roads and streets.

Dr Gilbert Skene, of Aberdeen, commented on the behaviour of people panicked by the plague:

'Every one is become so detestable to the other, which is to be lamented, and specially the poor in the sight of the rich, as if they were not equal with them touching their creation, but rather without soul or spirit, as beast degenerate from mankind.'

205

He was well aware of the causes of the plague which he lists simply: corruption, stink, and filth. But between the visitations of the plague, the clearing away of the middens and dirt was neglected, making more certain the return of the disease. Nor was any other attempt made to improve the sanitation.

The custom of 'gardyloo' added to the general foulness of the streets. In Edinburgh, the sounding of the ten o'clock bell from St Giles's church was followed by the emptying of all nightsoil and household rubbish into the streets from the house windows. The householders throwing out their filth were supposed to shout 'Gardy loo!' (*garde à l'eau*). Passing travellers, anxious to avoid having their clothes ruined, were in self defence supposed to shout 'Hold your hand!' Doubtless too late. Attempts were made to suppress this custom, but as late as the eighteenth century, Smollett commented on the unattractive habit.

By the beginning of the new century, King James VI was still complaining about the dirt in 'the streets, wynds, and closes'. Orders were issued that the citizens should at least clean up their own mess. But for a century or two few people took any notice.

Venereal disease was another infection which spread rapidly throughout Europe. It is supposed to have been brought back from the Middle East by the Crusaders, and the first mention of it in Scotland was late in the fifteenth century. The cause of the disease was known, and it was remarked that 'the infirmity came out of France, and strange parts. So all light women were charged and ordained to desist from their vices and sin of venery, and their booths and houses dismantled, and they to pass and work for their sustenance under pain of a key of hot iron on their cheeks and banishment from the town.'

The dignitaries of the Church were not considered to be free of the disease, and Mary Stuart even remarked about the baptism of her son, James, that she would not have a poxy priest spitting in her child's mouth.

As with leprosy, attempts were made to keep the infected people away from the 'clean folk'. At the end of the century, Glasgow had a house for women 'affected with the Glengore' (syphilis). The doctors of the city were called together to try to find a remedy but although some doctors claimed to have cured it, the spread of the disease was not halted.

The Medical Profession

Doctors were few during the sixteenth century, and their knowledge scanty. The Queen, Mary Stuart, aware perhaps that they needed time to study, granted before her marriage to Bothwell a letter

'to the cunning men of the occupation and craft of chirugeons freeing them from attending military service and inquests and assizes in order that they might have the greater occasion to study the perfection of the said craft to the uttermost of their abilities'.

From her earliest years Mary Stuart's health had given concern, so possibly she was more aware of the necessity for good doctors and hygiene than the Scots.

As early as 1548 there was correspondence between Giovanni Ferrerio and the Bishop of Orkney about the appointment of a Scottish doctor for the child Queen. The Bishop was a diplomat who had represented Scotland at the courts of France, England and Italy.

Ferrerio writes to his patron about the necessity of taking care of

'the little lass your Queen . . . enquiries are being made about a doctor . . . many Frenchmen desire the post, but most of them do not take their art seriously, or are little fit to understand the Scottish constitution. One only is a Scot, William Boig, M.D. . . . beyond being of your nation Dr Boig is a skilled physician and apothecary, and above all a lover of religion and his country's freedom'.

Unfortunately Dr Boig did not get his appointment as official apothecary and physician.

There seems, as always, even in our own time, to have been a certain grave suspicion of foreign doctors and remedies. John Knox, when writing of the death of the Scottish envoys in France, hints darkly that their deaths may well have been due to French remedies, 'for whitter it was by an italian posset, or by french fogges, or by the potage of thare potingar [apothecary] he was a Frenchman, thare departit fra this lyef.'

In 1566, Queen Elizabeth, having had smallpox, wrote to the Scots' Queen asking how she had managed to save her complexion when she had had smallpox in childhood. Mary Stuart replied:

'Randolph [English Envoy to Scotland] begged me to send you some recipe to keep it from showing, which I could not have done as I would wish, for he who dressed me is dead, and was called Fernel, First Physician to the King: and he would never tell me the recipe for the water which he put on my face, after having opened it all with a lancet; and after all, it would be too late to use it. What they did for me after, you will see in this memoir. I am very sorry I did not know it sooner, for I would have sent you him whom I consider most excellent for this, who was my man, assuring you that I would never know of anything that would serve you but that I would do it as a good sister should, so long as I know my love rewarded by such affection.'

Even for Queens, doctors were few, and if they had remedies they liked to keep their mystic secrets to themselves.

But gradually the towns tried to attract doctors. Aberdeen, as early as 1503, offered fishing rights to a doctor if he would settle in the town. Glasgow and Edinburgh, perhaps under the panic produced by the plague, were offering monetary inducements.

At this time there were no more than six surgeons, one doctor, and a couple of midwives in Glasgow. But Glasgow seems to have early been conscious of the necessity of doctors, and a Faculty of Physicians and Surgeons was established there in 1599.

There seems to have been a degree of specialization. Some surgeons were licensed to cut for the 'stone', while others, possibly the barber surgeons, were only allowed to perform minor surgery.

Scottish surgeons may or may not have been particularly skilled, but they were concerned that foreign doctors should not usurp their privileges. At the end of the century a complaint was made to the town council of Edinburgh by the corporation of surgeons against a M. Awin, a French surgeon, 'for practising his art within the liberties of the city'. He was ordered to stop practising, 'except for the cutting for the stone, curing of ruptures, couching of cataracts, curing the pestilence, and diseases of women consequent on childbirth'. This clearly narrowed his chances of success.

Diet

A certain amount of interest was paid to diet, although in the case of the poor, it could be said that the lack of food was more a cause of disease than the wrong food.

Judging by the constant laws limiting the diet of the monks and the nobles, overeating was commonplace among the rich. In an early comedy, called *Philotus*, there is drawn a picture of the life led by a fashionable lady in the sixteenth century.

On getting up she has a glass of Malvoisie wine sweetened with sugar. For 'disjune' (luncheon) a pair of plovers, a partridge, and a quail washed down with a cup of sack. From the number of meals listed in the play it is obvious that the fashionable lady managed to survive on around five meals a day. Some contemporary writers, no doubt well fed, say that 'surfeit killed more than the sword'.

There was, however, some sensible medical advice on diet:

'Who would take rest upon the night,
The supper should be short and light
The stomach has a great full pain
When at supper much is ta'en.'

Among the things to be avoided are flat drinks, and 'mixed meats'. Salt meat is not good for the health for it is the 'worst of ony fude', and 'does great oppression to feeble stomachs that nocht refrane, for things contrary to thyn complexious of gredy throttis the stomokis has grit pane.'

The general advice proffered was simple: not to eat until the previous meal has been digested. Even a modern dietician would not disagree. 'That nourishes best which savours best.' 'Clear air and walking makes good digestion.'

Things to be avoided are:

'Nodding heads and candle light.' And for some reason the combing of the hair at night is not considered to be good for the health. Sleeping at noon is also bad, it causes 'great sweirness' (disinclination for work). Sleeping on the back can cause sudden death.

A good thing to do when sleeping is to cover the head, which will 'protect us from mists black, and air of pestilence'. In the morning a good fire, and at night a bed 'closely curtained', are also good for the health.

General advice which still holds good was:

'Where thy own governance may hold thine health
Press never with medicines for to deal.'

Magic and Healing

Because of the lack of medical knowledge which had much scientific basis, the belief in magic, and the magical properties of wells, springs, and rivers was prevalent.

Under the Roman Catholic regime in Scotland, former pagan wells and springs took on the name of the local saints. Each spring was dedicated to a particular saint who gave it special qualities of healing. Many of these spring waters had an unpleasant taste, or were slightly warm. This probably added to the idea of their efficacy, being an early example of something which tastes nasty doing you good.

St Corbet's well near Stirling gave a promise of life for at least a year. But the reputation of this holy well was downgraded when some of the local inhabitants started to mix whisky in the water. At St Fillan's Well, in Strathfillan, the insane were subjected to a cure which was more in the nature of an ordeal. The person who had lost his wits was thrown into the pool, then bound up, and left in the chapel for the night. If there was any hope of his recovery he would be found to be free the following morning.

At Musselburgh the well was dedicated to our Lady of Loretto, and expectant mothers sent their 'childbed linen' to be sprinkled with its waters and then consecrated by the priest.

Other wells cured whooping cough, and at Strathnaven a small loch was alleged to have healing properties—the people who wished to be cured immersed themselves in the water, left a coin, and then walked out without looking back. One wonders how shallow the waters of the loch were, and whether there was a human guardian-spirit who benefited from these tributes to the spirit of the loch.

Amber beads were used in the curing of blindness. Other cures could be effected by drinking the water in which certain charmed stones had been dipped. Other stones cured sterility in women. A writer on folk lore in Scotland instances a large rock, which if a pregnant woman climbed it, would give a speedy and successful delivery. This may well have been the case.

Other childbirth superstitions were linked with witchcraft. It was believed that the pains of childbirth could be transferred. Lady Reres, who is supposed to have been the go-between for Bothwell and Mary Stuart, was found to be ill in Edinburgh Castle. Asked what ailed her, she answered, 'she was never so troubled with no bairn that ever she bare, for the Lady Atholl had cast all the pain of childbirth upon her'. As Lady Atholl was supposed to have magical gifts, it was taken for granted that she had been able to do this.

Naturally the Reformers were against all forms of superstition, including 'well-worshippings, enchantments, and the vain practices which are carried on with various spells and stones'. But in the middle of the seventeenth century they were still trying to stamp out these old customs.

The 'stones' were supposed to have magical qualities, and many old families owned and used them. In the introduction to *The Talisman*, Sir Walter Scott refers to the Lee Penny. This was a stone which was dipped in water, which then had curative properties and was supposed to keep wounds uninfected, charm away fevers, and exercise a benevolent influence over the destiny of those who drank it.

In fact, the Lee Penny was enquired into by the Synod of the Presbyterian Church:

'The Synod found no ground for drastic action against the use of the penny though they admonished the Laird of Lee in the using of the said stone to take heed that it be used hereafter with the least scandal that possibly may be.'

This makes it clear that the use of these stones and the superstitions connected with them died hard.

Other stones were supposed to cure sterility in women. The Devil's Needle, in the Aberdeenshire Dee, was considered a magic stone. Sterile women crawled through the hole in the centre of the stone and were supposed then to become pregnant. The magical quality of water may possibly have had some connexion with fertility. Another stone, on the Isle of Rona, 'provided speedy delivery to a woman in travail'.

In the Isle of Skye this superstition connected with stones continued until recent times. A stone was made red hot and cooled in water or milk and the patient, whether man or beast, was given the water or milk to drink to effect a cure.

The Powerful Magic of Doctors

Though in theory the doctors of the sixteenth century were supposed to have scientific knowledge, much of their practice could be said to lie not far from the realm of powerful magic. Medieval and Renaissance medical knowledge was scanty. After the burning of the library at Alexandria the whole of the medical knowledge of the Egyptians, the Greeks, and the Romans had been lost, and doctors were labouring in darkness.

Originally the practice of medicine was in the hands of the priests, and many monasteries carried on this tradition. Continental countries were more advanced than either England or Scotland in this respect. Sir Walter Scott immortalized one Michael Scott in the *Lay of the Last Minstrel*. His medicine was supposed to be so efficient that he was regarded as a wizard capable of curing anything, and producing miracles. Apparently he perfected a pill whose ingredients were aloes, rhubarb, and extracts of fruit and flowers. This was regarded as a cure-all. The list of miracles this pill was supposed to perform reads like the advertisement for some patent medicine formerly sold at fairs. His pill was said 'to relieve headache, purge the humours wonderfully, produce joyfulness, brighten the intellect, improve the vision, sharpen hearing, preserve youth, and retard baldness'.

The kings of Scotland always had apothecaries attached to the court. The apothecaries also carried out minor operations, if they could do this without the Company of Barber Surgeons objecting. The grandfather of Mary Queen of Scots, James IV, took an interest in medicine, and even carried out interesting operations himself. In the Lord High Treasurer's account appear items which prove that he paid his patients to undergo his scientific experiments: '17s to allow the King to let blood, 18s for allowing the King to pull a tooth, and 13s to a blind woman to have her eye shorn.' (The last was possibly an operation for cataract.)

Illegitimacy, and the Treatment of Orphans

In the middle of the sixteenth century more than a quarter of the births in Aberdeen were illegitimate. In Perth, in 1580, forty per cent of the children who were baptised were illegitimate.

The ruling classes contributed largely to the illegitimacy rate. But the rules for them were different than for the poor. The princes of the Church openly endowed their illegitimate daughters on their marriages, and very often married them off to rich landowners. The Synod of Edinburgh, in 1558, enacted that church dignitaries should not make over more than £100 yearly from the Church's funds as dowry to their illegitimate daughters.

Although the bishops were apt to regard provision for their own children seriously, the general attitude of the Church towards illegitimacy could be said to be harsh, and no particular care was given to the welfare of the unfortunate children.

A system also existed whereby if 'beggars' bairns between the ages of five and fourteen shall be liked by any subject of the realm of honest estate, such a person might have the bairn by direction of the magistrates' to the age of twenty-four for a male child, and twenty-eight for a female child. In 1597, the Act extended the period of servitude to a lifetime. Although these laws, which were authorizing nothing less than selling children into slavery, made pious gestures about the necessity of educating the children, the emphasis of the laws was more on servitude than education.

Education

Before the Reformation there were two kinds of school in Scotland. The first was the lecture school, where children were taught in the vernacular. These were not numerous. The higher category of school was the grammar school, where pupils were taught Latin, and the humanities generally. The Latin teaching schools were usually attached to the monasteries, or were situated in the royal burghs.

In the early part of the century, Edinburgh did have schools for the instruction of children, but there was a bias in favour of grammar schools which seem to have had the monopoly of teachers. There are also records of women teaching in schools. But in 1520 Edinburgh Town Council enacted 'that no inhabitant of the town should put their children to any school in the burgh but to the principal grammar school to be taught in any science except only grace book, primar, and plain duty under a fine of 10s'. This seems to indicate either that the standard of schools, other than grammar schools, was to be officially kept low, or that the authorities had no faith in the other schools.

In the early sixteenth century, Edinburgh had two or more grammar schools, one in the Canongate. The town council is recorded as having paid the master of the Grammar School various lump sums as well as annual fees. In 1555, the town paid ten merks to the master of a French school for teaching French in the burgh, and there are records of other grammar schools teaching French as part of the general education.

Most of the principal towns in Scotland boasted grammar schools which were under the control of the Church before the Reformation and these continued under the control of churchmen afterwards. The most outstanding grammar schools were those of Glasgow,

Dunfermline, Perth, Stirling, Linlithgow, and Dundee, although others such as Haddington had a good reputation.

Even on the eve of the Reformation there were still Catholic churchmen such as Ninian Winzet, who opposed Knox, holding posts in grammar schools. Winzet was finally driven out of Linlithgow by the power of the Reformers, and complained 'so little respect has never been paid to the grammar schools'. No doubt his remarks were somewhat biased due to his sorrow at being forced to leave his 'kindly town'.

The teaching in the Catholic grammar schools naturally favoured Latin and subjects connected with religion, which was the dominating influence in the education of the period. But even after the Reformation there was still a marked bias in favour of religious teaching, for the wave of revolution lay in the sphere of religion and morals.

General scientific knowledge in the sixteenth century was very scanty, but although the education could be said to be narrow in scope it produced a logical way of thought. The emphasis on disputation and argument helped to mould the Scottish character, for instruction in the truths of religion took place in all places of instruction in Scotland from the smallest village school to the great universities. The result of this has been to form that delight in argument which is a very Scottish trait.

The Reformed clergy took a greater interest in the spread of education and began to establish schools in the parishes. In 1578, a new High School was built in Edinburgh on the site of the Black Friars Monastery, and various other educational reforms were begun including the projected standardization of the teaching of grammar.

Universities

St Andrews was the first university to be founded in Scotland, and dates from 1512. It was under the control of John Hepburn, the Prior of the Abbey, and its teachers were always drawn from the monastery. The original intention of this university was to 'educate 20 poor scholars'. The first college was St Leonard's. But in 1537 the College of St Mary was founded by Archbishop Beaton and the building of the college, although carried on by his successor, was not completed till 1554, by Archbishop Hamilton. The studies including grammar, logic, theology, medicine, canon and civil law, as well as lectures on the Bible, ethics, physics, and mathematics. The teachers, regents, and students wore caps 'after the Parisian fashion', and all the students, 'nobles as well as the bursars had to wear gowns tied by a girdle, although the bursars added a black hood'.

During the upsets caused by the Reformation the number of students at St Andrews diminished, but although the teaching of the Roman Catholic form of religion was removed from the curriculum, the rest of the studies remained the same. The length of study at St Andrew's University was four years, but it could be shortened to three and a half years.

All scholars entering university for the first time were put under the tuition of a regent. The regent was responsible for their studies over the whole curriculum. His class was assembled for three hours each day. During this time he explained the books of Aristotle, beginning with dialectics, ethics, and physics, and the course was concluded with mathematics, and metaphysics. During the course the students were expected to engage in disputation and declamation, both in front of their class and also in public session before the whole university.

The principal of the university also gave public lectures on the more advanced grades of philosophy to the top students, and in the middle of his third year a student who had a certificate of regular attention and good behaviour from his regent, and from the principal of the college, was admitted to 'trials for the degree of bachelor'. The faculty of the university elected three of the regents as examiners, and students trying for their degree had to answer questions mainly in logic and morals.

John Knox put up a scheme for the entire re-casting of university education, in his *First Book of Discipline*, but this was never adopted.

The Reformation and the Universities

The impact of the Reformation on the universities caused a great deal of disruption. Glasgow University was nearly ruined by this disorganization. But in 1563, Mary Stuart granted the university some land, houses, and rents which had been the property of the friars. The money and properties granted by the Queen were used to found bursaries for 'five poor scholars'. Later that year the Queen was presented with a petition 'in the name of all that within this realm are desirous that learning and letters may flourish'.

The nub of the petition was that 'the patrimony of some of the foundations in the colleges, especially those of St Andrews were wasted, and the sciences that were most necessary, the tongues and humanity, were very imperfectly taught in them which was equally injurious to the people, to their children, and to posterity'. As a result of the petition, Parliament appointed a committee to enquire into the state of the universities and the teaching, and to report on the best way of improving education. There is no record of this committee's report; possibly like many committees, its efforts were soon dissipated in talk.

However, there were many attempts at university improvements over the period of the Reformation. In 1572, the town council in Glasgow was granted lands, houses, and rents to support fifteen scholars, and Andrew Melville, a man of energy and ability, was appointed principal of Glasgow University in 1574.

It was realized that the universities were in urgent need of re-organization after the upheavals of the revolution, but like many new brooms, the Reformers soon found their own reform projects hard and slow going. In 1576, commissioners were appointed to enquire into the state of things at St Andrew's University, but nothing was done, and three years later the General Assembly was still talking about the necessity for reform.

Most of the trouble about reorganization sprang from the fact that, like their predecessors, the Catholic priests and monks, the Reformers were more concerned with keeping the morals and faith of the students pure than they were with the actual teaching of the subjects in hand.

A purge in Aberdeen University started in 1561, when Knox and other leading Reformers held a conference about it. They were inevitably more concerned with the knotty topics of faith and morals, rather than with soiling their minds with secular subjects. The net result of their deliberations was that the principal of Aberdeen University, his sub-principal, and three regents were all deprived of their offices, ordered to leave the university, and were in addition banned from teaching publicly or privately in any part of Scotland. Presumably neither their way of teaching, nor their faith and morals came up to the standards of the new purity.

Edinburgh University was started in 1581, the site being some old houses near the spot where Darnley was murdered. Students were expected to live in the college during the course of their studies.

From 1581 till the end of the century, a period of nearly twenty years, the number of students who graduated from Edinburgh was about 322, the average attendance not exceeding 150. From St Andrews the numbers in the last half of the century were 200, and the numbers at Glasgow and Aberdeen were somewhat less.

Although the teaching of religion had changed at the universities, the curriculum was still narrow. The aim of education was the acquisition of a good knowledge of Latin, an ability to read Roman authors, translate Latin exercises, and also do cross-translation of Latin into Greek and Greek into Latin.

Once the students had become conversant with the Latin authors, could translate and read them freely, knew the rules of formal logic, as well as the ethics of Aristotle, they were considered to have received a full and liberal education.

But the fact that numerous sons of the aristocracy were sent abroad to be educated seems to indicate that to many a foreign education was considered to be better than the native product. James Hepburn, Earl of Bothwell, afterwards Mary Stuart's husband, was educated in France. Many others of similar background were either attached to the French court, or else went to schools and universities in the Low Countries, which enjoyed not only a higher level of education and learning than Scotland, but also a better cultural background and standard of living.

Learning had an international aspect, and there were Scots professors at Cambridge, and in France, and Frenchmen, as we have seen, teaching in schools in Scotland. After the Reformation many of the leading churchmen who were previously concerned in teaching and lecturing went to schools, universities, and monasteries overseas. Winzet was amongst those who escaped abroad.

Among the scholars who helped to restore learning in Scotland after the Reformation was James Melville, nephew of Andrew Melville. James Melville is supposed to have been the first regent in Scotland to read the Greek authors to his students at Glasgow University in the original. In his *Memoirs* he gives a vivid picture of his own schooldays at Montrose:

'My father put my eldest and only Brother David, about a year and a half in age above me, together to a kinsman and brother in the ministry of his to school. A good learned kind man which for thankfulness I name, Mr William Gray, Minister at Logic Montrose. He had a sister, a godly and honest matron, ruler of his house, who often remembered me of my mother, and was a very loving mother to me indeed. There was a good number of gentle and honest man's bairns of the country about, well trained both in letters, godliness and exercise of honest games. There we learned to read the Catechism, Prayers and Scripture; to rehearse the Catechism and prayers par coeur; also make notes of Scripture after the reading thereof; and there first I found (blessed be my Good God for it!) that spirit of sanctification beginning to work some motions in my heart, even about the eighth or ninth year of my age; to pray going to bed and rising, and being in the fields alone to say over the prayers with a sweet moving of my heart and to abhor swearing . . . Whereunto the example of that godly matron who was given to pray and read in her bed did much profit me. For I lay in her chamber and heard her exercises.

'We learned the rudiments of the Latin grammar with the vocabularies in Latin and French; also divers speeches in French with the reading and right pronunciation of the tongue. We proceeded further to the etymology of Lillius and his syntax . . . therewith we joined Hunter's Nomenclature, Erasmus, the Eclogues of Virgil, the Epistles of Horace, also Cicero. He had a very good and profitable form of resolving the authors he taught gramatically both according to the Etymology and Syntax.'

It is apparent that Melville had a good all round education, and in addition, the development of the body was not neglected: 'There also we had the air good and fields reasonably far, and by our master were taught to handle the bow for archery, the club for golf, the batons for fencing, also to run, to leap, to swim, to wrestle, to practise all exploits by everyone having his match and antagonist—both in our lessons and play.' There seems to have been a very healthy spirit of competition in the school, and no quest for egality.

Melville goes on nostalgically:

'A happy and golden time indeed if our negligence and unthankfulness had not moved God to shorten it partly by the decaying of the numbers which caused the master to weary, and partly of a pest which the Lord for sin and contempt of his Gospel sent upon Montrose distant from Over Logie but two miles; so that the school broke up and we were all sent for and brought home. I was at that school the space of almost five years in which time of public news I remember I heard of the Marriage of Henry and Marie, the King and Queen of Scots, Seignour Davies slaughter, of the King's murder at the Kirk of Field, of the Queen's taking at Carberry and the Langside Field. Also I remember how we passed to the head of the moor to see the fire of joy burning upon the steeple head of Montrose at the day of the King's birth.'

The Reformers Reform
At the end of the century a Royal Commission was set up under the tutors of King James, George Buchanan and Peter Young. The Commission included the headmasters of the grammar schools at Edinburgh, Stirling, Dunbar, Haddington, Glasgow and St Andrews. It was decided that the school books were not up to the required standard, and consequently a new grammar was ordered to be written. By the end of the century in 1593 this had been done, and the Privy Council ordered the new grammar to be proclaimed at all the market crosses, and afterwards it was ordered to be in general use all over Scotland:

'Foreasmuch as it is understood by the King's Majesty and Lords of Secret Council that the masters of schools and pedagogues have this many years bygone chosen to themselves such writings of the arts of grammar as have been commended unto them by booksellers, which they have learned themselves or else been accustomed to teach, or such as upon the occasion of the time, and place come readiest to their hands; whereby it often comes to pass that the best and most profitable form for advancing of the studies of the youth has not been taught, both such as they find to be most easy for sparing and retaining their work, and likewise there by many and diverse grammars are brought in and taught in the country as there are teachers of that art; so that when scholars changed from place to place at the arbitrement of their parents they are newlings to begin that art where they have spent some years before, and are rather charged there to forget, nor repeat that which they have learned, to the great hindering of their proceedings and the confounding of their memories and intelligence.'

The Scots seem early to have come to the conclusion that learning is not only important in itself, but that the books which the scholars use must be sensible and standardised.

Apart from university education, John Knox also interested

himself in the teaching of children, and, when Mary was imprisoned in Lochleven, in 1567, a Commission of the Articles, in which he took part, decided as follows:

'Item that all scholars both in burghs and in the country and colleges to be reformed and that none be permitted to have the charge thereof or to instruct the youth privately or publicly but such as shall be tryit by the Superintendents and visitators of the Kirk and admitted by them to their charges.'

Like the Jesuits, John Knox believed in starting at the beginning —with the education of children.

Trouble With Sit-ins

The truism that there is nothing new under the sun is shown in tales of recalcitrance by the pupils at Aberdeen Grammar School. It was apparently an old custom that for two weeks at Christmas the pupils took possession of the school 'to the exclusion of their masters and all authority'. Obviously the pupils of Misrule took over the school for some Yuletide fun. But in 1580-1 the magistrates were at work trying to prove that this assumed privilege of the boys 'had been abrogated'. They agreed, however, that the vacation should be made up, and that there could be three holidays at the beginning of every quarter, making twelve in all for the year. The idea of a long vacation did not exist in the sixteenth century.

But the magistrates' rules were not obeyed, for at the beginning of 1604 the 'school disorder' at Yule is mentioned as being very violent, 'the boys keeping and holding the school against their masters with swords, guns, pistols, and other weapons, spulying [despoiling] and taking of poor folks gear, such as geese, fowls, peats [magpies] and other vivres during the holding thereof'. The magistrates ordered that to avoid 'such disorders in future no boy from without the town shall be admitted without a caution for his good behaviour'. As is usual, strangers were blamed for the little local difficulties.

This trouble with armed schoolboys does not seem to have been a new problem, for in the middle of the century the town council of Edinburgh was involved in an armed affray with the 'scholars and gentlemen's sons of the High School of Edinburgh'. The scholars were complaining about the shortening of their holidays. Apparently the headmaster was favourable. But the town council,

stubborn as town councils often are, and standing upon the letter of
their own law, 'bore down and abused the headmaster'.

As a result the scholars

'resolved to make a mutiny and one day the master being on necessary business a mile or two off the town, they came in the evening
with all necessary provisions, entered the school, manned the same,
took in with them some fencible weapons with powder and bullet,
and reinforced the doors refusing to let any man come there either
master or magistrate until their privilege was granted'.

A night passed and the next morning some men of the town came
to these scholars

'desiring them to give over and to come forth . . . affirming that they
should intervene to obtain them the licence of eight days playing.
But the scholars replied that they were mocked of the first eight
days privilege . . . they would either have the residue of the days
granted for their pastime or else they would not give over. This
answer was consulted upon, and notified by the Magistrates to the
ministers.'

There was a hurried consultation, some gave their opinion that
it would be better to leave the schoolboys alone, and others that they
should be starved out. But after a day's to-ing and fro-ing the
bailies lost patience, and

'headed by Bailie John Macmoran and attended by a posse of
officers they came to the school. . . . The bailie at first called on the
boys to open the doors. They refused. . . . The bailies began to be
angry and called for a great joist to prize up the back door. The
scholars bade them beware and wished them to desist and leave off
that violence or else, they vowed to God, they would put a pair of
bullets through the best of their cheeks. The bailies, believing they
durst not shoot continued still to prize the door boasting with many
threatening words. The scholars perceived nothing but extremity,
one Sinclair, the Chancellor of Caithness's son presented a gun from
a window direct opposite the bailies' faces boasting them, and
calling them buttery carles. Off goeth the charge gun. The bullet
pierced John Macmoran through his head and presently killed him
so that he fell backward straight to the ground without speech
at all.'

The upshot of this affray was that Sinclair was accused of the murder, but he denied it. 'Divers friends convened and assisted him ...'; other friends

'threatened death to all the people of Edinburgh if they did the child any harm saying they were not wise that meddled with the scholars, especially gentlemen's sons. They should have committed that charge to the master who knew best the truest remedy without any harm at all.'

The influential relatives of the culprit and his fellow scholars then rallied to the cause. Lord Sinclair and others came forward. At first the main culprit and his seven fellow scholars were imprisoned with a view to bringing them before a 'fair assize'. But various objections were then thought up—for example, should the assize be composed of citizens it was alleged that these could 'be partial against the boys'.

The King then commanded that an assize of gentlemen should be chosen, and in the end the boys managed to get off scot free—a phrase which could be applied literally to the case.

The main culprit lived to become Sir William Sinclair of Mey and married a Miss Catherine Ross.

These pictures of armed students seem to give a very different view from that of Melville with his fond remembrance of the classic authors and quiet games of golf. But no doubt the discipline in a school depended on the character of the masters running it, which is true in all times and all places.

CHAPTER ELEVEN

CRIME AND PUNISHMENT

It is difficult to understand the logic and sometimes the cruelty of some of the punishments meted out in the Scotland of this period, unless one considers them alongside the general violence of the country and in the context of the age. Although some people were punished severely a great many committed numbers of murders, and were never punished at all. In some cases, if they were pursuing some feud, or if the murder was on the side of the Sovereign, they could even be commended.

In 1541, Sir Thomas Wharton wrote a recommendation of Douglas of Drumlanrig, to Henry VIII. Douglas had fled south and Sir Thomas was writing in explanation: 'His offence was very little, being only accused as accessory of a murder.'

The same attitude is taken by John Knox with regard to the murder of David Riccio, and the narrow escape of Mary Stuart and her unborn child:

'That poltroon and vile knave Davie was justly punished . . . by the counsel and hands of James Douglas, Earl of Morton, Patrick Lindsay, and the Lord Ruthven, with other assisters in their company, who all, for their just act and most worthy of all praise are not unworthily left of their brethren, and suffer the bitterness of banishment and exile.'

It all depended on the politics of the person murdered whether the murder was regarded as bloody, or simply a reasonable punishment for previous faults.

Enormous discrepancies also lay in the realm of the game laws. These were harsh and savage, but very often owing to the extended nature of the country and the lack of transport it was not possible to enforce them, and as most of the Highlanders followed their own laws under their own chieftains, they could hardly be said to be observed all over the country.

The penalties for stealing a horse or an ox could be death or mutilation or a large fine, depending upon where the illegal hunting had been done. If it were in a park, which was an especially protected place, then the penalty would be heavier. As was previously mentioned, cutting off of ears was considered a reasonable punishment for infringement of the game laws. In 1567, death was not mentioned in connexion with the game laws, but the cutting off of the right hand was the punishment for a second offence.

There were simple attempts to protect the propagation of the game—deer, hares, and rabbits must not be 'taken in time of snow'. Game were not to be taken by shooting at them with 'hagbuts, hand guns, cross bows, or pistols'. As it was also forbidden to catch hares and rabbits with gins and nets, it is difficult to see how they could be caught, which was doubtless the object of the laws.

By the end of the century the game laws had been modified, and sheriffs were told to put the offenders in the stocks for forty-eight hours or 'as ofte as they be apprehended'. This was probably the rub—it was not so easy to apprehend them.

The records of the burgh court of Dundee from 1550 to 1568 give an impression of judicial conditions in the country. For although the state of the country was one of civil disturbance and war, the burgh magistrates certainly tried to preserve law and order in their primitive fashion.

The general administration of the laws seems to prove that while many of the punishments are severe and cruel, yet the idea of the courts was an attempt to be paternal and corrective, and to make peace between litigants whenever this was possible. A point to be observed is that the magistrates took it for granted that the offenders had a sense of shame, and that they held the good opinion of their fellow men in some regard.

Brawls and quarrels were not unusual, but theft was not common. Because the country was poor, and goods were hard to come by, possibly theft may have been worse regarded in the sixteenth century than in later times. Another point which is made clear by the records is that most burghs tended to 'off-load' their offenders on other towns; banishment was very frequent. Drunkenness was not usual, for whisky was not in general use in the country until much later. Wine drinking was common, but wines, being imported and expensive were not drunk by the general run of the population.

Owing to the irascible nature of the Scots of the period, the prevalence of feuds, and the idea that 'honour' could be avenged

14. *Top:* Three witches

centre: An execution of witches

bottom: Swimming a witch

15. *Top:* Craigievar Castle, the Great Hall *bottom:* Stirling Palace, the Outer Court

by any weapon which happened to be handy, personal insults were a major cause of trouble leading to lawsuits and summonses.

Typical examples of this were a man called Riche Crag, a baker, who falsely accused a town officer of using false weights. The baker had been indicted for selling underweight bread. The punishment was that the baker must come to the church on Sunday next 'in time of High Mass there to offer a candle of a pound of wax and to ask the officer's forgiveness and say that the word he said was false'. This accusation was obviously made by the baker before the Reformation, although the Reformers also carried on the idea of offenders being made to do public penance in church.

Blaspheming was another common offence of the period. James Denman, 'having blasphemed a notary has to ask his forgiveness and to pay to the master of the hospital 20s to be given to the poor, and if he again offended he would be banished the burgh for a year and a day'. John Robertson and his wife, who had slandered Katrine Butcher, had 'to come instantly to the Mercat Cross and there ask Katrine's forgiveness upon their knees'.

Another woman, for 'wrangeous mispersoning of Will Gibson's wife', was made to go to the Mercat Cross and with 'beads about her neck to say "My tongue lee it" and then walk through the town in penitence'.

The object of the cuckstool (or pillory) was repentance by public humiliation. A woman, Bess Spans, was threatened with a day on the cuckstool in a public place if she is found 'flyting' (quarrelling) with her neighbour. But Bess apparently got her own back, for some time later she herself accused one Allan Sowtar with troubling her husband and herself 'under silence of the night'. He was fined, and if he was found to commit the fault again he was to be 'banishit'.

Many of the quarrels between men ended in grievous blows, and if the aggressor was found guilty he could be ordered to pay a heavy fine. Punishments were carried out on the spot, and the modern idea of imprisoning men for long periods away from their normal occupations was rare. Banishment was a heavy punishment because it was difficult to earn a living once a person had become a vagabond, and other towns were not prepared to offer asylum to the riff-raff thrown out by neighbouring burghs.

Nor was banishing a light punishment, or to be easily ignored.

'Alexander Clark and Elizabeth Stevenson being banished this burgh for their demerits, pykerie [stealing] and sumptuous spending by night, has contemptuously come to the town, contrary to the statutes; wherefore they are adjudged sound to be nailed to the tron by the ear, and Elizabeth burned upon the cheek and they be again banished for all the days of their life. And if ever they be found within this burgh, or any of them, to be put to death.'

In another case death by drowning was ordered for a woman returning to the burgh after being banished.

Great importance was attached to restitution or compensation in cases of theft, and if there were aggravating circumstances the thief could be punished by flogging. Nor was it necessary to have absolute proof of stealing. What was called 'vehement suspicion' was enough:

'James Richardson, tailor, being accused of pykerie is adjudged to be punished with twelve strokes with a double belt because there could be no sufficient proof gotten, but vehement suspicion, and afterwards to be banished this burgh for a year and a day.'

The universal habit of wearing sword and daggers led to a great many fights ending in woundings, and general affrays. Occasionally the offenders who had started the fights were forbidden to wear swords. But the policy of making the punishment fit the crime seemed to have achieved results, and perhaps more modern criminologists could learn something from the ways of our ancestors.

The 'enforced reconciliation' of Jonkyn Davidson and John Jack is such a case. Davidson 'hurt and wounded John Jack in his body with a whinger to the effusion of his blood in great quantity'. The bailies decided on the punishment.

'That upon Saturday next Jonkyn shall come to the Mercat Cross in his sark [shirt] alone, his head discovered and upon his knees, take his whinger by the point and deliver the same to John; and thereafter the officer shall affix it in the place whereof those are affixed that commit tulzie within the burgh. And Jonkyn shall ask mercy and forgiveness at John for God's sake for his crime; and then shall act himself to be true friend to John and shall never hear nor see his hurt nor skaith, but will take part with him in all lawful things; and shall never draw a whinger hereafter on any inhabitant under pain of banishing this burgh for ever.'

Jonkyn was also ordered to pay John £100. On the day named, Jonkyn at the Market Cross, made the atonement demanded, 'and then John received him in favour, embraced him in his arms and

226

forgave him the crime'. Possibly the £100, being a great deal of money, was one reason, though a minor one, why John 'embraced him in his arms and forgave him'. But these simple adjudications and penalties seemed to be effective.

Penalties for Immorality
Work started early in the old Scottish burghs, and the wakener with his bell was often about by four o'clock in the morning. In the same way the ringing of the ten o'clock bell was a call for the general clearance of streets and alehouses. This was the signal that the burgh had entered 'the silence of the night'.

It was a serious matter, for under the Act,

'No person walking in the night season privately or openly in the streets or gaits of the burgh or drinking in any ale or wine tavern after ten hours of the night under pain of 40s for the first fault and for the second fault to be banished.'

So night life was in short supply and much frowned on. Banishment was the punishment most used for combating both drunkenness and immorality. Keepers of houses of ill-fame facing the same punishment.

Other unchaste conduct seems to have had a sliding scale of punishment. The first offence merited a severe reprobation, admonishment by the preachers, and the showing of repentance publicly in the presence of the whole congregation of the church. This usually consisted of appearing in a coarse white garment, and sitting on a stool of repentance in the centre of the local church. The second offence rated three hours in the 'gyves' and to be 'thrice dunked in the sea'. After that life banishment was the lot of a lady of light virtue.

But should a woman be pregnant the life of the coming child was not to be endangered. In this case the woman's hair was cut off, and she was nailed to the cuckstool, and had then to make public repentance in the kirk.

Thus the idea of humiliating offenders and subjecting them to popular derision was very common—the stocks, the cuckstool, and the stool of repentance being all used. A variation was the 'joug'. This was a hinged iron band for the neck which could be attached to any public place, the market cross, the gatepost of the church, or the tolbooth. The guilty person was chained there, and the offence

227

which he had committed was written on a notice in large letters, and either hung over his head or attached to his body.

The jugg, or 'joug', was the punishment usually meted out to people who had cheated in the market. They were taken by the executioner to the market cross, or whatever place had been chosen. Their necks were made fast by the iron collar. Apart from the disgrace of the punishment and the public humiliation attached to it, it was extremely painful, for the staple of the joug was fixed at a distance from the ground which had been carefully judged so that the offender could neither sit, stand, or even lean.

This punishment was taken over by the Reformers who used it for cleaning up the morals of the town, and attached 'jougs' to the doors of churches.

In October of 1555 the town council of Dundee appointed the treasurer and three citizens to clean up the 'dunking hole' in the North Loch and to repair the pulleys. They also asked the magistrates to put all 'adulterers and fornicators in prison—there to be fed for the space of one month on bread and water'. For a second offence both the man and the woman 'were to be scourged at the cart arse and banished the town'. In 1564, any woman charged with 'impurity' should be brought to the market cross, have her hair shorn, and nailed upon the cuckstool. For a second offence, her hair should again be shorn, and she should be carried through all parts of the town in a cart.

Adulterer's Tragedy

In 1574, Robert Drummond, called Dr Handie who had been very eager in the smelling out and persecution of 'papists' was punished for adultery by being exposed in the church and banished from the City of Edinburgh. He was pardoned and allowed to return to the city, but on returning repeated the offence. This time he was exposed in the stocks at the market cross along with his mistress, and then branded on the cheek.

While he was being branded, there being a great press of people around him,

'Dr Handie being in a great fury said: "What wonder ye? I shall give you more occasion to wonder." So suddenly he took his own knife and struck himself three or four times in the heart with the which he departed. This done the magistrates caused him to be

228

hauled in a cart through the town, and the bloody knife born behind in his hand; and on the following morning hauled in the same manner to the gallows on the Burghmuir where he was buried.'

Punishment of a Homosexual

In the words of a Victorian chronicler, 'Paul Methven, a baker in Dundee afterwards Minister of Jedburgh was excommunicated for immorality of a gross kind'. He offered to undergo any punishment which the Kirk might impose on him 'even if it were to lose any member of his body'.

After some years of difficulties, he induced the Kirk to look leniently on his offence.

'It was ordained that he present himself before the Church Assembly, and being entered prostrate himself before the whole brethren with weeping and howling, and being commanded to rise, might not express farther his request being as appeared so sore troubled with anguish of heart.'

The Reformers then imposed the penitence.

'The said Paul upon the two preaching days between the Sundays shall come to the kirk door of Edinburgh when the second bell rings, clad in sackcloth, bareheaded and barefooted and there remain until he be brought in to the sermon and placed in the public spectacle above the people . . . in the next Sunday after shall declare signs of his inward repentance to the people, humbly requiring the kirk's forgiveness, which done he shall be clad in his own apparel and received in the society of the kirk as a lively member therefore.'

Handing Over the Lease

The kind of punishments meted out to try to keep order in towns must be viewed against the general background of cruelty in the country and the period. For example, Gilbert, Earl of Cassillis, in 1570 was anxious to get hold of the lease of the abbey of Cross-raguel. The earl invited the abbot to dine, and not being able to talk him into handing over the lease, he proceeded to use more persuasive methods.

The dialogue still has a certain grisly punch: The earl said: 'my lord abbot it will please you to confess here that with your own consent you remain in my company because you dare not commit yourself to the hands of others.'

The abbot replied: 'Would you, my lord, that I should make a manifest leasing for your pleasure? The truth is, my lord, it is against my will that I am here; neither yet have I any pleasure in your company.'

The earl said, 'You must then obey me', and presented the abbot with a five-year lease, a nineteen-year lease, and a charter for all the abbey lands, in order that he might sign them over to him.

'After that the earl espied repugnance and that he could not come to his purpose by fair means, he commanded his cooks to prepare the banquet. And so first they flayed the sheep [i.e. took off the abbot's clothes] even to his skin; next they bound him to the chimney, his legs to one end, and his arms to the other; and so they began to beat the fire sometimes to his buttocks, sometimes to his legs, sometimes to his shoulders and arms. And that the roast should not burn, but that it might roast in sop, they spared not flamming with oil.'

In the account given by Bannantyne the story ends with the earl saying: 'You are the most obstinate man that I ever saw! If I had known that you had been so stubborn, I would not for a thousand crowns have handled you so. I never did so to man before you.'

The abbot gave a different account, and said that he had yielded to the earl's desires to save his life and free himself from pain. He then signed the papers. 'Which being done the earl caused the tormentors of me swear upon a bible never to reveal one word of this my unmerciful handling to any person or persons.' Against this background of violence, the punishments imposed for civil offences pale into insignificance.

Perhaps because it was comparatively rare, drunkenness seems to have merited a rising scale of fines: first time—'five merks unforgiven'; second time—'ten merks'; third time—£10, to be taken up by the deacons and distributed to the poor.

After that, the drunkard was classed with the keeper of the house of ill-fame, and the brawler, and could be banished for a year and a day, and not received back without 'open repentance'.

Imprisonment was not widely used, as it was wasteful of man-power, but should offenders be unable to pay their fines they could be put into the 'thief's hole'. If the dungeons in commodious castles are anything to go by, the 'thief's hole' would have seemed a place to be avoided.

There were, of course, especially under the Reformers, a number of offences against ecclesiastical discipline. One William Craig was fined 10 merks (about £7) for being absent from 'his kirk this long time by-gone, and obliged to keep his kirk on a Sunday to hear God's word'. Similar disciplines were used for ministers who did not keep to the correct prayers.

Common blasphemers tended to be treated in a similar way to drunkards with a rising scale of fines. But in flagrant cases the blasphemer was dragged off and put for an hour in the 'choks'. This was another instrument of punishment which included a gag which stopped the victim's mouth. The Reformers recommended people should keep their own private 'choks' for keeping the language clean at home among their own families and domestic staff. This punishment was also known as branking, and it was a customary one for scolds, and slanderers. The head was enclosed in an iron frame from which projected a kind of iron spike.

Counterfeiting

Because of the continuing decline in Scottish currency, counterfeiting was a crime to be seriously combated. Thomas Peebles, a goldsmith in Edinburgh, was convicted of 'forging coin stamps and uttering false coin'. Apparently he had passed false money to a woman in exchange for some coal.

With this money she came to the market to buy some necessary articles and was instantly challenged for passing false coin.

'The said Thomas being said by her to be her warrant, delivered of the said false coin to her, David Symmer and other bailies of the burgh of Edinburgh come with her to the said Thomas's chamber to search him for trial of the verity. He held the door of his said chamber close upon him, and would not suffer them to enter till they broke up the door thereof upon him and entered perforce therein; and the said Thomas, being inquired if he had given the said poor woman the said lions [coins], for the price of her coals, confessed the same and his chamber being searched there was divers of the said irons as well sunken and unsunken together with the said false testons [another coin] found in the same and confessed to be made and graven by him and his colleagues. Thomas was condemned to be hanged and have his property confiscated to the Queen.'

In 1567 there is another account of the hanging of a man for currency offences: 'Robert Jack, merchant and burgess of Dundee, was hanged and quartered for false coin called Hardheads, which he had brought out of Flanders.' The account mentions, 'False lions called hardheads, placks, bawbees, and other false money'.

The hardhead was a French copper coin, and was valued at about 1½d in Scottish money. It was often further debased by the Scottish rulers as a means of raising revenue. Knox in 1559 complains, 'daily there were such numbers of lions [alias hardheads] printed, that the baseness thereof made all things exceeding dear'. The Regent Morton did not add to his popularity by bringing down the value of hardheads from 1½d to a penny, and the plack piece from fourpence to twopence.

It is quite possible that Robert Jack, the indicted merchant, had been importing foreign money. Great importance was attached to his being taken prisoner because it is reported: 'Payment. Jan. 28th 1567 to George Monro, of Dalcartie, for expenses made by him, upon six horsemen and four footmen for the sure conveying of Robert Jack being apprehended in Ross for false cunyie.'

Obviously tampering with currency was considered to be one of the sins 'crying to heaven for vengeance' since it debased and threatened the livelihood of the people, and in a country which mistrusted its own money and was inclined to trade for goods, or other foreign currencies, anyone who engaged in this kind of crime was adding to the burdens of the poor, and the difficulties of the trading community.

Keeping Order

Each corporation employed one or two civic officers. They were used to carry the halberds on state occasions and attend the magistrates at the courts. In early times the various trade guilds were supposed to be responsible for keeping order in the city, but the craftsmen were unequal to this herculean task. The system of 'watching and warding' proved difficult to carry out, and sometimes at a period of public disorder, which was not infrequent—in Edinburgh, for example—soldiers from the castle were used to restore reasonable peace to the City.

But the burgh magistrates had fairly extensive powers, and were allowed to repress crime by summary jurisdiction. Every burgh had its public executioner. It was he who carried out corporal punishment, and even hanging, if that should be necessary. Scourging, ducking and the various other disciplinary measures which were in use at the time were all carried out by the public executioner.

Witchcraft
It is a curious fact that although the Roman Church concerned itself to some degree with witches, and with superstitious practices of all kinds, the prosecutions of witches seem to have risen rather than diminished at the time of the Reformation.

Shakespeare is supposed to have written the three witches into the play *Macbeth* at the request of James I and VI, who had a firm belief in both witchcraft and witches.

In 1563, the Estates passed an Act 'that no person take upon hand to use any manner of witchcrafts, sorcery or necromancy, nor give themselves forth to have any such craft or knowledge therefore, therethrough abusing the people and that no person seek any help, response or consultation at any such uses or abusers of witchcraft under pain of death'.

Against the dark background of this law many perfectly innocent women (and men) were condemned to horrible deaths.

In 1576, a middle-aged woman called Bessie Dunlop, of Lyne in Ayrshire, was tried for witchcraft. The trial has a curious naïvety. For Bessie had done no evil to anyone but merely attempted to cure various illnesses or to find missing things. 'She herself had no art nor science so to do', and she said that her information 'came from one Tom Reid who died at Pinkie' a battle which took place nearly thirty years before.

She was asked what kind of man this Tom Reid was.

'She declared he was an honest, well, elderly man, grey bearded and had a coat with Lombard sleeves of the old fashion, a pair of grey breeks, and white stockings gartered above the knee, a black bonnet on his head close behind and plain before, with silken laces drawn through the lips therefore, and a white wand in his hand.'

Tom apparently predicted that her child would die but her husband would get better, which made her 'somewhat blither'. According to Bessie, Tom then promised her gear, horses, and cows

233

if she would deny her Christendom and the faith she took at her baptism which she refused to do.

Bessie also declared that she had seen a dozen other spirits when in Tom's company, and that he had tried to entice her away to Elfland which she had refused. She answered, 'That she dwelt with her own husband and bairns and could not leave them'.

But in spite of her obvious simplicity, and hallucinations, and the fact that she had done no one any harm, Bessie was found guilty of sorcery 'and other evil arts laid to her charge and consigned to the flames'.

Nor were the fighting men immune from a belief in the Evil One. After a skirmish in the early part of the century, the son of the Earl of Surrey, Commander at Flodden, wrote:

'I dare not write the wonder that my Lord Dacre and all his company do say they saw that night, six times, of spirits and fearful sights. And universally, all their company say plainly the devil that night was in among them six times which misfortune hath blemished the best journey that was made in Scotland for many years.'

Possibly a night attack by the Scots was best blamed on supernatural forces.

John Knox was concerned with the hunting of witches as well as papists, and James Melville writes in his diary: 'The first execution that ever I saw was a witch in St Andrews against the which Mr Knox dealt from the pulpit, she being set up at a pillar before him.'

One of the ancestors of James Boswell was not without stain when it came to witchcraft:

'John Boswell of Auchinleck not only has oft and divers times consulted with witches but also by himself practised witchcraft, sorcery, enchantment, and other devilish practices to the dishonour of God, slander of his Word, and great contempt of His Highness, his authority and laws.'

It is thought that possibly the doctrine of predestination, that some were born to be saved and some were eternally damned, gave the cult of satanism a certain attraction. If the saved were saved whatever they did, then the ungodly might as well draw some benefit from their dealings with the devil.

Some accused witches would purchase their freedom by indicting others:

'Margaret Aitken, the great witch of Balwearie, being examined touching her associates in that trade, she named a few, and perceiving her declarations found credit, made offer to detect all of that sort, and to purge the country of them so that she might have her life granted. For the reason of her knowledge she said that they had a secret mark in their eyes whereby she could surely tell whether they were witches or not.'

As a result of this many innocent people were accused of witchcraft, but at her trial she had better thoughts, for 'she affirmed all to be false that she had confessed either of herself or others, and persisted in this to her death'.

Sometimes accusations of witchcraft were brought in order to get hold of property illegally. In 1596, the Earl of Orkney alleged that his brother, John Stewart, was plotting his murder with the help of a witch named Alison Balfour. When the case was settled Alison was dead, and in her dying declaration at the place of her execution she had declared her complete innocence. The Master of Orkney, John Stewart, gave the declaration:

'She in presence of me and witnesses declared and took upon her soul and conscience as she would answer at the day of Judgement when the secrets of all hearts shall be disclosed that she was innocent and would die as innocent of any point of witchcraft as a babe new born. And being inquired upon her soul and conscience to declare what she knew of the Laird of Stenhouse and to what effect he gave to her the wax that was found in her purse? The wretched woman said that she knew nothing of the Laird of Stenhouse but honestly, and that his lady being subject to the colic willed the Laird to give her a piece of wax, a four year bygone to make a plaster to be employed by her to his lady for remedy of her said disease and in no other way, as she would answer to the living God of Heaven and Earth; and said then plainly that she would die with the same confession.'

On being asked why this varied from her first deposition, made in the castle of Kirkwall, she answered that at that time she was 'tortured divers and several times . . . and sundry times taken out dead and out of all rememberance either of good or evil; as likewise her good man being in the long irons of fifty stone weight and her daughter (aged seven) tortured by the thumbscrews wherewith she and they were vexed and tormented' she had confessed to 'eschew any greater torment and punishment.' For her false confession she 'asked the Lord's forgiveness and constantly died thereat'. It is not always possible to find the truth with torture.

There was also the case of Thomas Lorn, obviously an errant husband, who was brought before the Provost of Aberdeen accused of 'hearing of spirits, and wavering oft-times from his wife, bairns and family by the space of seven weeks, they not knowing where he has been during the said space'. Mr Lorn agreed that he would not go away in this manner again, without giving warning, and if he did was prepared to suffer death 'as a guilty person, dealer with spirits'.

But many learned men of the time fully believed in demoniac possession and marvels. Andrew Melville presided at a discussion in the theological hall of St Mary's College, St Andrews, and the subject was:

'Whether by divining or diabolical force of witches and hags, bodies may be transported or transformed or souls released for a time from bodies, or whether this transportation or transformation of bodies, or resemblance of a projected corpse without sense and motion, as if the soul were banished, be a simple lethargy, or a certain evidence of execrable demonomania?'

In King James's book on demonology he talks of

'witches . . . being carried by the force of the spirit . . . either above the earth or above the sea swiftly to the place where they meet . . . or being transported in the likeness of a little beast or fowl, they will come and pierce through whatsoever house or church, though all passages be closed. And some say that their bodies lying still, as in an ecstasy, their spirits will be ravished out of their bodies and carried to such places; and for verifying thereof will give evident tokens, as well by witnesses that have seen their body lying senseless in the meantime.'

Monsters and Others
People who believed so firmly in witches were also prone to believe in other extra-terrestrial happenings.

An intensive search is still being made today for the Loch Ness monster, but in the sixteenth century the monster was in Loch Fyne, possibly living on a diet of the famous Loch Fyne herrings.

'In this time there was a monstrous fish in Loch Fyne having great eyes in the head thereof and at some times would stand above the water as high as the mast of a ship, and the said had upon the head therefore two crowns, the one above little, the downmost crown large; which was reported by wise men that the same was a sign and tokening of a sudden alteration in the realm.'

The prediction drawn from the appearance of the monster was hardly startling in the Scotland of the time.

In 1575, it was reported that 'there was a calf calved at Roslin with one head, four eyes, three ears, one in the middle and one on each side, and two mouths'.

At the beginning of the seventeenth century it was reported that

'a cow brought forth fourteen great dog whelps instead of calves. Another after the calving became stark mad . . . a 3rd brought forth a calf with two heads. One of the Earl of Argyll's servants being sick, vomited two toads and a serpent, and so convalesced, but vomited after a number of little toads.'

Although in modern context there might be an inclination to smile at such strange beliefs and the odd credulity of the period, this would be a misplaced superiority. It is not so long since the TV teams were investigating the monster in Loch Ness (not Loch Fyne)—and there are people who firmly believe in flying saucers.

CHAPTER TWELVE

THE ARTS
LITERATURE, PAINTING, SCULPTURE, MUSIC AND ARCHITECTURE

A country which is engaged in constant wars, both internal and external, does not provide good ground in which the arts may flourish. In the Scotland of Mary Stuart many aspects of art, especially architecture, woodcarving, sculpture, music, and even literature were connected with that great international organization of the period, the Roman Catholic Church. This meant that when the religious split came there was a consequent decline in many aspects of these arts.

Literature was the first of the arts to break out of the straitjacket of Holy Mother Church. Many of the writers of the early part of the century took the abuses of the church as their theme and were instrumental in drawing the attention of people to the immoralities, follies, and stupidities of churchmen. Much of the literature of Scotland in the early periods was written in Latin which was the cultured tongue of the educated, and for this reason literature tended to be divorced from the general life of the country.

But as this literature was written for an international audience, it was not strictly speaking a literature which had any connexion with Scotland. Another difficulty in Scotland at the time was the lack of printing presses.

In 1507, James IV, Mary Stuart's grandfather, granted a patent to Walter Chepman and Andrew Myllar by which they were to print 'the books of our laws, acts of Parliament, chronicles and mass books'. Both these men were burgesses of Edinburgh, Chepman being a merchant who traded in wood, cloth, and other imports and exports. He seems to have been a man of wealth and possibly had some connexion with the King's household.

Myllar was a bookseller and a supplier of books to the King. This meant, in effect, that he was an importer of books from England and the Continent. Then these two men started their own printing presses in the Blackfriars Wynd in Edinburgh. They printed a number of short romances, some school books, and the *Aberdeen Breviary*, which became the chief church service book for Scotland. But after the death of Chepman the art of printing appears to have lapsed in Scotland, and books were again imported from England and the Continent.

A year or two before the birth of Mary Stuart, Thomas Davidson started printing again in Scotland, and in 1541 he was commissioned to print the *Acts of Parliament of James V*, by order of the Lord Clerk Register, and so became the King's printer. The best work produced by his press was Bellenden's translation of Boece's *History of Scotland*. This history had first been published in Paris in 1526, and was translated into the Scottish vernacular by Bellenden, who explains his reasons for the translation to King James V:

'I that has been your humble servitor since your first infancy has translated the History of Scotland since the first beginning thereof in your vulgar language that your highness may know the valiant and noble deeds done by your progenitors and have cogniscence how this realm has been governed these one thousand and eight hundred years bygone; which was never subdued to uncouth empire but only to the native princes thereof; howbeit the same has sustained great trouble by wars of Romans, Englishmen and Danes with sundry changes of fortune.'

John Bellenden was a Catholic churchman who attained the rank of Archdeacon of Moray. While engaged on his translation he was subsidized by the Treasury. This translation is supposed to have been printed by Davidson about 1540.

Another early work which gives familiar pictures of the country, the seaside, and the general state of the country is *The Complaynt of Scotland*. The author of this work is unknown, but it has been deduced from the fact that the church is not attacked in quite such strong terms as in other works of the period, that like Bellenden, he may have also been a Roman Catholic churchman, and a supporter of the French alliance. The work was dedicated to the Regent, Mary of Guise Lorraine.

The first part of the work is devoted to drawing a general picture of the state of the kingdom. 'Dame Scotia' complains about her three sons—the three estates—the clergy, the nobility, and the burgesses. In the event Dame Scotia seems to have found little to praise in the state of the kingdom. The author reproaches his countrymen for sacrificing the country to their own selfish interests, to the ruin of the kingdom. Some of them have even sold themselves to the English and 'become vile slaves'.

True to his belief in the French alliance, he says that the English and the Scottish should have no truck with one another as 'familiarity between enemies is sure to beget treason'. He castigates the Scottish for their feuds, and in his work, Catholic author or not, the peasantry pour forth their lamentations against their oppressors— the clergy and the nobility who are described as 'more cruel than the English invaders'. The kingdom was misgoverned and the people had been brought low as a consequence. 'How baseless is the boast of blood. Let it be tested.' The author then goes on to state quite logically 'the stock of the first genealogy of nobles since the world began has been—poor labourers and mechanical craftsmen'. With a quick prayer for their reform, he then points out: 'In the past all conspiracies have been originated and fomented by the great, as treason is impossible amongst the poor.'

But the writer of the *Complaynt* does not take a particularly rosy view of the common people either. They are described as dull asses, kicked and goaded, and made the burden of every dart. Their meetings were often scenes of uproar, 'where they scolded and barked without rhyme or reason all day long'. Their judgement is described as worthless, and 'they are worse than the brute beasts, intemperate, lustful, and steady only when forced'. He does not seem to think that a rising standard of living improves them either: 'When any of them rise in the world they become much worse than the higher classes and their children are ignorant, vain, prodigal and arrogant.'

The unknown author lashes out thus at the upper classes:

'I see nothing among gentlemen but vice. For honesty is spotted, ignorance praised, prudence scorned and chastity banished; the nights are too short for gentlemen to commit their lecheries, and the days too short for them to commit extortions upon the poor people. . . . A man is not reputed for a gentleman unless he expends more on his horses and dogs than he does on his wife and children.'

Like all satirists in all centuries, he brandishes the skull and crossbones:

'As they must all return to their common and general mother the earth, and she makes no acceptation of persons nor differences of qualities between gentlemen and mechanics but receives them all indifferently in her domicile and receptacle. Then, when the corrupted flesh is consumed from the bones, no man can distinguish a prince from a beggar.'

The armorial bearings of gentlemen should be dust, ashes and earth. The usual picture of a golden age free, naturally, from drink, lechery and rich food, is painted. Every age sees every other age as golden.

The clergy get off rather more lightly in the *Complaynt* and are mostly reproached for schism, and told to reform themselves, and not to persecute others before they have achieved this. Otherwise, executing and punishing schismatics will be 'like unto a man casting oil on a burning fire in the hope of extinguishing it'. In the last thought, the anonymous author spoke more truly than he knew, since every execution of a Protestant for professing the new faith only lit another torch to burn brightly for the Reformers.

Sir David Lyndsay of the Mount, who wrote the play *The Three Estates*, another satire on Scotland, was less lenient with the clergy.

A speech in this play, written for the abbot, who is asked how he has kept his three vows of poverty, chastity, and obedience, gives the attacking flavour of it:

'Indeed right well . . .
Then did I live as did my predecessor,
My paramours are both as fat and fair
As any wench until the town of Ayr,
I send my sons to Paris to the Schools,
I trust in God that they shall be no fools,
And all my daughters I have well provided,
Now judge ye if my office be well guided.'

Sir David Lyndsay died in 1555, before the Reformed Party had the reins of power in their hands, and it is uncertain whether he gave up the Catholic faith. He had been employed at the Scottish court for the greater part of his life.

A Victorian commentator of the work of Sir David Lyndsay remarks: 'He had a fund of genuine humour and his satire is often pungent and stinging, but his taste was rather coarse which was partly the fault of his age, and sprang out of the state of society.' The fact that *The Three Estates* has been given at the Edinburgh Festival in the last few years may show that the sixteenth-century theatre had more in common with modern theatre than with the theatre of previous ages. Coarseness is not a quality which troubles the modern critic.

After Lyndsay's death collections of his writings were published in France in 1558. From that date until 1614, fourteen editions of his writings were published, including two French and three English ones. His works were popular not only in Scotland but also in England, France, Holland and Ireland.

Other authors also satirized the Church. Killor, a friar who was burned for heresy, wrote a tragedy about the Crucifixion in which he attacked the clergy. James Stewart, son of Lord Methven, also wrote poems and ballads attacking the Church.

Popular 'street' literature used the Church as a target. It was the habit during the transition from Catholicism to Protestantism to take rude popular songs and their airs, and sing them to sacred subjects. The 'Good and Godly Ballads' also took popular tunes and substituted the original words for attacks on the Catholic Church, including in their subjects of satire, relics, the reverencing of statues, indulgences, and the Mass. The author of these ballads is unknown but they have been credited to James Wedderburn, or his brothers, John and Robert.

The writing of poetry was a courtly accomplishment, and there are many minor poets of this time, including Mary Stuart herself who also wrote poetry in French. As a young woman, she had been a pupil of Ronsard, and like her father James V, she showed some facility and sensitivity for verse. Her son, James VI and I, was equally anxious to prove himself a poet. At the age of eighteen, in 1584, his first work in this field was published, called *Essays of a Prentice in the Divine Art of Poesie*. Although it was not generally considered to be of high merit, like the autobiographies of celebrities in our own time, it was highly praised.

James VI and I also contributed to a Cambridge collection of poems on the death of Sir Philip Sidney in 1587. Over-fond of displaying his learning, he had a deep and complicated knowledge of that favourite subject of the Scots, theology. One critic demolishes poor James's pretensions with a short sharp blast: 'It may at once be stated that his books have contributed nothing to the advancement of an enlightened and liberal policy of government, nor to the progress of civilization.'

The largest collection of early Scottish poems is that carefully put together by George Bannantyne. This collection of 800 pages was made during the three months of plague in Edinburgh in 1568, and it is through his labours that poets such as Alexander Scott have survived.

Many of the court poets wrote for their own and others' amusement and the idea of printing their works never occurred to them. Making poems was an accomplishment like singing, and many of the little ballads written at the time were planned to be sung.

John Knox was a good firm prose writer. His history of the Reformation was begun in 1559 and the fourth book was finished in 1566. The last book was finished after Knox's death, from his own notes. His *First Blast of the Trumpet against the Monstrous Regiment of Women* which caused some difficulties with Queen Elizabeth, shows a good round invective style mixed with a touch of the Old Testament prophet:

'To promote a woman to bear rule, superiority, dominion, or empire above any realm, nation, or city, is repugnant to nature, contumely to God, a thing most contrarious to His revealed will and approved ordinance and finally it is the subversion of good order, of all equity and justice. . . . For who can deny that it repugneth nature that the blind shall be appointed to lead and conduct such as do see? That the weak, the sick and impotent persons shall nourish and keep the whole and the strong? And finally, that the foolish, mad, and phrenetic shall govern the discreet and give counsel to such as are sober of mind? And such be all women compared unto man in bearing of authority.'

A week or two before Mary Stuart's arrival in Scotland, he wrote to Elizabeth trying to explain and justify the *Blast*. He casts a few sly slurs on Mary.

'To wit that neither doth our Sovereign so greatly fear her own state by reason of that book, neither yet doth she so greatly favour the tranquillity of Your Majesty's reign and realm that she would take so great and earnest pains, unless that her crafty counsel shot at a further mark.'

George Buchanan, sometime classical tutor to Mary Stuart, and afterwards one of James VI and I's tutors, originally taught one of James V's natural sons. Born in 1506, he was educated in Paris, and for many years taught in Italy, France and Lisbon. He returned to Scotland in 1561 after an absence of over twenty years. Buchanan wrote many Latin works both in prose and poetry, as well as a *History of Scotland* in twenty books. At Queen Mary's court he was the interpreter of documents written in foreign languages. He seems, before his joining the Reformers, to have joined in the court past-time of poetry-making and wrote several poems to Queen Mary—one on the birth of her son.

He also wrote graceful little pieces to her court ladies. These are lines addressed to Mary Beaton, one of the four Marys:

'Winter is fierce, the meadows are not bright, nor the gardens full of flowers, when I might seek to make ready an offering for my lady. So also that garden of my mind and thought, once fertile in the worship of the Muses, is bound by winter in the cold of age. Yet still, of the warm west wind, Betonian airs, should blow on it, there should abound the succour of the spring.'

Once the wind had changed George Buchanan joined the Reformers, and was the author of a scurrilous book attacking the Queen, *The Tyrannous Reign of Mary Stewart*. The soft strains of the lutes were forgotten and the trumpet of righteousness was sounding.

Another collection of early Scottish poems was compiled by Sir Richard Maitland of Lethington. He had been a lawyer, Lord of Session, and Privy Councillor in the reign of Mary Stuart. His collection of early Scottish poems, 272 pieces in two volumes, is more famous than his own poems. He died in 1586 at the age of ninety and all his verse was written after the age of sixty.

His mature eye did not gaze myopically at the Reformers and his is one of the few moderate voices of the time. Whether it was the old Church, or the new, the people professing the doctrines with such vigour were equally culpable in his eyes, and is to be regarded with a certain cynical detachment:

'They think it well if they the Pope do call
The Anti-Christ and Mass idolatry
And guzzle flesh upon the Fridays all,
That they serve God right well accordingly,

Though in all things they live most wickedly,
But God commanded us His Law to keep
First honour Him, and then have charity
With our neighbour, and for our sins to weep.'

It is the view of one who has seen the programme round once before. Corruption is corruption no matter which banner it hides behind.

One of the classics of early Scottish writing is Sir James Melville's *Memoirs*,

'containing an impartial account of the most remarkable affairs of state during the sixteenth century, not mentioned by other Historians: more particularly relating to the Kingdoms of England and Scotland, under the Reigns of Queen Elizabeth, Mary Queen of Scots, and King James. In most of which transactions the Author was personally concerned.'

Sir James Melville lived from 1535 to 1617, and consequently was over eighty when he died, an immense age for the period. It is thought that the memoirs were written in the 1590s, when he was already an old man. The manuscript was discovered in 1660, and considerably 'edited' by his grandson, George Scott of Pitlochrie. The original was then lost, and not rediscovered until 1827 when a new edition was made for the Bannantyne Club.

Like most diaries and memoirs James Melville's bring the small everyday things to life in a way that grander biographies concerned with the great sweep of events do not do. In the passages where he relates, 'such things as I myself was employed in, or where I was present and heard with my own ears', the narrative gives a sidelight on history. Melville, possibly because he was already an old man when he wrote the book, is inclined to remember 'with advantages' the things he did. This is particularly true of the short, sharp talks he recounts having given to the queens, Elizabeth and Mary, as well as the appendix, 'Melville's Advice to King James'. Old men certainly remember 'with advantages' the things they said, whether it is modern politicians, or a courtier at Holyrood in the sixteenth century.

But while during the last days of Catholic supremacy in Scotland, the art of satire flourished wild and free, the coming of the Reformers put an end to this kind of writing. In 1551, a law was passed against

245

the press which 'teemed with lewd rhymes and ballads with scandalous songs and tragedies, and must be subjected to the censorship'. Every printer was compelled to obtain a licence from the Queen and the Governor.

After the triumph of the Reformation, the power of Latin civilization over Scottish literature was broken. Numbers of books of sermons began to be published, and because the Bible had been published widely in English, it also contributed to the decline of the native 'Scottis' writing. The general trend of writing after the Reform was towards the improvement of the soul, and the hard hand of puritanism fell heavily on all forms of frivolous literature.

There had been one or two defenders of the old Faith, one of whom was Ninian Winzet. He was a schoolmaster in the grammar school at Linlithgow, being appointed about 1552. As already mentioned, Winzet was first driven from his teaching post for making an attack on the Reformers, 'being expelled and shut out of that my kindly town and from my tender friends there whose perpetual kindness I hoped that I had conquest'.

In 1552, Winzet asked Mary Stuart's permission to put certain questions to Knox and his fellow Reformers. As a result he wrote a tract called *Is John Knox a lawful Minister?* Knox did not deign to reply in writing but preached one of his sermons, no doubt 'dinging the pulpit to splinters' in his usual way. Winzet then published the *Last Blast of the Trumpet of God's Word against the usurped authorities of John Knox and his Calvinistic brethren intruding preachers etc. put forth to the Congregation of the Protestants in Scotland by Ninian Winzet a Catholic priest born in Renfrew.*

Unfortunately for Winzet the last blast of the trumpet was turned against himself. His defence of Catholicism was published in Edinburgh in July 1562, but the printer of the book was seized and imprisoned. Winzet managed to escape, and took a ship bound for Flanders. He went to Antwerp and subsequently taught at the University of Louvain. Another of his writings, *A Book of Four Score and Three Questions*, was published in Antwerp in 1563. Only a fragment of the *Last Blast of the Trumpet* remains; presumably the copies were destroyed at the time of his flight.

In 1577 Winzet became Abbot of the Benedictine monastery at Ratisbon, and there he died, in exile, at the age of seventy-five in 1592.

246

Music

Before the Reformation singing was taught throughout Scotland, and no doubt, as is still the case, the cathedrals and monasteries had choirs attached to them. James Melville seems to corroborate this.

'I learned my music, wherein I took greater delight than in law, of one Alexander Smith, servant to the Head of our College who had been trained up amongst the monks in the Abbey. I learned of the scales, plain song and many of the trebles of the Psalms whereof some I could well sing in the Kirk; but my natural turn and easy learning by the ear made me the more unsolid and unready to use the form of the art. I loved singing and playing on instruments passing well, and would gladly spend time where the exercise thereof was within the College; for two or three of our co-pupils played extremely well on the virginals and another on the lute and githorn [guitar]. Our Regent also had the spinet in his chamber and learned something and I after him, both perceiving me to be much carried away with it, he gave up the practice and left off. It was the great mercy of my God that kept me from any great progress in singing and playing on instruments, for if I had attained to any reasonable address therein, I had never done good otherwise, in respect of my amorous disposition.'

Melville's attitude to his music shows a good Puritan tendency to treat it as a frivolous pursuit.

Brantôme, who accompanied Mary Stuart from France to Scotland, did not take so generous a view of Scottish music. Having described Mary's entrée into Edinburgh, when the guilds and corporations of Edinburgh lined the route and played their musical instruments, and celebrated their Queen's return with fireworks, he adds,

'And worst of all, that at night when she wished to sleep, being lodged in the Abbey, there came under her window five or six hundred rogues from the town giving her a serenade of evil violins ... and began to sing psalms very badly.'

As commentators the French do not gloss over their opinions. This serenade is described in Knox's history as a 'company of most honest men, with instruments of music, and with musicians gave their salutations at her chamber windows, and that the Queen said

247

that the melody liked her well, and she wished the same to be continued some nights after'. Either Knox was taking a rosy view of Scottish music, or the Queen was exercising a superhuman tact.

But the Queen is believed to have taken a great interest in Highland music when she had occasion to visit the Highlands. It was also reported that there was a competition of harpists, and the Robertsons of Lude possessed a harp supposed to have been the prize given by Queen Mary to Beatrix Gardyn.

The harp appears to have been the most ancient instrument amongst the Highlanders, and was as much used as it was in Ireland.

'They delight much in music, but chiefly in harps and clarischoes of their own fashion. The strings of the clarischoes are of brass wire, and the strings of the harps of sinews which strings they strike either with their nayles growing long, or else with an instrument appointed for that use. They take pleasure to deck their harps and clarischoes with silver and precious stones, and poor ones that cannot attain hereunto deck them with crystall.'

In the early sixteenth century the Lord High Treasurer's accounts include items for payment to musicians.

May 10th 1503 to Mackberty, the clairsha to pass to the Isles —10s.
Sept. 3rd 1506—Item to Mackleans clairsha 1 9s.
Duncan Campbell's bard—5s.

The Lords of the Exchequer, when engaged on their weighty deliberations, liked to have a little music while they worked, for when they met to edit the accounts, minstrels and players were provided at the public expense. But later in the sixteenth century, under the Reformation, minstrels had fallen from popularity and attempts were made to put them down by law. They were described in round terms as 'idle persons without lawful calling as pipers, fiddlers, songsters, sorners, pleasants, and stray beggars'.

In 1568, in Dundee a rule was laid down that 'none was to come out of his house after 9 p.m. to use any kind of dancing, playing, or such vain exercise under punishment of breaking the musician's instruments, and a fine of 20s to be given to the poor'. There seems little point in bringing your harp to the party if the night watch is going to break it up afterwards.

Other instruments which are mentioned in the records of the

period are the fiddle, the whistle, the flute, and pipes of several kinds. One set of pipes is said to include a drone bag, so it was probably an early type of bagpipe.

In spite of Sunday grave faces, song and dance was popular in sixteenth-century Scotland. The dances started usually with two low bows and then a kiss. This is possibly the reference which John Knox made to Mary Stuart kissing Chastelard 'in the neck' and then adding 'and this was honest enough; for it was the gentle entreatment of a stranger'.

In 1553, the town council of Edinburgh gave a licence to James Lauder, the prebendary of their choir, to go to England and France and 'remain for a year, and learn better music, and more aptitude on musical instruments', which might have been more tactfully phrased. The following year the dean of guild was ordered by the council to repair the 'song school in the churchyard so that the bairns may enter and attend it'. The magistrates also engaged one Alexander Stevenson to sing in the choir every festival day at the masses of Our Lady, and the Holy Blood. His salary to be 20 merks a year. Musicians were also said to play during the sitting of Parliament, and to play before the image of St Giles. While in 1556 Jacques, and his sons, were paid for playing on 'All Hallowe'en and all the time of the fair, twice in the day through the town'.

But all this playing and singing in churches and at fairs was slowed down at the time of the Reformation. Indeed by 1579, the adverse effect of so much gravity had begun to be perceived. An Act of Parliament was passed which stated that 'the teaching of the youth in the art of music and singing had begun to be neglected'. It went on to say 'that the instruction of the children in music and singing had almost decayed and must decay altogether if a timely remedy was not provided'.

The provosts and councils of the burghs throughout the kingdom, and the patrons and provosts of collegers were 'enjoined to repair and set a going the song schools, and to appoint qualified masters to instruct the young in the science of music'.

But unfortunately the general atmosphere of the Reformers and their attitude towards music was not conducive either to the writing or to the practising of music. Although it was customary to sing psalms and sometimes hymns in the reformed churches, both organs and any other form of instrumental music were banned from public worship. The prosecutions of pipers at weddings, and the general discouragement of music, did not form a background which would enable this art to flourish, and indeed many forms of music were definitely discouraged as leading to levity, and possibly, what Knox calls dulciness. Dancing, which is so often an accompaniment to music and its co-partner, was frowned on as a sin. It is difficult to encourage music as an art if at the drop of a Reformer's black hat a couple can be prosecuted for dancing at their own wedding.

Painting

There remain very few paintings of this period in Scotland. Those portraits which are in the Scottish National Portrait Gallery and in private collections are either by Arnold von Bronkhorst, or by that well-known character 'artist unknown'. It could well be that many of the early portraits were either painted in France or the Low Countries, or, if painted in Scotland, by travelling French or Flemish artists. There are, as far as is known, no portraits of Mary Stuart painted while she was in Scotland. Although there is supposed to have been a picture of her painted in Highland dress, this has disappeared.

Among the portraits which remain are that of the fifth Lord Seton, painted in the costume of the Master of the Queen's Household. The quality of the painting shows that in spite of the fact that the costume is Scottish, it must have been painted in France. Mary of Guise Lorraine was also painted by a French artist, Claude Corneille de Lyon. The two very attractive twin miniatures of Bothwell and his wife, Jean Gordon, are also anonymous. Painted against a background of sharp green, the tawny colouring of the two Scots is thrown into brilliant relief.

The famous picture of James I and VI, as a child, holding the hawk, is attributed to Arnold von Bronkhorst. Hans Eworth painted the Earl of Moray and his wife; these portraits, thought to have been painted in France at the request of Queen Elizabeth, hang in Darnaway Castle. Eworth was a Fleming, born in Antwerp, and was a fashionable portrait painter of the period. Among his sitters were Mary Tudor, Queen Elizabeth I, and many leading members of prominent Tudor families.

Other good portraits are those of Lady Helen Leslie, the wife of Mark Ker of Newbattle. Her brothers were concerned in the murder of Cardinal Beaton, and her dress shows a suitably neat puritan style. The two regents, Moray and Mar, are well painted,

and depict them showing their stern reforming faces to the dangerous world they lived in.

The engravings which were made from the portraits of the period also mostly emanated from the Low Countries. Typical examples are the twin engravings of François II and Mary Stuart (*c.* 1530) by Pieter van der Heyden, who was born in Antwerp. These two belong to a series called *Royal Personages*, published by Hieronymus Cock in Antwerp in the mid-sixteenth century.

In 1585 there is a record of a Dutch painter called Adrian Vanyone who was made a burgess in Edinburgh to be 'employed in his craft in the town and to instruct apprentices'. This painter had obviously been induced to come to Scotland to teach painting in much the same way that Flemish weavers were encouraged to go to Scotland to teach the art of weaving to local talent.

John Mackintosh, writing at the end of the nineteenth century about Scottish art, dismisses it in a few devastating sentences:

'Painting and sculpture are almost a blank in Scotland [i.e. at this period]. The remarkable revival of Renaissance Italy had little effect on this northern corner of Europe. Indeed painting may be said to be an importation for us. With a few exceptions Scotland had no painters till a recent period. It is not, however, to be supposed that the Scots made no attempts at the figurative arts, only their efforts in this department were so crude as to place them nearly beyond criticism.'

The black and white portrait of Mary Stuart, supposed to have been painted by a Scot during the Queen's imprisonment in England, would, by the crudity of its painting, seem to bear out this criticism.

From the inventories of the period amongst the rich burgesses, it is apparent that paintings were imported from Flanders, and that they were beginning to replace hangings in the houses of the rich bourgeoisie.

The inventory of the goods of Francis Spottiswood, a cloth merchant trading in Flanders, who died around 1540, included a gilded picture of Our Lady, also folding pictures of St John and St James. Other inventories (1561) included 'a hanging brod [picture] of oil colours' as well as 'other painted brods, Doctors of Almaine'. These are believed to have been early instances of oil paintings in private houses. In other account books there is an entry, 'John Meill promised a fine gilt brod with a picture how soon he passes to France'. 'Thomas Young is owing me 2 painted over-gilt brods at his coming home from Flanders.' In the Royal Inventory is included the item, 'Brod of the picture of the Queen Regent brought out of France.'

The very word 'board' seems to point the difference between the idea of a picture on a hard background, and the painted or embroidered hangings which up till that time had been the sole wall decorations.

It could be said the merchants were the pioneers in the art of importing paintings, because they travelled to the Continent and were more in touch with the new ideas than the majority of the aristocracy of the period, whose concentration on the twin arts of war and feuds did not make for the development of peaceful art.

Influence of the Church on Art
Woodcarving was originally an art strictly confined to the church and monastic buildings. Another factor which militated against the spread of this minor art in Scotland was the scarcity of oak.

There was very little wood carving in private houses, and such wood carving and panelling as remains has been much mutilated by alterations, on being moved from one place to another. There is one panel from this period which depicts the monks as foxes and swine, and it is thought that this may have been local Scottish work carved nearer to the date of the Reformation, and, like the scurrilous ballads current at the time, a comment on the *mœurs* of the period.

Embroidery and needlework were much used in church banners, and indeed embroidery was one of the minor arts which flourished amongst the fashionable ladies of the period. Catherine de Médicis, Queen Elizabeth I, and Mary Stuart were all accomplished embroideresses. But they were dependent on professional artists to draw their designs for them. During her imprisonment in Loch Leven, Nicholas Throckmorton reports to Queen Elizabeth that the Queen of Scots had applied for 'an imbroderer to draw further works as she would be occupied about'. Just before her execution, one of the minor tyrannies used against Mary Stuart by Sir Amyas Paulet was to take away from her '*son brodeur* Charles Plouvert'.

The embroiderer or 'brodstar' was a regular servant of a royal retinue. Amongst his employments were the keeping of the chapel vestments in repair, mending the tapestry hangings, and many other jobs very necessary to keep embroideries in good order in the houses and churches of the period which must have been exceedingly damp. Before the general spread of the use of paintings in churches and houses, these embroidered hangings were not only used as altar decorations, but also as banners in processions, whether processions of church dignitaries, or of the guilds who each had banners of their patron saints. Unfortunately many of the hangings of this period disappeared during the despoiling of the churches at the Reformation, as all such 'trumpery stuff' as banners was considered to be of popish origin and therefore not in keeping with the simplicity of the new creed. The Fetternear Banner is a solitary surviving example of this art. The banner, which was never finished, is thought to have been made for the Confraternity of the Holy Blood, and shows Our Lord with the instruments of his Passion surmounted with the heads of Judas and a mocking Jew. The embroidery which is carried out on linen is of great delicacy and is considered to be a fine example of early Scottish craftsmanship. It is believed to have survived possibly because it was not finished, and remained in the Leslie family, by whom it was hung in the local Catholic Church in the Fetternear district. It was not until 1955 that its antiquity was discovered, as previously to that it had been thought to be a family rather than an ecclesiastical banner.

After the decay of church embroidery as a form of art, it became the custom to use embroidered panels in private houses. This could have been because there was a fashion for wood panelling during the sixteenth century, and colourful hangings were needed to lighten the darkness of the wood. Possibly also many of the old tapestries from churches and monasteries had found their way into private houses, and this led to a fashion for this kind of secular embroidery. The Oxbrugh hangings which were carried out by Bess of Hardwick and Mary Stuart during the Queen's imprisonment are typical of this type of work. Very often the pieces of embroidery were part of a series designed to run round the room like a continuous frieze. The designs were actually drawn on the canvas, and not previously traced out on squared paper. Each panel was fairly small—less than two feet high—but varying in length, as obviously the length depended on the size of the room. Embroidered panels were also used as bed hangings, and again these were in panels. Most of the embroidery of this early period is in *gros point*. The Oxbrugh hangings are fairly crude in design and consist of squares of embroidery showing mythical and allegorical birds and beasts, coats of arms and ciphers.

Architecture

Scotland had as great a richness of heritage of churches, abbeys and castles as England. From the twelfth to the beginning of the sixteenth century the abbeys and cathedrals, particularly, were constantly enlarged and adorned as they were in other countries. Church architecture was European in context. Many of the architects of the abbeys and churches are unknown, although it is thought by some writers that priests assisted by master masons were responsible for some of the beautiful abbeys which still remain as gaunt ruins to show the beauty that once was. Father Forbes Leith S.J. writing on pre-Reformation scholars says categorically that

'The clergy were the architects of many of the churches and public works of the sixteenth century. . . . It was to bishops that Scotland owed her most notable bridges. The bridge over the Clyde at Glasgow, described in the Privy Council Register as one of the most remarkable monuments within the kingdom; that over the Don at Aberdeen; the Guard Bridge in Fife, and that over the Tay at Perth. All were directly or indirectly due to the pious care of Scottish bishops.'

The same writer also mentions that the Parliament Hall with its great window within the castle of Stirling is due to these early churchman architects, and 'the delicacy of the outline bespeaks an admirable type of Gothic design'.

He quotes

'A precept made to Maister Leonard Logy for his good and thankful service done and to be done to the King's highness and specially for his diligent and great labour made by him in the bigging of the palace beside the Abbey of Holy Cross of the sum of £40 of the usual money of the realm to be paid to him of the King's coffers yearly, for all the days of his life, or until he be benefited of a hundred merks.'

This was dated Edinburgh September 10, 1503.

But other writers point to the French Renaissance influence which comes out very strongly in much of the domestic architecture of the period. From the beginning of the sixteenth century until the two crowns became merged under James VI and I, the French influence is clearly revealed. In fact the typical style now known rather contemptuously as 'Scottish baronial' is in fact a blending of the Gothic with the influence of French architects and master masons. The little, rounded fairy-tale turrets so typical of French architecture are seen all over Scotland of this period. In Falkland Palace can be seen one of the best samples of the French Renaissance influence in Scotland. Stirling was also partially rebuilt under James V, using French master masons and architects. Much of the architecture of early sixteenth-century Scotland has the distinct flavour of the châteaux of the Loire on a smaller and less sophisticated scale.

During the nineteenth century, Robert William Billings produced an exhaustive study of Scottish baronial and ecclesiastical architecture in Scotland. Illustrated with nearly three hundred engravings, these volumes give a very good picture of the state of these buildings in the nineteenth century. Incidentally they also throw a sidelight on the taste of the mid-nineteenth century period with its passion for the pure Gothic unsullied by the soft influence of the Renaissance.

Writing about the satyrs and grotesques which ornament Stirling Castle, Billings says:

'The exterior of the Palace . . . is profusely decorated with statuary, in some respects of a very peculiar kind. On the other side of the edifice, reached by rounding the corner to the left, there is a row of sculptural efforts, the fruits of an imagination luxuriant but revolting, and indicating abominations that can be but indistinctly traced through the effects of injuries which appear to have been inflicted more from disgust than a love of mischief. It is rather when contemplating these obscene groups, than when looking on the symmetrical architecture or the smiling landscape, that one remembers how this fair scene has been stained with blood.'

Writing about Falkland Palace also charmingly added to by French architects, Billings says

'On a near approach, the lover of art who can tolerate the northern renovation of classical architecture, in the blending of the Palladian with the Gothic and the stunted baronial architecture of Scotland will find much to enjoy in this fragment.'

255

A later critic, Mark Girouard, finds Falkland to be a 'display of early Renaissance architecture without parallel in the British Isles'. The front and gatehouse which flanks the street in Falkland shows the usual pepper-pot turrets so typical of Scottish architecture both in the sixteenth century and in later periods.

Unfortunately for Scottish castles the passion of the late eighteenth century and early nineteenth century for renovations and 'improvements' has altered many of the older buildings completely. The nineteenth-century passion for the 'horrid' and the Gothic has transformed buildings which were once formidable fortifications into pleasant gentlemen's residences. Although some of these improvements date from much earlier: at Glamis Castle, for example, many alterations were made in the seventeenth century. Scott remarked about these 'improvements':

'The huge old tower of Glammis whose birth tradition notes not once showed its lordly head above seven circles of defensive boundaries, through which the friendly guests were admitted and at each of which a suspicious person was unquestionably put to his answer. A disciple of Kent had the cruelty to render this splendid old mansion (the more modern part of which was the work of Inigo Jones) more 'parkish' as he was pleased to call it; to raze all those exterior defences, and to bring his mean and paltry gravel-walk up to the very door from which we might have imagined Lady Macbeth (with the form and features of Siddons) issuing forth to receive King Duncan.'

The impact of the Reformers on architecture, and especially on church architecture, was destructive. Billings defends Knox on this count saying, 'Doubtless there is much truly laid to the charge of that great star of the Reformation, and to his satellites; but their wrath was not against the Church, it was against what they considered the idolatrous part of her doctrines.' He goes on to say

'The actions went beyond their intentions; but what reformer could ever stop the career of his followers? Could stem the torrent at a moment's notice? Doubtless the power set in motion by the Scottish Reformation leaders went rapidly beyond their control, and ended in destruction.'

Billings then goes on to quote the order for the demolition of Dunkeld: 'And fail not, but ye take good heed that neither the desks, winnocks, nor doors, be any ways hurt or broken, either stone work, glass work, or iron work.'

But, once the mobs are in the street, it is too late to start worrying about the preservation of art treasures. No revolution preserves; they all destroy. But John Knox cannot be blamed for all the destruction of the medieval treasures of Scotland. Many of them, after the destruction of the monasteries, were pulled down piece by piece and the stones were used elsewhere.

One of the most beautifully ruined cathedrals in Scotland is Elgin. This was set on fire by Alexander Stewart the 'Wolf of Badenoch', in the fourteenth century. At the same time, for good measure, he destroyed the houses of the canons attached to the Cathedral, as well as a good part of the town. Although the Cathedral is also supposed to have been destroyed by fire in the thirteenth century. It was partially rebuilt during the fifteenth and sixteenth centuries. But in 1568 the lead was stripped from the roof 'for the sustentation of the men of war'. This lead was sent to Holland to be sold, but unfortunately the ship carrying the cargo was sunk. Without its protecting lead roof, the interior crumbled away, Billings says that some of the mural paintings of the Mater Dolorosa. the Crucifixion and other relics of Catholicism were still in existence in the cathedral until the seventeenth century, and were still reverenced by those of the old faith. But 'some zealous reformers, headed by the Lairds of Innes and Brodie, and by some of the neighbouring clergy, proceeded to the ruins . . . and demolished the "symbols of idolatry" with the rood screen which still remained'.

So the destruction commenced by wars and feuds was completed by prejudice.

A typical example of Scottish defensive architecture was the motte or square tower. The plan of these was simple. The lower room was a kind of vault for protecting the owner's cattle against 'reavers'. The upper floors formed the house of the laird and usually consisted of two or three rooms, with other small apartments which were built into the thickness of the tower's walls. The upper floors—again for defensive purposes—could only be reached by means of a ladder. Once the alarm had been given the cattle were enclosed, and the inhabitants retreated to the upper floors pulling up the ladder. The windows of these towers are small, having more the appearance of port holes to be used for defence by means of bows and arrows or muskets. Because Scotland was a more primitive and

I

disturbed country than England, the building of large houses purely for pleasure came at a later date.

Borthwick Castle is a more complicated example of this kind of castle tower. It was, according to Billings, restored in the mid-nineteenth century, having been previously unoccupied for nearly a century. The main portions of the castle date from the fifteenth century, and it was from Borthwick that Mary Stuart escaped 'booted and spurred' at the time when the Lords rose against her and Bothwell. In the great hall of Borthwick there remains a great hooded fireplace worthy of any château of the Loire. Comparison of Billings' engraving of this fireplace with a modern photograph seems to show that in the nineteenth century the room was ruinous—for he shows the fallen masonry inhabited by an owl and a jackdaw. The modern room has been opened up to let in the light, and turned into a pleasant room. As with other towers the first floor was reached by a bridge from the curtain wall, but it now has a stone staircase.

The three streams of influence on Scottish architecture were firstly the Church, secondly the impact of the French with the 'auld alliance', and thirdly the necessity for dwellings which acted as watch towers, a protection against marauders and a secure place to live.

Domestic architecture in the towns as has already been mentioned was one of the simplest, many of the houses of even rich burgesses being wooden structures with thatched roofs. In the country there were no cottages, but merely hovels of turf and stones which could be speedily erected again should they be demolished by raiders. It was not until the pacification of the Highlands and the spread of a more settled way of life that other forms of domestic architecture were able to develop in Scotland.

SELECTED BIBLIOGRAPHY

Billings, R. W., *Baronial and Ecclesiastical Antiquities of Scotland*, W. Blackwood & Sons, Edinburgh, 1845–52.

Brown, P. Hume, *Scotland in the Time of Queen Mary*, Methuen & Co., London, 1904.

Burton, John Hill, *History of Scotland*, W. Blackwood & Sons, Edinburgh, 1867, 1870.

Chambers, William, *The Book of Scotland*, William Hunter, Edinburgh; Longman & Co., London, 1830.

Clark, Robert (ed.), *Golf—a Royal and Ancient Game*, Macmillan & Co., London, 1893.

Domestic Annals of Scotland from the Reformation to the Revolution, W. & R. Chambers, Edinburgh, 1858.

Dunbar, J. T. and Annette Kok, *History of Highland Dress*, Oliver & Boyd, Edinburgh, 1962.

Ferguson, Thomas, *The Dawn of Scottish Social Welfare*, Thomas Nelson & Sons, London, 1948.

Fittis, Robert Scott, *Sports and Pastimes in Scotland*, Paisley, 1891.

Forman, Sheila, *Scottish Country Houses and Castles*, Collins, Glasgow, 1967.

Gordon, Seton, *Highways and Byways in the Central Highlands*, Macmillan & Co., London, 1948.

Grant, I. F., *Social and Economic Development of Scotland before 1603*, Oliver & Boyd, Edinburgh, 1930.

Grant, I. F., *Everyday Life in Old Scotland*, G. Allen & Unwin, London, 1931.

Henderson, T. F., *Old-World Scotland*, London, 1893.

Knox, John, *History of the Reformation in Scotland* (ed. W. C. Dickinson), Thomas Nelson & Sons, London, 1949.

Lawson, Robb, *Story of the Scots' Stage* (ed. Alexander Gardner), 1917.

Leith, W. Forbes, *Pre-Reformation Scholars in Scotland in the XVIth Century*, James Maclehose & Sons, Glasgow, 1915.

Mackenzie, Agnes Mure, *The Scotland of Queen Mary and Religious Wars*, 1513–1638, A. Maclehose & Co., London, 1936.

Mackenzie, Agnes Mure (ed.), *Scottish Pageant*, Oliver & Boyd, Edinburgh, 1948–50.

Mackintosh, John, *The History of Civilisation in Scotland*, A. Gardner, Paisley, 1892–96.

McNeill, F. Marion, *Scots Kitchen: Recipes*, Blackie, Glasgow, 1929.

Maxwell, David, *Bygone Scotland: Historical and Social*, W. Bryce, Edinburgh, 1894.

Maxwell, Stuart and Robin Hutchinson, *Scottish Costume* 1550–1850, A. & C. Black, London, 1958.

Rogers, Charles, *Social Life in Scotland*, W. Paterson, Edinburgh, 1884–86.

Skene, William, *The Highlanders of Scotland*, John Murray, London, 1837.

Stewart, David, *Sketches of Character, Manners, and Present State of the Highlanders of Scotland*, Edinburgh, 1822.

Tytler, Patrick Fraser, *History of Scotland*, W. Tait, Edinburgh, 1845.

Warrack, Alexander, *A Scots Dialect Dictionary*, W. & R. Chambers, London and Edinburgh, 1911.

Warrack, John, *Domestic Life in Scotland*, 1488–1688, Methuen & Co., London, 1920.

INDEX

GEORGE ALLEN & UNWIN LTD
Head Office:
40 Museum Street, London, W.C.1
Telephone: 01-405 8577

Sales, Distribution and Accounts Departments
Park Lane, Hemel Hempstead, Herts.
Telephone: 0442 3244

Athens: 7 Stadiou Street, Athens 125
Auckland: P.O. Box 36013, Auckland 9
Barbados: Rockley New Road, St. Lawrence 4
Bombay: 103/5 Fort Street, Bombay 1
Calcutta: 285J Bepin Behari Ganguli Street, Calcutta 12
Dacca: Alico Building, 18 Motijheel, Dacca 2
Hornsby, N.S.W.: Cnr. Bridge Road and Jersey Street, 2077
Ibadan: P.O. Box 62
Johannesburg: P.O. Box 23134, Joubert Park
Karachi: Karachi Chambers, McLeod Road, Karachi 2
Lahore: 22 Falettis' Hotel, Egerton Road
Madras: 2/18 Mount Road, Madras 2
Manila: P.O. Box 157, Quezon City, D-502
Mexico: Serapio Rendon 125, Mexico 4, D.F.
Nairobi: P.O. Box 30583
New Delhi: 4/21-22B Asaf Ali Road, New Delhi 1
Ontario, 2330 Midland Avenue, Agincourt
Rio de Janeiro: Caixa Postal 2537-ZC-00
Singapore: 248C-6 Orchard Road, Singapore 9
Tokyo: C.P.O. Box 1728, Tokyo 100-91